ROSA.

Collaborative Internationalization
of Small and Medium-sized
Enterprises

Poul Houman Andersen

Collaborative Internationalization of Small and Medium-sized Enterprises

SMEs Participation in the International Division of Labour

Jurist- og Økonomforbundets Forlag
DJØF Publishing Copenhagen
1995

Collaborative Internationalization
of Small and Medium-sized
Enterprises
First Edition 1995

© 1995 by Jurist- og Økonomforbundets Forlag
DJØF Publishing Copenhagen

DJØF Publishing is a company of the
Association of Danish Lawyers and Economists

Cover design: Henning Jensen

Printed in Denmark 1995
by Narayana Press, Gylling

ISBN 87-574-7390-0

TABLE OF CONTENTS

Foreword

This book addresses a highly interesting but largely overlooked paradox in the Danish economy: Small and medium-sized enterprises (SMEs) control comparatively small resources and are unable to reap the competitive advantages of scale and scope internally as compared to larger firms. Nevertheless, Danish SMEs as well as SMEs in other countries are able to organize world-wide activities in competition with much larger companies. This book is an attempt to investigate how SMEs organize their international activities, and to reveal the underlying rationale in this form of organization. This effort leads to drawing some central implications for theory as well as for managerial practice.

Collaboration is a central aspect of SMEs internationalization, as well as in the making of this book. I would like to thank everybody who has helped me writing it. Especially, I will mention Professor Poul R. Christensen who has been a major supporter of this work and who has backed me up throughout the entire research and writing process, Ph.D. students and professors at Uppsala University, who have also been extremely supportive. Finally, my father who has functioned as critical reader and corrected my worst grammatical blunders.

Last but not least my family has cheered me up and borne over with me in my manic as well as in my moody periods. I therefore dedicate this book to Kirsten and our daughter Emma.

Poul Houman Andersen

Spring 1995

CHAPTER 1
Introduction

In terms of size and company-controlled resources, the structure of Danish industry has generally been seen as inferior in a world of increasing globalization and large-scale advantages. Economists and business theorists agree that, in order to achieve efficient forms of exchange, an international competitive position requires substantial direct foreign investments in both production and marketing. Since successful international activity is linked to achieving "critical mass", the internatio-nalization of firms is simultaneously equated with organizational growth (Forsgren & Johanson, 1992). Firms are expected to follow a specific path of investment, in which they gradually increase their international engagement by building up managerial competences and internalizing value-adding activities (Johanson & Vahlne, 1977 & 1990).

Chapter one will take a closer look at these axioms concerning the organization of international engagement. The first section explains the rationale for regarding SMEs as a specific type of firm. This is followed by an overview of the literature on the internationalization of the economy and the expected impact on the competitive-ness of Danish small and medium-sized enterprises (SMEs). Next, this is compared with the economic situation of these companies. This overview leads to a discussion of the internationalization theory underpinning the debate. Finally, the chapter presents the aims of the present thesis.

1. SMEs: Distinctive Characteristics

The persistent interest of theorists and politicians in SMEs implies that they constitute a special phenomenon. Scholars have emphasized that small firms differ from large ones and should not be analysed or discussed according to the same concepts (Brytting, 1991; Dandrigde, 1979). In spite of this interest, the concept of SMEs is still only vaguely defined, and it is not possible to find any universal agreement on the specific qualities of SMEs and how these should be distinguished from large enterprises (LEs). An investigation of the literature underlies the situation-dependent and eclectic nature of existing definitions (Davidson, 1991). In order to justify the special interest in small firms vis-à-vis large ones, however, we must first be clear about how SMEs differ from LEs. The purpose of this section is to present some of the traditional definitions, and indicate how SMEs differ from large enterprises from the perspective of the present study.

SMEs are often defined in quantitative terms, most commonly by number of employees[1]. The problem with quantitative definitions, however, is that they tend to overlook the unique features of SMEs. The idea of "Small" versus "Large" enterprises implies a relativity. But firms are not small or large independent of their context. One way of illustrating this is by comparing the definitions of SMEs and LEs in various European countries and the EEC Commission:

---

[1]   Other definitions include turnover (Christensen 1981) and fixed assets (EEC, 1991).

Table 1.1: Various definitions of SMEs and LEs (no. of employees)

Country	SME	LE
Denmark	0 - 99	≥100
EEC	0 - 499	≥500
Finland	0 - 499	≥500
France	0 - 499	≥500
Sweden	0 - 199	≥200
United Kingdom	0 - 199	≥200

As table 1.1 shows, there is considerable disagreement between the definitions commonly used, irrespective of whether the country is a member of the EU or not. These differences are also evident in industries where the size distribution varies greatly. Since the present study concerns Danish firms, and takes a starting point in the Danish discussion of these firms' future prospects in the perspective of a widening world economy, the Danish definition of SMEs will be used here.

Based solely on the above definitions, it is doubtful whether SMEs can be isolated as a distinctive type of firm. A number of other characteristics distinguish the two types of firms, however. Firstly, LEs have an elaborate formal structure which influences both the employer-employee relationship and the decision-making process. A formal structure is the framework for the division of responsibility, and also influences the allocation of resources. Resources are thus allocated on different terms in large firms than in small firms, since the claim on resources is legitimized through other channels and is unaffected by the institutions which are normally associated with lending and borrowing capital. Moreover, LEs are active in other markets than SMEs, e.g. the stock market. This also influences the organization of activity, as described by scholars focusing on the long- and short-term interests of stock market capitalists. Meyer & Rowan (1977) have emphasized that myths of rationality penetrate large firms through the medium of managerial professions, forcing these to act in unequivocal ways in order to legitimize their existence in the eyes of the institutions on which they depend (Dimaggio & Powell, 1983; Chandler,

1977). LEs are managed by people trained to recognize organizational problems from an administrative point of view and frame problems accordingly.

By comparison, managers of SMEs tend to represent themselves more than their organization. To a larger extent, therefore, SMEs can also be seen as an extension of the personality of the manager/entrepreneur (Johanisson, 1988). This also means that SMEs tend more to follow the objectives of the manager than market-driven demands. As several authors have pointed out, therefore, autonomy and other existential objectives are more likely to be found on the business agenda in SMEs than in LEs (Gouldner, 1958; Brytting, 1991; Borch, 1992). This has ramifications for the organization of economic activity in and among SMEs. If efficiency is no longer the single dominant objective of the firm, then many of the traditional managerial concepts and doctrines in the business literature are either obsolete or misplaced. There is therefore clearly a need to study the business practices of this type of firm.

2. The Internationalization of the World Economy and the Competitiveness of SMEs

Directly or indirectly, internationalization is a major issue in the public debate, and is discussed in relation to a wide range of other issues. National borders no longer separate human activities to the extent they used to, and international events increasingly influence everyday life. Civil war, immigration, and pollution are all examples of issues which are increasingly treated as global problems rather than the problems of separate nation-states. The development of international business reflects this. The conduct of international business is facilitated by increasing numbers of agreements on cross-border flows of people, goods and capital. To illustrate the interrelatedness of the world economy, the Uruguay round of the GATT is expected to result in a global growth of 4.5 per cent of GP (DRI, 1993). This is also underlined by the increasing number of direct foreign investments and the growing interrelation of production systems, as intra-industry trade between firms in global trade and supply networks increases (OECD 1992, 1993).

Researchers in the field of international business generally agree that increased internationalization will primarily benefit large companies. Within the EU, the removal of trade barriers is predicted to have a profound influence on the structure of European industry (Quelch et al., 1990; Bradley, 1991), leading to a competitive shake-out and the dominance of large companies. The argumentation is more or less as follows: The removal of trade barriers will increase the benefits of large-scale production and hence increase the competitive strength of major firms, as opposed to nationally-oriented producers. No longer able to operate in protected markets, these firms will become competitively inferior. By analogy with Darwin's theory of the survival of the fittest, increased competition is expected to transform the structure of industry into one of large enterprises, competing on a global, rather than a local, scale. The superiority of LEs is mainly related to their possession of resources, since it is especially these firms which have the means for investing in research and development and for influencing exchange activities through ownership rather than market control. Thus, the opening of the internal market, "Europe 92", is expected to lead to a consolidation, in which

> *"manufacturing and distribution activities are being combined into fewer, larger facilities [and] industries are becoming more concentrated, and will become more so via mergers and acquisitions."*(Quelch et al., 1990, p.62-63)

2.1 Scenarios of the impact of increased competition on the structure of Danish industry

Since Denmark has an open economy and is also a member of the EU, this development will naturally have a considerable impact on the structure of Danish industry. As shown in table 1.2 below, the size of Danish firms reveals an industrial structure heavily dependent on small production units, and in which only a few firms control large resources. This is also reflected in the average assets controlled by each firm (Finansredegørelsen 1992, 1993). As measured by the amount of company-controlled resources, therefore, most Danish firms must be considered as resource-weak.

Table 1.2: Distribution of firms and production units by number of employees		
Number of employees	Number of firms, in per cent	Number of production units, in per cent
6-19	47,9	48,6
20-99	39,7	40,8
100-200	6,0	6,0
200-500	3,7	3,6
> 500	1,7	1,2

Source: OECD1993

As seen from table 1.2, Denmark has only a few large firms. Compared with similar-sized economies, such as The Netherlands and Sweden, the size composition is remarkable. Moreover, most Danish firms are in industries characterized by mature technologies and small growth potential. This has led some academics to predict a gloomy future for Denmark as an industrial nation. We will address some of these predictions in the following.

According to Rasmussen et al. (1988), Danish industry is facing problems in the internal market, due to the lack of large industries which can act as engines of growth. The small size of Danish industry is a problem, because no single investor has the capacity to invest in basic research. (See also Rasmussen, 1993.) Moreover, most research carried out in Danish industry is related to product innovation rather than new inventions, which the authors call "defensive R&D" (Rasmussen et al., 1988, p. 23). Furthermore, they claim that:

> "A number of the most important Danish firms are in what can be labelled a 'danger zone' - that is, they do not have the necessary size and position in their respective market to compete internationally. They miss the necessary 'critical mass'." (Rasmussen et al., op. cit., p.48)

It is therefore to be expected that several Danish firms with international potential will be taken over by foreign investors, thus placing the locus of decision-making outside Denmark.

Other reports take into consideration the weak position of SMEs as regards growing international competition. Rasmussen (1991) foresees that:

> *"Many small and medium-sized firms in Denmark risk being outdone in the coming years, due to an increasingly competitive international business climate and a weak economic situation. This especially holds for the approximately 3.500 companies with a staff between 20 and 200 .. The small and medium-sized firms in the Danish industry holds great expectations to the formation of the '92 internal market. Unfortunately, these companies' ability to meet the intensified competition on domestic and foreign markets related to the removal of trade barriers is questionable."*
> (Rasmussen, 1991, p.2)

Apart from firms' lack of critical mass, which affects their ability to compete, both in terms of scale (e.g. production) and scope (e.g. R&D), firms also lack international competence, which mainly relates to their choice of mode of international operation (Strandskov et al., 1988; Rasmussen, 1991). Surveys have shown that the greater part of the international turnover of Danish firms is generated either through direct exports or via foreign intermediaries (Strandskov, 1987; DTI, 1991). The distribution of export versus market entry modes is illustrated in figure 1.1.

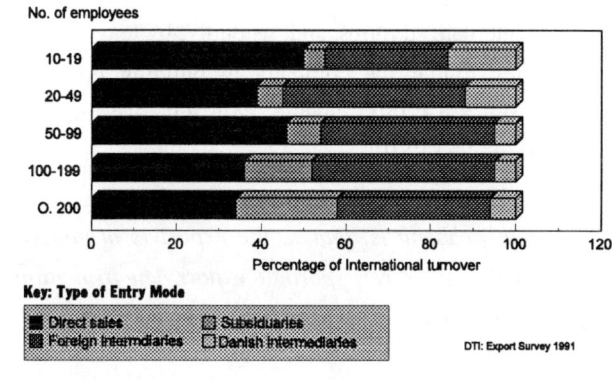

Figure 1.1: Various channels of International distribution according to firm size

The inferiority of Danish SMEs is especially associated with exportation as a mode of international operation. Organizing international activity through exportation

15

indicates insufficient international orientation. There are two main reasons for this. Firstly, through this mode, the firm lacks the possibility for controlling its market operations, since transactions are governed by the market mechanism. Secondly, leaving sales in the hands of exporters reduces direct market contact, and with it the possibilities to achieve international competence (Strandskov et al., 1988; Rasmussen 1991). With the growing competitiveness of the international business environment, these factors are increasing in importance. The relationship of this increasing competitiveness to the organization of international activity has received much attention in the literature.

Strandskov et al. (1988) argue that, with the increasingly sophisticated nature of demand, international markets are changing in character. Consequently, immaterial parameters such as product design and brand names are increasing in importance. This also means that the locus of power within the value-adding chain is moving towards organizations responsible for downstream activities, such as distribution, marketing and services. Thus: *"It is becoming necessary for the firm to escort the product a longer way to the end-user"* (Strandskov et al., 1988, p.8). The bulk of the international activities of Danish firms is still organized through traditional exportation modes, however, which is considered inadequate in light of the coming international competition. This is because there is little control over the functions responsible for marketing and services. Firstly, intermediaries are seen as being less controllable than internalized forms, and, secondly, by leaving this function to other organizations, they hinder the company in building up its own international competence. Rasmussen (1991) concurs with this, especially with regard to the international activities of SMEs, and adds:

> *"The main problem is, that ... the export is organized through foreign agents or through direct sporadic export. The firm gains consequently no important international skills."* (Rasmussen 1991)

The general conclusion of these reports is that the international competitive environment of the future will benefit those large-scale, vertically integrated companies, which are able to take advantage of diminishing entry barriers, such as those associated with the establishment of the EU's internal market. Consequently, international development will put SMEs and the Danish economy at a disadvantage. This is emphasized by Rasmussen as follows:

> *"Many SMEs in Denmark risk being outdone in the coming years, due to a strongly increasing international competitive climate and a weak financial position. This especially holds for the approximately 3.500 companies with a staff between 20 and 200, which forms the Danish industrial underwood."* (op.cit., p.2)

2.2 Beyond the internal market: The competitive situation of Danish SMEs

Despite the above discussion, international developments have yet to yield the expected effects in major areas of industry. Hand in hand with a steady consolidation of the Danish economy, including an annual balance of trade surplus for the past 8 years, the number of firms with less than 500 employees and the ratio of SMEs to total employment has increased. (Finansredegørelsen, 1992; Erhvervs-redegørelsen, 1993)

This growth can hardly be explained by the existence of a protected home market. On the contrary, with only five million inhabitants, Denmark is a small market for most companies, and exports are therefore necessary in order to achieve and maintain a sufficient turnover. In addition, one of the world's highest taxes on personal income, combined with a generally restrictive financial policy (nicknamed the "potato diet"), has depressed both private and public demand for more than five years. In spite of this, it can be shown that SMEs are actively engaged in the international division of labour. This is illustrated in figure 1.2, where both private and public production is distributed according to the cross-border component of inbound and outbound activities.

Export-import Relations
in Danish production

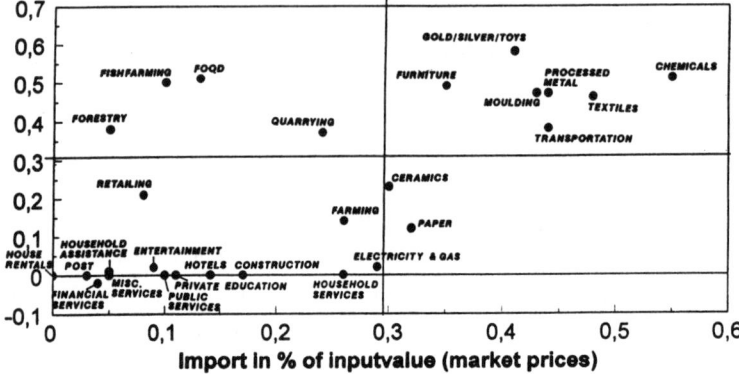

Export percentage of production value (basic value)

Import in % of inputvalue (market prices)

Figure 1. 2: Distribution of Danish industry according to particiption in the international division of labour (1989 figures)

Figure 1.2 illustrates the way in which Danish firms participate in the international division of labour. Three groups can be distinguished: (1) The lower-left segment contains industries whose output is not directly exportable. These are the service industries, such as restaurants and hotels, education and household services. Also included in this group are industries whose products or services are strictly national, such as producers of government services, including communication; (2) The upper-left segment contains firms with a high degree of outbound activity based on country-specific production factors. These industries include: forestry, fishing, and food and beverage manufacturers; (3) The upper-right segment contains firms actively engaged in international activity with respect to both inbound and outbound activities. These industries include textiles, timber products, chemicals, and manaufacturers of fabricated metal products, such as machines. These companies are characterized by a heavy engagement in the international division of labour, both as regards incoming and outgoing activities.

On average, Danish manufacturing exporters imported almost 36 per cent of their production value in 1988. These imports were not only due to the lack of natural

18

resources, however. Almost 70 per cent of Danish imports consist of semi-manufactured goods competing or supplementing national production. This suggests a strong international orientation on the supply side.

As figure 1.2 shows, those industries most heavily engaged in importation are also those which have the highest ratio of exports to total output. Furthermore, as shown in table 1.3, these industries are dominated by SMEs.

Table 1.3: Importance and internationalization of SMEs in selected industries (1991)			
Manufacturing industries	Average no. of employees **)	SME -% (SME < 200) *)	% of total industrial employment *)
Chemical Industry	56.8	87%	9%
Iron, Metal, Machinery	40.8	90%	43%
Textile, Clothing	26.7	97%	6%
Furniture	27.4	97%	9%
Paper, Printing	23.3	93%	8%

Source.: *) OECD (1993); **) DTI 1991

Industries such as the furniture and textile industries and producers of metal products have been able to win market shares in OECD countries despite the general maturity and recession of these markets, which, according to traditional product-life-cycle arguments, should support scale advantages, and hence capital-intensive firms (Erhvervsredegørelsen, 1993).

The success of SMEs as exporters, despite economic integration, suggests that our knowledge of the organization of international activity in these firms, and how it is affected by the growing internationalization, is limited. In the following pages, this will be examined from the point of view of the theory of the organization of international activity.

3. Internationalization Theory - An overview of selected schools

While the internationalization of economic activity is a major topic within the field of business studies, there is little agreement on the content, what should be studied, and on which grounds. The field has developed in line with the shifting focus on various issues, and contains numerous perspectives. Consequently, the concept of internationalization is fuzzy and ill-defined (Forsgren, 1989; Strandskov, 1994). According to Welch and Loustarinen (1988), internationalization *"roughly describes the outward movement in an individual firm's or a larger grouping's international operations"*.

Internationalization theory can hardly be called a well-organized discipline. Rather, it can be characterized as "confusing, pluralistic and non-integrating" (Hawkins, 1984). However, as pointed out by Strandskov (1994), this may, in fact, be typical of young scientific disciplines in which specific theories have not yet come to dominate the field. Notwithstanding, three theoretical schools, mainly inspired by economic theory, play an important role and have also supplied most of the underlying assumptions of the above debate. These schools are:

- ◆ Transaction Cost Economics
- ◆ Strategic Competition
- ◆ Organizational Learning

The following presents a brief outline of these theories. A more detailed description of contributions and concepts is given in chapter 9.

3.1 Transaction Cost Economics
In seeking to develop a theory of the existence of exchange structures, such as firms, within the general theoretical framework of equilibrium economics, institutional economists are inspired by neoclassical economists . These scholars attempt to explain the organization of activity from an economic perspective.

In transaction cost theory, the organization of market entry is commonly discussed as entry modes. Root (1987, p.5) defines an entry mode as *"An institutional arrangement that makes possible the entry of a company's products and other resources into a foreign country"*. From this point of view, organizing international activity consists in the development of an entry mode which organizes international transactions most efficiently (Buckley & Casson, 1976). The analytical unit is the single transaction, and the focus is on the factors which inhibit the emergence of specific exchange structures for their control and coordination. Williamson (1975, 1981) calls these **governance structures**. In situations of perfect competition, the market is assumed to be the most efficient interface for conducting transactions, since, overall, the invisible hand of the market mechanism results in the most beneficial allocation of resources. The premises for perfect competition are often corrupted, however, which results in market failure. Scholars distinguish between three generic types of entry mode, divided according to management's relative possibility to extend ownership-based control (and therefore to suffer ownership-based risk): Export entry modes, Contractual Entry modes, and Direct Entry Modes (Porter, 1985; Root, 1987). The efficiency of these transaction modes depends on the relative degree of market failure, which in turn depends on such factors as small-numbers bargaining, complexity, opportunism, and bounded rationality (Williamson, 1975). This general framework has been used by several authors (Anderson & Gatignon, 1986; Klein et al., 1990; Hennart, 1986; Ried, 1983).

An increase in any one of these factors will increase the likelihood of opportunistic behaviour, and thus constitutes an inducement to internalize transactions. Since conducting international activities must be considered a relatively more complex task than doing business in the domestic market, international activities are expected to have a propensity towards internalization.

In short, internationalization - as a process - can be described as the successive adjustment of institutional modes resulting from a development in the factors causing market failure (Andersen & Gatignon, 1986; Hansen, 1990; Hennart, 1986). From a transaction cost perspective, Hansen (1990) briefly describes internationalization as the change from externalization to internalization, through which the assessment and control of market transactions are transformed into the control and assessment of hierarchical transactions.

3.2 Organizational Learning

The focus of organizational learning is the management process and the factors influencing managerial decision-making. The fundamental assumption of this theoretical framework is based on the behavioural theory of organization associated with Simon & March (1958). Management is considered boundedly rational due to the limited mental capacity of decision-makers. Adjustment to environmental conditions is limited by the mental capacities of human perception, and managers' choices are based on their mental model of the situation. As managers are not capable of calculating optimal solutions, they attempt to make satisfactory decisions aimed at achieving results above a certain level of aspiration. Management is therefore characterized by risk-reducing rather than profit-maximizing behaviour. The nature of managerial judgement is the outcome of several factors, relating to both personal and organizational characteristics. These may change, however, due to individuals' and organizations' ability to memorize and learn through experience, and programme this experience into their behaviour (March & Simon, 1958).

From this perspective, internationalization is seen by the so-called Uppsala school as a process of knowledge development and increasing foreign market commitment. Johanson & Vahlne (1977 & 1990) see managers as boundedly rational. Since international activity takes place under unfamiliar environmental conditions (as opposed to the home market), conducting business in foreign countries is perceived as risky. Commitment to foreign market activities is contingent on the perception of uncertainty, and the resource commitment is usually low during the early stages of internationalization. As the internationalization process moves forward, management gathers knowledge and increases its experience of foreign market conditions, which again leads to a reduction of perceived uncertainty. Reduced uncertainty contributes towards perceptions of business opportunities, thus encouraging commitment decisions. This again speeds up the process of internationalization. This pattern describes internationalization as a sequential process - it is the result of a series of incremental decisions, or "small steps". Thus, two patterns of internationalization behaviour can be observed: a) international market expansion, and b) organizational development. Internationalization proceeds via a) towards markets with successively greater psychic distance (Slipsager, 1969; Vahlne & Wiedersheim-Paul, 1973), and, consequently, increasingly heterogeneous business environments. But internationalization also proceeds via b) as an increasing commitment of resources in support of international business activity, following the successive pattern of an *establishment chain*. The establishment chain expresses the gradual change in organizational structure towards increasing internationalization. Since internationalization and organizational learning are intimately linked, the phases may be seen as a consequence of the relation between experience gathering and resource commitment. No actual commitment is made in the initial stages of internationalization, and international activity is conducted on an ad hoc basis on the initiative of foreign customers. The experience gained from these orders leads to a more active search for international business opportunities. However, since the company is still unexperienced, and therefore also highly ambiguous about foreign business, this activity is entrusted to someone who "knows the ropes" (Hymer, 1976), i.e. an independent intermediary. Both domestic and foreign intermediaries are used in the early stages of internationalization, where risk perception is high and market knowledge low. By using intermediaries, the exporter can gain access to knowledge resources not found within the organization. As the firm develops international competence, uncertainty is reduced, thus allowing a larger resource commitment. Now, however, with a larger and larger share of turnover being generated from exports, the intermediary is increasingly seen as providing superficial information about market conditions, hindering the direct flow of information. Consequently, the firm replaces intermediaries with ownership-controlled sales subsidiaries, thus extending organizational operations to foreign markets as well. This in turn allows for closer market contact and increases the development of international competence. Finally, as more and more knowledge is accumulated about factor markets, sales subsidiaries are supplemented with foreign production facilities. This marks the final stage of organizational development according to the Uppsala model.

3.3 Strategic Competition

This perspective focuses on the underlying economic structure which determines business conditions within a task environment, such as an industry. Inspired by industrial economics, the strategic competition perspective attempts to explain the structure and performance of industries from their structural conditions (Bain, 1958; Porter, 1980, 1985). Another source of inspiration is the contingency school of organization theory, as represented by Chandler (1962) and Lawrence & Lorsch (1967), who have explained the internal organization of firms from an environment-strategy-structure point of view. Following this, organizations adapt to their environment through strategy. Organizational strategy is thus a reflection of environmental conditions, an effort by management to achieve the proper "fit" between the organization and external conditions, in which competitive conditions play a chief role.

Central to the explanation of the competitive situation are the forces which narrow or broaden the competitive scope within an industry. Since several of these forces relate to the nation-state (e.g. legislative conditions, political factors, language, taxation, etc.), this perspective offers a framework for understanding the development of international business conditions, and how changes in these conditions encourage or hinder specific forms of international organization.

Several factors related to the internationalization of the task environment of companies can be identified. Levitt (1983) and Ohmae (1987) have pointed to the universalization of consumer tastes as a factor expected to lever a large-scale marketing economy. The penetration rate of mass media such as radio, television and newspapers in both the OECD and the NICs is creating an information structure for global marketing communication, which is leading to increasingly homogeneous consumer preferences. Quelch et al. (1990) have focused on the removal of trade barriers as a factor contributing to advantages of both scale and scope. The harmonization of trade and legal conditions reduces the diversity of international market conditions, which further spurs the development of international activities. Other writers, such as Ohmae (1987), have focused on the period in which inventions give firms a competitive advantage. If inventions are only short-lived, the payback of R&D investment must be achieved through a simultaneous product launch in several companies, leading to an increasingly rapid international expansion. Ohmae also points to the increased productivity arising from the capital-intensive automatization of plants. Such plants also demand rapid internationalization in order to pay back investments, however.

In general, the internationalization of competitive conditions is expected to benefit large companies, since these possess the resources required both to overcome the disadvantages and exploit the advantages of the new rules in global competition.

24

According to Douglas & Craig (1989), these advantages are related to at least three types of economies:

i) Economies of scale are achieved when investments are made in specialized, capital-intensive plants which reduce production unit costs, and which are only economic with a sufficient "market mass", which is realized as markets are internationalized. Uniform marketing advantages are another type of advantage related to scale economies.

ii) Economies of scope concern the possibilities of broadening the use of administrative resources and utilizing these in different task environments, such as international product launch, thus spreading administrative costs across a comparatively larger sales volume.

iii) Synergetic economies relate to the effects of attaining and distributing increased know-how developed in various national contexts, through learning curve effects.

The forces of change outlined above are expected to transform the industry structure into larger integrated resource units, either through mergers and acquisitions or through close collaboration in strategic alliances or joint ventures in such activities as procurement, R&D, production, etc.

3.4 Summary: Theoretical Influences on Industrial Policy

The influence of the various theoretical perspectives on the debate concerning the international activities of Danish firms is relatively clear. Moreover, these perspectives are complementary, in the sense that their underlying assumptions concerning the nature of firms and markets are similar. The contention is that firms are rational optimizers, and that markets are driven by the forces of instrumental utilitarianism. While the firm is perceived as being intendedly - but only to a limited extent from an organizational learning point of view - it does not change the basic notion of firms as seeking to optimize the allocation of resources, given the constraints of the human mind. Humans are intendedly rational, but only to a limited extent (Simon 1948).

The common assumptions of the above perspectives can be outlined as follows:

- Internationalization as organizational evolution in objectively defined environments
- Firms as solitary decision units
- Ownership structure as a reflection of authority structure

There is general support from all perspectives for the first point, which sees internationalization as organizational evolution or growth, achieved by internalizing competencies and extending organizational boundaries to include the control of coordination of activities across national borders. In relation to this, the firm is seen as an independent unit allocating resources in isolation. In addition, control and coordination are expected to follow lines of formal authority, underpinned by ownership. The command and ownership structures are expected to co-variate, since they express both the arena and the principle of the allocation of resources in the organization of activity (Imai & Itami, 1984).

The main question is: Do these assumptions provide any clues for understanding the organization and development of international activity in Danish SMEs? This will be discussed below by means of a framework for understanding SMEs as business organizers, and comparing these with the above assumptions. As will be shown, several studies suggest that the business reality of Danish SMEs diverges radically from the theoretical assumptions outlined here, and, in the case of SMEs, the organization of international activity must start with some radically different assumptions of such phenomena as firms and markets.

4. Main characteristics of SMEs as international business organizers

The organizational characteristics of SMEs have been the subject of various studies. These have characterized SMEs as entrepreneurial and flexible, and depending heavily on their external relations (Brytting, 1991; Mønsted, 1985). Such studies are not sufficient, however, as they normally take place in a social vacuum, considering these characteristics as universal. But it is also important to include the socioeconomic institutions in which this activity takes place. This approach especially stresses the interdependence of economic activity and social institutions. Economic relations are increasingly seen as embedded in social structures (Granovetter, 1985; Meyer & Rowan, 1977). Scholars are looking more and more at the socially constructed nature of markets as well as firms, by stressing the importance of institutionalized roles and world views in structuring and legitimizing specific patterns of organization (DiMaggio & Powell, 1991; Whitley, 1992; Graheber, 1992).

SMEs play an important, and growing, role in the Danish economy. At the end of the 1980s, SMEs with 6-499 employees accounted for 78% of total employment. SMEs also have a major share of the total of value added Danish production. As such, most Danish manufacturing industries are dominated by companies with fewer than 200 employees.

The size distribution shown is similar to that of other European countries like The Netherlands and Italy, with the crucial difference that, compared with other European countries, Denmark has only a few large firms. Furthermore, firms with more than 500 employees are, on average, smaller than similar firms in both Italy and The Netherlands. This has a major effect on intra-industrial competition and collaboration, as well as on the institutional settings developed.

The internationalization of the Danish industrial structure seems to be characterized by two main features: a small home market, and a small-scale-oriented supportive infrastructure.

Due to the small size of both the resource base and the home market, Danish companies are quickly exposed to international competition with regard to the procurement of production factors and the generation of sufficient demand. This relation between the size of the home market and the internationalization of SMEs has been confirmed in a recent study (UN, 1993).

As regards output conditions, the possibilities of generating sufficient turnover in Denmark are limited, not least for highly specialized products. Limitations of the home market thus encourages international expansion. This is reflected by

27

developments in the furniture industry. In 1988, the domestic market absorbed 47 per cent of manufacturers' output; in 1992, this had fallen to 35 per cent. The consequences of a limited domestic market are reflected in the fact that the exports of new furniture manufacturers started between 1985-1989 amounted on average to more than DKK 163,000 during their first year of existence (Industri- & Handels-styrelsen, 1992).

Specialization in production is a major competitive parameter used by SMEs. A lack of internal resources tends to make them specialize and rely on their own capacity to build up relations with external actors. SMEs are thus engaged in an extensive division of labour. They participate in several business activities by using their competencies in various resource chains. One main vehicle of support is contact with other SMEs. As such, SMEs extensively use and are used as subcontractors. This creates a high degree of interwovenness in the industry, in which organizational boundaries are crossed by means of shared skills, mutual knowledge, and patterns of interaction. The competencies of SMEs are developed in close interaction with other firms. This pattern is also evident in SMEs involved in direct foreign investments, where SMEs have a stronger propensity to engage in joint ventures and other forms of collaborative arrangements than LEs.

The lack of large-scale engines of industrial growth also contributes to the special business conditions in the Danish economy. In contrast to subcontractors in other countries, Danish SMEs probably depend less on their ability as vendors to larger firms - what has been described as arm´s length relationships and zero-sum games. The advantages of "strategic networks" thus accrue to hub firms, at the expense of more peripheral firms, through arm´s length relations and competitive manufac-turing. Porter (1983) has described these mechanisms at length in a study of the automobile industry. On the other hand, Danish SMEs often depend on a host of relations to other SMEs. Subcontracting thus takes place in an atmosphere of interdependence, which increases the mutual orientation of the companies in terms of shared knowledge, willingness to interact, etc. Therefore, the exchange environment in small-business interaction is characterized by collaboration and mutual trust.

4.1 Consequences for research on SME internationalization

Compared with the assumptions of current internationalization theory, it seems that Danish SMEs diverge radically from the norm. Firstly, since the firm is dependent on external relations, managerial action largely takes place within a collective frame. In other words, management is expected to take the path of collaboration rather than direction. As advocated by Christensen (1991):

> *"The export start and the expansion process are not only a task of directing and coordinating internal resources of the exporting firm. To a very high extent, it is also a task of finding, committing, directing, coordinating and evaluating external resources in favour of export activity."* (Christensen, 1991, p. 63)

This implies that, in the case of SMEs, internationalization is a collective venture of development, in which the international position of the individual decision unit depends on its position in a business network. The implication is that internationalization should be seen more as a process of change than one of automatic evolution (Strandskov, 1994).

Moreover, this point of view gives subjective and collective roles and trajectories developed over time a decisive role in determining how international activity should be carried out in small firms. As implied by the nature of exchange activity between SMEs described above, international business activity can be expected to have a more "thick" and interactive nature than that implied by the theoretical perspectives and research studies reviewed so far. These relationships give a picture of collaborative development (Christensen, 1992), and are characterized by an organizational, rather than a market mode (Imai & Itami, 1984). Furthermore, through the generation of expected behaviour, these relationships may even prove to be superior to authority relations in discouraging malfeasance and hindering market failure (Grannovetter, 1985; Thorelli, 1986).

Most business theories implicitly assume that growth is the basic driving force of business activity. Firms are defined by means of ownership, and their basic function is to optimize economic rent, in competition with other owners of capital. All business activity, including internationalization, is therefore conceived as actions directed towards achieving organizational development in terms of developing internal resources. Since information on foreign markets is not free, they cannot function optimally, and international markets are therefore characterized by market failure. An important prerequisite of international growth is thus the development of internal competencies to overcome perceived market barriers.

The assumption of universal development paths for firms has been challenged on several points. It has been argued that it is not possible to generalize company heuristics, since these very much depend on the context of the firm (Ried, 1983; Whitley, 1991). "Firms" and "markets" are not universal mechanisms, where behaviour can be decided on the ground of external contingencies. Rather, both markets and firms are embedded in social structures such as traditions and other types of market institutions.

The deterministic flavour of the assumption behind internationalization theory can also be questioned. By regarding internationalization as a process following a specific path, little room is left to managerial decision-making. However, this underemphasizes the role of managerial and strategic choice in deciding the development of the company (Child, 1972). It seems an unrealistic assumption to regard managerial action to achieve the proper fit between firm and environment as nothing more than a response to internal or external contingencies. Managers are known to take chances, and to decide according to their interpretation of the situation, or in their own self-interest (Aharoni, 1966). The mechanistic relation between knowledge-gathering and international organization also seems to be an oversimplification.

In addition, identifying internationalization with organizational growth risks a circular argumentation, since the lack of organizational growth becomes equal to the lack of international orientation. International orientation in resource commitment may also take other forms, however, depending on the choices made by management. Therefore, internationalization does not necessarily follow a predefined order of gradual extension of organizational boundaries across national borders.

Another implicit assumption is that the environment is objectively given and defined by forces outside the organization. In other words, firms adapt to environmental conditions and play no role in defining them. Scholars criticize the idea of business environments as existing objectively, however (Pfeffer & Salancick, 1978). Environments are not "out there" in any physical sense, and they cannot be unequivocally defined independently of the decision-maker. Rather, environments are interpreted by decision-makers (Weick, 1979), or negotiated with interest groups (Pfeffer & Salancick, 1978; Cyert & March, 1963; Astley, 1984). Consequently, through processes of interpretation and action, the firm plays an active role in defining its environment.

The perspectives discussed above regard firms as independent decision units, acting in anonymous environments. The firm is defined though its ownership-controlled resources, over which it has exclusive rights. This implies a sharp boundary between what belongs inside and outside the organization. This firm/market dichotomy is questionable, however, as the present research on Danish SMEs shows.

5. The topic

Following the lines of the business system developed above, it is to be expected that, in the case of Danish SMEs, internationalization is characterized by a large degree of both externalization, coordination and configuration, through which the SMEs organize their activities. International business can be seen as an activity carried out by an international resource chain of specialized companies, which, through their joint activity, manufacture, distribute and administer - in short, organize the activity. Far from being organizational structures characterized by stability, present research paints a picture of SMEs as involved in an ongoing process of complex interaction between independent, but also interdependent, firms. In view of the extent of international activity which SMEs are involved in, this seems to function relatively well. Moreover, several SMEs have achieved a certain position in international markets, reflecting some sort of international competitive advantage. The interesting question is how this has been achieved.

The international organization of activity reflects a channel of value added in which various flows are dispatched and activities concluded through the co-alignement of functional units. This co-alignement of activity essentially reflects an international division of labour between several functional units. All units participating in the activities associated with the flow of goods and services can be integrated within the boundaries of a single firm with foreign sales subsidiaries, as in international firms, or organized by formally independent economic actors, as with exporters and intermediaries, or exporters and industrial customers or end-users.

The fulfilment of the channel flow continuously calls for some form of organization to combine the activities of dispersed actors into a concerted activity, which repeatedly dispatches commodities and/or services from producers to users. The purpose of the present investigation is to discover whether there are difficulties in using non-hierarchical means for organizing business activity, and how SMEs overcome the difficulties of organizing international activity. The investigation is thus primarily concerned with the organization of activity between organizations in different countries. Research questions related to this activity include: What are the mechanisms for configuring and integrating distinct resources in a feasible activity structure? How are coordination and control achieved? How are competencies established and developed in relation to the organization and development of international activity? **In short, this book is a study of the practices by which SMEs participate and develop their position in the international division of labour.**

Little is known about the organization and development of international activity between SMEs and foreign intermediaries beyond the descriptive level. The aim of this thesis is therefore to shed some light on this by studying the organization of international activity and the relations to foreign intermediaries.

The book is divided into three parts: Part I gives a preliminary understanding of the phenomenon based on a search of the literature; Part II consists of four case studies of SMEs and the organization of international activity in which they participate; Part III contains analyses of the assumptions in Part I and the four case studies.

The rationale behind the above structure is a methodological one. Thus, the paradigmatic standpoint of the thesis and the research strategy followed is given in chapter 2, which forms the groundwork of the dissertation. The present chapter (chapter 1) outlines the research topic and the background for the investigation. The theoretical framework described in chapter 3 specifies the assumptions underlying the field study, and, at the same time, constructs a theoretical language in which the findings of the field study can be expressed. The case studies in the following four chapters describe the development and business profile of an SME and how it participates in the organization of international activity. In chapter 8, the findings of the cases are compared with the conceptual framework presented in chapter 3. Finally, chapter 9 discusses the theoretical and managerial implications of the study.

CHAPTER 2

Methodological Considerations

Ever since the seminal work of Kuhn (1970) on the role of paradigms in science, it has been generally agreed that there are several "routes" for carrying out social research, depending on the paradigmatic stance of the researcher, and that theories and research strategies should be seen as parts of an overriding perspective. This means that data generation methods cannot be treated as a question of which "tools" to select from a "tool box" containing an array of techniques for handling qualitative or quantitative data (Smircich & Morgan, 1980). Some academic circles regard concern about the issue of methodology as exaggerated (Koch, 1993). Notwithstanding, ontological assumptions about the construction of the social world cannot be separated from speculations about how it should be systematically investigated.

In principle, methodological considerations are the most important part of conducting research. By deciding which methodological principles to follow, a number of other choices are also automatically made. The methodology contains the principles of the approach adopted in the study. It embraces the assumptions, purposes, expectations and dispositions of the research. It is also through methodology that the researcher relates his work to a scientific community and subjects it to the community's standards and traditions for conducting scientific research.

The choice of research strategy is a process of clarifying the interpretation of reality. In formulating a research strategy, the paradigm acts as the underlying guideline for what is considered 'useful' for creating knowledge. Since the choice of method is closely intertwined with the conception of reality, the choice of research strategy is not merely to define which method is the most appropriate in the specific context, but to clarify the implications of one's core beliefs to the investigative method used.

34

The purpose of this chapter is to present the paradigmatic basis of the present study and relate it to the interpretive tradition for conducting social science. One way of doing this is to place the study in relation to the meta-theoretical assumptions underlying the social sciences, which group researchers into specific scientific communities, research programmes, etc. This involves an excursion into the philosophy of science. While this may seem unwarranted at first, it can be justified by the fact that it serves a multitude of purposes for the present study. Firstly, an outline of the paradigmatic assumptions underlying the study explicitly expresses a point of view with which the reader may agree or disagree. Secondly, it relates the research to a specific scientific tradition, one with which its core assumptions are compatible, and against which the scientific quality of the study should be judged. At the same time, it distances the study from other scientific traditions which base their techniques and heuristics on entirely different assumptions.

1. The paradigm concept

The paradigm perspective was originally suggested by Kuhn (1970), who found scientific investigation clustered around specific ontological and epistemological assumptions which were taken for granted by scientists. These assumptions function as shared perspectives or tacit knowledge, and are not questioned in the scientific community. Paradigms can be defined as:

> *"Basic meta-theoretical assumptions, in relation to the nature of science and society."* (Astley & Van de Ven, 1983, p.246).

Basic assumptions are those which are not questioned in daily research activities, but which form a common ground of shared beliefs within a specific group of researchers. Together they form an interrelated and coherent approach to the area of inquiry. As such, paradigms determine which questions to ask, what a discipline should study, and which methods to apply. This is called "normal science" (Kuhn, 1970). In this sense, paradigms also have a social dimension, in that they connect the individual scientist with a particular scientific community (Fast, 1992; Andersen et al., 1992). A paradigm is therefore rooted in a social context. A research effort is not a simple interaction between a researcher, a research problem, theory, data, and a limited budget. The research society is not a democratic community, but a reputational system, in which there are several sources of power and authority (Whitley, 1989). The challenge therefore, is to discover the subtle (or tacit) relations between the social and the theoretical field. Theoretical choices have consequences for social affiliation in a community of scientists and vice versa.

1.1 Paradigms within the Social Sciences

According to Kuhn (op. cit.), a normal science paradigm rules until it is destroyed by inner contradictions, or new scientific breakthroughs challenge the assumptions on which the scientific results of the paradigm are based. It should be remembered, however, that Kuhn developed the concept through studies of the natural sciences.

The social sciences have been called multi-paradigmatical or a-paradigmatical, and it has been argued that it is impossible to find a single period of "normal science" in social science (Knudsen, 1984). In spite of this, business students have found the concept useful for disentangling the structural foundations of research contributions within a specific discipline.

The success of the paradigm concept within the social sciences may be due to the fact that the core assumptions, or meta-theoretical underpinning, of the field has been under debate ever since social studies, as a field, became "worthy" of scientific endeavour (Swedberg & Granovetter, 1992). The meta-theoretical assumptions of the social sciences have been debated with varying degrees of intensity throughout the 20th century. This debate received renewed attention after the introduction of the paradigm concept, which presented new opportunities for putting scientific investigation into perspective and creating an overview of scientific activities.

Within business studies, Burrell and Morgan's (1979) study of the sociological paradigms underlying organizational analysis has achieved widespread influence, and has also been adopted in studies of other disciplines (Morgan, 1980; Astley & Van de Ven, 1983). This suggests that the study's proposals have general merits for the study of business issues.

36

Burrell and Morgan (op. cit.) have established an overview of the philosophical basis of social science. Based on their analytical framework, two paradigms can be identified in the social sciences which especially relate to the field of business studies: The *functionalist* and the *interpretive* paradigm. These paradigms largely follow a fundamental debate which can be traced throughout the history of philosophy, namely whether any form of knowledge can be attained independent of the subjective individual. This has elsewhere been called the objective versus the subjective stance of social science (Schutz, 1970). These paradigms are juxtapositions of what can be regarded as valid assumptions in the production of science. This means that research which conforms to the scientific standards of one paradigm is unacceptable to the other.

The **Functionalist Paradigm** can be related to the positivist ideal of science, which has dominated business research for some time (Mintzberg, 1979). Positivist epistemology in the social sciences seeks to free the study of society from "mysticism". According to the positivist philosophy of science, the task of the scientist is to develop universal knowledge by observing reality without preconceptions. Positivists hope to establish guidelines which can guide the scientist through the epistemic fallacies of subjectivism to the objective, empirical world, and thus construct truths of the same consistency and durability as the laws of physics. This is achieved by adopting the same epistemological guidelines as those used in the natural sciences. Only that which can be observed and verified by others can be objective, and therefore scientific. The impact of subjective interpretations is reduced through rules of validity and reliability. What cannot be directly observed and verified is termed metaphysics, and is outside the realm of "pure" science.

Business research based on the **Interpretive Paradigm** is a recent phenomenon. The interpretive scientist believes that the social world cannot be studied on the same grounds as the natural sciences. The social world is constituted by human beings capable of reasoning, and their actions and interpretations are derived from complex patterns of reasoning.

The interpretive researcher starts from the ontological assumption that the social world, unlike the physical world, is socially constructed. Social reality evolves according to complex patterns of reasoning and meaning-giving. These patterns are partly individual and partly shared. Far from being static, they are constantly evolving and changing, through human action and interaction, as individuals take the actions of others into account, ascribe a specific meaning to them, and act accordingly.

> *"I determine a line of action, act overtly. The other (alter) acts overtly toward me, and I interpret what that act means (represents) ... We interpret each other and we communicate to the other, and the other, in turn, must interpret, communicate, and alter his or her action. This is a constant, never-ending process."* (Charon, 1989, p. 141)

The development of shared world views has been described by Berger & Luckmann (1966) as a process of converting subjective assumptions into collective constructions of institutionalized reality. Their framework, which is depicted below in figure 2.1, shows the transfer process of individually interpreted frames into collectively shared perspectives. According to Berger & Luckmann (op. cit.), this process takes place in four stages.

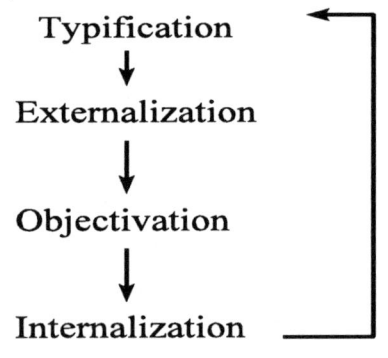

Figur 2.1: The Social Construction of Reality

Typification is the process of generating subjective knowledge, through typifying, or categorizing experiences as explained above. In categorizing events, actions relating to the typfication are also given. If for example, an export manager typifies the delayed response from an intermediary as a way signalling lack of interest toward his products or services, he may assign a set of activities accordingly.

38

Processes of organizing emanate from individual experience. Individual experiences are externalized symbolic interchange, or communication among a collection of individuals. Dialogues are communicative acts through which shared grammars emerge, as phenomena are labelled and the relation between a label and a phenomenon is enacted and more widely accepted. This is the process of **Externalization.** Externalization processes are collectively developed, and are shared by a larger group of individuals. Through externalization, the typification becomes collectively accepted: a legitimized term with a specific meaning which relates and fits into the existing organizational grammar; a part of an institutionalized reality belonging to a group of individuals. Grammar thus serves essentially as a code which ensures quick access to a shared definition of a situation, ascribing to it a specific pattern of activity or routine. Studies of organizational cultures have found rituals, symbols and artefacts to serve such communicative purposes (Morgan, 1986; Smircich, 1983).

Objectivation turns intersubjective typologies into social facts. They become part of a collective interpretive frame shared among a number of persons, called an organization, which can, for example, be a profession or a culture. The framing of reality influences, and is in turn influenced by, the meaning-shaping reality of an organization. In this sense, organizations are socially constructed institutions which construct individual conceptions of reality through processes of socialization. One example of this process was demonstrated in a study of economics students at Cornell University, where a proxy for "honesty" was used for measuring changes in perceptions among economics students at different points in their education. The results showed that students' conceptions of honesty changed according to their accommodation and their training in the interpretive schemes of economic theory (Frank, Gilovich & Regan, 1993).

Social reality can thus be pictured as an ever-changing field of force. The inner logic of a phenomenon only reveals itself to the researcher through interaction. Research must therefore be grounded in direct interaction with the phenomenon under study.

1.2 The functional versus the interpretive approach - an epistemological comparison

The ontological assumptions outlined above make it clear that the perspectives also diverge radically on epistemological assumptions.

According to the positivist foundation of the functional approach, social reality has an objective existence, which it is the task of the social sciences to reveal. The purpose of research is therefore to contribute to this stock of knowledge, either by verifying postulated cause-effect relations or by rejecting hypothesized assumptions derived from existing theory. Thus, verification plays a central role in the functionalistic approach.

Positivist philosophers have developed a set of premises which makes it possible to evaluate whether new findings can be validated as scientific results. Validity is ascertained through principles for collecting and analysing data, the purpose of which is to remove subjective bias from the results and ensure that the empirical data represents the population they are intended to. These guidelines are generally known as validity, reliability and representativity.

Validity is concerned with the truth of the findings, and whether they actually correspond to the reality they claim to portray. Validity is an overriding principle for ensuring the quality of research, and both the claim of representativity and reliability can be seen as tests of the validity of the research.

Representativity refers to whether the data sample has been taken from a population which reflects similar qualities to the population which the findings relate to, and the extent to which the findings can be generalized to other phenomena. Reliability means that the results can be replicated either by the researcher (intrasubjective reliability) or by other researchers (intersubjective reliability). However, this also means that researchers must restrict their investigations to what is measurable, and refrain from metaphysical speculation, since this includes the speculations and subjective interpretations of the researcher.

From an interpretive point of view, it is misleading to claim that social reality can be studied using guidelines similar to those of the natural sciences, and even an attempt to do this would be erroneous. The scientific ideal of the natural sciences relates to the study of objects incapable of reasoning. Humans reason, however, and their individual and collective actions reflect these patterns of reasoning. It is therefore impossible to detach any observable behaviour from the context of meaning which it relates to. Schutz (1970) has illustrated this through the example of anthropologists watching a tribal dance. What the anthropologists observe is behaviour, but this behaviour cannot be detached from the meaning it has for the dancers. Thus the dance could both symbolize a celebration of the coming of spring and a declaration of war. The study of social phenomena involves an act of interpretation, which is essentially subjective and therefore incompatible with positivistic claims of reliability. Furthermore, scholars from both the social and natural sciences have called for an "objective" stance on reality. Scholars contend that investigations are driven - and therefore also affected - by some form of intentionality. Thus, the study of any phenomenon is not independent of the theoretical framework in which it is studied. Therefore it is essentially misleading to discuss the empirical and the theoretical world as two separate spheres.

While interpretive social research acknowledges the researcher as indivisible from the research object, validity obviously has another meaning than just to ensure universal truth. In departing from the correspondence criterion of truth associated with the positivist ideal of science, therefore, validity becomes context-specific. The purpose of investigation within the interpretive approach is to develop a theoretical language to capture and comprehend complex social phenomena, and to communicate this language to others in order to enhance their understanding of their situation and its possibilities (Brunsson, 1981). The construction of a language is thus more important than the verification of findings. This does not mean that there are no quality requirements for the development of theoretical languages, however. The validity of the research relates to how well it is capable of generating useful theory, as seen from the community's interest in the research. Scholars therefore speak of communicative validity as a central claim of scientific investigation (Giddens, 1984; Kvale, 1989). As expressed by Rorty: *"conversation is the ultimate context within which knowledge is to be understood"* (Rorty, 1979, p. 389). Thus, one claim of the validation of social research relates to whether the actors studied find the language and ideas developed useful and relevant in portraying the reality in which they find themselves. Pragmatic value is not the only claim that should be raised for scientific research, however, although this is precisely what has been suggested by scholars associated with the school of action research (Gummesson, 1987). Clearly, an investigation can lead to results which, while accepted by a community, do not challenge their preconceptions. An investigation can also lead to the development of a language which holds genuine insights for the actors involved, but which for some reason or another they choose to ignore or reject. In order to make an investigation scientifically valid, therefore, it must also by characterized by some form of rational argumentation. Social research must therefore contain a chain of reasoning in order to convince the reader of the accuracy of its findings.

1.3 Paradigms, metaphors and methodology

Following the paradigm concept, it can be argued that theories are basically perspectives, or metaphors, used to capture aspects of the real world. The field of business studies can be arranged according to the underlying metaphors on which this insight is based. These metaphors embody assumptions regarding the nature of reality and the methods that are useful for addressing this reality. Smircich & Morgan (1980) have attempted to give an overview of these assumptions, and to show how ontology, metaphors and research methods are intertwined.

In discussing the relevance of data types and research strategies, scholars have tended to limit the debate to the issue of quantitative versus qualitative data. Data is referred to as "belonging" to either the functionalistic or the interpretive paradigm. This discussion is based on a misunderstanding, however. What matters is not so much whether the data is qualitative or quantitative, but how it can and cannot be used for achieving knowledge within different conceptions of science. For example, it is misleading to take account of respondents' metaphysical speculations collected through unstructured research interviews when the researcher's own axioms are to be found within the positivist canons of science. Rather than limiting research to one or the other type of data, researchers must consider their usefulness, given the imperatives of the scientific standpoint. The interpretive researcher can gather information from a company's balance sheet or export ratio and interpret this information within his own frame of reference.

Business studies are mostly dominated by the metaphors and research techniques of the objective, functional approach to social science (Mittroff & Killmann, 1978; Mills, 1959; Burrell & Morgan, 1979; Østergaard, 1992; Whitley, 1984). There is a growing concern about the limitations of this approach, however. It is argued that the concern for validity based on principles applicable in the study of both physical and social phenomena has disabled the social scientist working within this research tradition.

In principle, human cognition is beyond the reach of the positivistic scientist, because it is not measurable. What can be measured, however, and used in theorizing, is human behaviour. In the positivist approach to social science, humans "behave" according to objective structures, which, broadly speaking, can be termed "stimuli". Conventional economic theory sees human behaviour as driven by unlimited wants. A similar quest for universal principles of human behaviour can be found in Skinner (1953) and Maslow (1954). Social researchers question whether the positivist principles of science run counter to their original intentions, by biasing research towards verification rather than investigation (Mills, 1959). As argued by Mills, the most decisive result of adapting the positivist ideal of science within the social sciences:

> "... Has been a sort of methodological inhibition. By this I mean that the kind of problems that will be taken up and the way in which they are formulated are quite severely limited by the scientific method ... methodology in short seems to determine the problems." (Mills, 1959, p. 67)

The perspective of the present study is anchored firmly in the interpretive paradigm. Consequently, the present research is based on a scientific tradition which is gaining increasing ground within business studies. The number of recent and widely accepted publications containing this perspective seems to verify this assumption (see, for instance, Flyvbjerg, 1992; Weick, 1979; Morgan, 1986 & 1993; Peters & Waterman, 1982, and several recently published Ph.D. theses). The argumentation of and points made in theory discussion therefore reflect the "tacit" assumptions outlined in the present chapter.

2. Developing a research strategy for the present study

Although the phrase "research strategy" conjures up the image of a *plan,* i.e. an ordered set of sequential steps designed to lead the researcher from start to finish, the process of doing research often makes it necessary to see it as more of a *frame,* i.e. a series of iterative loops, through which some ideas disappear, new ideas emerge, and where the actual outcome, both in terms of the result and the process, is a consequence of the researcher's interaction with the research field.[2] For practical purposes, however, a schematic presentation of the research strategy is adequate. This is given below.

Textbooks on qualitative research often warn researchers against using their recommendations as cookbook recipes. If a research strategy is too rigidly followed, it could easily lose its initial purpose. Rather, various authors suggest their approach as a source of inspiration for developing research strategies tailored to the specific research situation. This advice has been followed in the present thesis. In the following, therefore, a research strategy for the present study is developed by drawing on various sources from the rich literature on qualitative research available.

The chapter is organized as follows: First, a general outline is given of the conceptual ideas behind a variety of interpretive research strategies. This is followed by a discussion of the choices behind the research strategy, with a focus on three broad phases of research: Preparation, field study, and data analysis (Andersen et al., 1992). Finally, the credibility claims of quality research strategies will be considered.

---

[2] The plan and frame metaphors have been adopted from Mintzberg (1983).

2.1 Interpretive research strategies for social inquiry - Background

Participation as a research strategy in social inquiry has been known from anthropological studies since the turn of the century. In the 1920s, interpretive methods were commonly used in research strategies by scholars associated with the Chicago school of sociology (Bogdan & Taylor, 1975).

As positivist-inspired research strategies came to dominate sociology in the postwar period, however, the influence of interpretive research methods in social inquiry declined. This later occurred in the study of business practices, too. However, interpretive research grew in importance during the 60s and 70s, partly as a result of the students' rebellion, where traditional sociological methods were seen as static, conservative, and as preserving the existing power structure in society (Due & Madsen, 1983). Interpretive research techniques became established as an alternative to the formal research procedures and the behavioralistic notions of human activity.

The emergence of subjective approaches to social science led to the development of theories to overcome the limitations of what has been called mainstream theory, or normal science. One important research strategy is field research. Among the many contributions are the works of Argyris (Action Science, 1987), Glaser & Strauss (Grounded Theory, 1967), and Nørreklit et al. (Actor's Approach, 1987). These approaches have several elements in common: Social actors as a starting point for inquiry; involvement rather than observation; and interpretation instead of explanation. These are briefly described in the following.

Social actors as a starting point for inquiry. Since social actors, rather than objective social structures, are seen as actively shaping their reality, their actions must be understood according to their own interpretation of their situation. Subjective logic (Nørreklit et. al, 1987), or theory-in-use (Argyris & Schön, 1978), deals with the commonsense evaluations which guide the actor in his actions. Applying these arguments in a business context, the actions of a manager cannot be understood solely by looking at the resource situation and other structural variables, which can be measured by an observer of the organization. The structural settings are only interesting to the extent that they are interpreted and have meaning to the actor. Therefore, the researcher must base his inquiries on understanding this logic rather than testing theoretical statements developed at a distance. In other words, it is the concept of strategic choice which should attract attention, not the structural constraints (Child, 1972).

Involvement rather than observation. According to the positivist approach, direct involvement will corrupt research because of the influence of the researcher's preassumptions on the object. This puts science at the mercy of metaphysical guessing. Preassumptions thus hinder the scientist in seeing the world clearly. Against this is the argument that all social actors, including researchers, actively construct reality through intentional activity. Scientific contributions thus cannot be value-free and free from the judgements of the researcher, and new insights cannot be achieved through formal techniques of inquiry. Data-gathering techniques, such as surveys, reproduce preconceptions by framing reality through predefined questions and categories (Morgan, 1983; Nørreklit, 1993). Ultimately, this could lead the researcher either to conduct research abstracted from the empirical world or to fit "round" data to "square" categories, and hence *"arouse the disbelief of both colleagues and laymen"* (Glaser & Strauss, p. 37). In summary, the observer status of the researcher found in positivist epistemology merely hinders the research effort, as social activity is best understood by exposure to the field.

Interpretation instead of explanation. Since individual and social activity are regarded as reflexive and intentional, any search for universal causes of individual and social behaviour is in vain. Rather than focusing on structural conditions as determinants for explaining individual and organizational behaviour, the focus should be directed towards actors' individual and collective strategies. Social research must consider both individual and social practices. The task of research and analysis becomes one of presenting and interpreting life in a way which shows how individuals express and construct their presence in the world, and how these form collective patterns of social conduct. Analysis must show how social life carries its own logic, sense of order and structure of meaning. The researcher must investigate reality, and, through his investigations, confirm or challenge theoretical predispositions. This can be described as the dialectical tension between field and theory, represented by the researcher (Andersen et al., 1993).

2.2. A schematic presentation of the research strategy

The research strategy developed for the present study follows three broad research phases:

✓ **Preparation Phase**
✓ **Field study Phase**
✓ **Analytical Phase**

These phases will be discussed in detail below.

2.2.1 The preparation phase

Ideally, the research process begins with an anomaly which cannot be explained by theory. However, an anomaly can also be due to the researcher's ignorance or lack of knowledge about existing research. The first phase of any scientific research process must therefore challenge a "raw" research question with the existing knowledge of the field, by studying present research and related theory. This serves several purposes. First, it gives an overview of relevant contributions necessary for relating the research endeavour to the overall discussion in the field. Second, it helps identify interesting research questions, and clarify the researcher's own position and the grounds on which the research questions are raised. Third, it leads to a generally more fruitful research endeavour from the point of view of the academic community, since it diminishes the risk of replicating existing research. This is called a *pre-understanding* of the phenomenon to be studied, analogous to Gadamer (Jensen, 1992). In addition to the development of a pre-understanding, issues concerning the research unit, as well as the amount of data to be collected, must also be considered. Moreover, the researcher must define the role he/she will play in the study.

The choices mentioned above are interrelated. As mentioned earlier, formulating research questions affects the data to be collected. However, in qualitative research, it is crucial to be open to impressions, and not be swayed by too-rigidly followed theoretical inspirations or empirical classifications. It is through the openness of the researcher that conventional ideas can be challenged and new knowledge acquired.

It is the "surprise" of the research that makes it interesting, rather than the trivial repetition of what is already known.

2.2.1.1 The role of theory in the preparation of field studies

A much-debated issue in qualitative research is whether the use of theory enslaves or inspires the researcher. Against the use of theory in scientific inquiry, it can be argued that theories "take control" of the researcher by imputing specific definitions and causal relationships a priori to his understanding of reality (Mills, 1959; Glaser & Strauss, 1967). In its favour, however, is that it flies in the face of "openness" in social inquiry not to consider alternative interpretations. At the same time, this would be a denial of the usefulness of existing knowledge. Nørreklit et al. (1987) regard the lack of presumptions as a question of attitude rather than "pureness". It is therefore also possible to develop conceptual frameworks which can be used in directing attention, and simultaneously abstract from theories in social inquiry.

Theories represent previous thought constructions, which, to a various extent, have value for understanding a specific phenomenon in a research situation. The role of theory in the preparation phase can therefore ideally be seen as one of inspiration. Theory serves the researcher in the pre-understanding phase in a variety of ways. It can provide the researcher with a technical language, help to refine his research design, and evaluate its strengths and limitations. Moreover, a theoretical overview might lead the researcher to unanswered questions, and direct attention toward areas which have not yet been researched. Finally, theories have a metaphorical value in the preparation phase. In general, the principles of using theories as frameworks for interpretation are widely accepted (Morgan, 1986; Morgan, 1993; Weick, 1993; Mintzberg, 1983; Strandskov, 1994).

The stance taken in this thesis is that, if treated metaphorically, present theory offers a fruitful source of inspiration. However, it is important to be aware of the ontological consequences of each view, and discuss theoretical frameworks in relation to the methodology used. As such, theory should not be used eclectically without considering the basic premises on which it is founded. Researchers should use theory as a source of inspiration rather than a means of compartmentalizing reality. A penchant for theory may beguile the researcher into viewing reality from a particular angle, blinding him to alternative interpretations. This will turn research into an inferior version of a hypothetical deductive study, in which the normal epistemological rules for theory-testing are not met.

2.2.1.2 Data considerations

Although one virtue of the qualitative research design is its avoidance of the premature "lock in" of data in predefined categories, some choices concerning data sampling must be made. There are several reasons for this. To some extent, research must be focused on a research question, otherwise it may lead to several problems: It can be difficult to obtain field data, because the researcher is unable to explain the objectives of the research to actors. In addition, even if questions are accepted by actors, it becomes difficult to establish a dialogue with them when the purpose of the field trip is not clear. At best, the person being interviewed may ask the researcher to return when his research questions are more clearly stated. Furthermore, research is often carried out under budgetary and time constraints. Data collection which has no explicit focus runs the risk of being inadequate and time-consuming, and may leave the researcher with a mass of "raw data" which are difficult to access and order in any fashion.

In short, the researcher must make his preassumptions explicit, both in terms of the focus of the research and in relation to the structural contingencies under which the research should be conducted. Broadly speaking, these involve two aspects: a) the kind of "sites" to choose, and b) the number of sites to study. We will address these in the following.

The kind of sites to choose

A "site" is basically a bounded context. It is a "piece of reality" whose boundaries are initially selected by the researcher. The choice of site can be addressed according to the actors, events, processes and outcomes which it encompasses (Miles & Huberman, 1984). In the following, the sites chosen for the present study will be discussed according to these dimensions.

The aim of the present study is to identify the ways in which SMEs arrange and develop the activities involved in conducting international affairs. This objective can be researched in various ways, based on the theoretical and ontological considerations of the researcher. If the researcher believes that social phenomena are best described through system theory, the focus should be on finding the discrete relations of the functional components (organizations, departments, actors) and their relation to the system as a whole. The first task would be to define the system by its structure and functions, in order to obtain a specific configuration of the organization of marketing within an interorganizational system. The next task would be to modify the model as the study evolves. [3]

The present investigation starts with the actors directly involved in organizing cross-border activities between SMEs and foreign intermediaries, together with the structure of the organization fields, which are a product of past acts. This means that persons from both SMEs and intermediaries are included. In addition, history is expected to play a role in explaining how actors frame reality and act accordingly. Consequently, the research design must also include actors who have a historical connection to the SME. This does not represent a complete research protocol, however. As pointed out by Glaser & Strauss (1967), apart from the initial collection of data, the collection of further data cannot be planned in advance, because it violates the investigative principle - that one must follow leads and hunches as they emerge "in the field". As such, research should be seen as an investigative process driven by qualified questioning, where additional actors will be involved to the extent that they are expected to increase the researcher's understanding.

The processes and outcomes studied here are primarily those related to the organizing of activity. By "organizing" is here meant activities related to outcome, or task fulfilment. The task of an organization is not objectively defined, but relates to how reality is framed by the individual actors. The essential feature of organizing activities, however, is that it is a collective act. This means that the person interviewed must relate both to the process of organizing cross-border business activity and the role that he/she and other actors have for the fulfillment of this

---

[3]   See Vestergaard (1992) for a good example of this research strategy.

activity. As such, the organization to which the person is related, in addition to other persons directly connected with the task of organizing international activities, are of key interest in the present study.

The number of sites to study
In principle, there is a choice of between one and numerous sites in qualitative research. In any type of site studies, however, considerations of sample size must be considered irrelevant, since the research does not aim at developing universally useful theories. But this does not mean that the researcher should be indifferent to the number of sites - the choice between a single-site and a multiple-site study is a trade-off situation.

Concentrating on one site instead of multiple sites enables the researcher to "follow" the field closely and let research evolve. The risk here, however, is that the researcher will get caught up by the idiosyncrasies of a one-site study, and thus be unable to perceive its peculiarities. Studying several sites allows comparison, and thus a reflective analysis. A multiple-site study has been chosen for the present investigation.

The selection of the sites must also be considered. Several parameters can guide this selection. Glaser & Strauss (1967) recommend that researchers should judge the inclusion of sites on the basis of their theoretical relevance for furthering the generation of "grounded theory". As such, sites should be included along with the development of theory, depending on their ability to increase the conceptual level of the "emerging" theory. They recommend maximizing the differences among the sites, since *"the similarities that occur through many diverse kinds of groups provide the most general form of uniformities"* (Glaser & Strauss, 1967, p. 56). Choosing widely different sites is expected to make the emerging theory more robust, and thus more universal in its scope.

In practice, the time constraints of most research projects requires some sort of organization of the field study. Appointments and arrangements must be made and field trips planned. The choice of sites, and how each site is further developed, is

51

inevitably influenced by some degree of practicability. While practical considerations can, to some extent, counter the intentions of the data-gathering logic in qualitative research strategies, they also represent idealistic models which are often impossible to follow slavishly. The question remains, however: does compromise substantially corrupt the initial idea of letting field studies "speak for themselves". Not necessarily. Normally, the researcher can return to the site and ask additional questions if the need arises.

2.2.2 In the field

Conducting field studies is an interactive process in which the researcher attempts to get in touch with the "locals". The main task of field studies, from an interpretive viewpoint, is to capture and understand the subjective logic which actors use to make sense out of their everyday activities, and to see how this leads to activities and further interaction. The quality of field study is therefore contingent on the researcher's ability to establish a relationship to actors and, by this means, acquire knowledge.

2.2.2.1 Field Dialogues

A dialogue is an interactive process in which both participants engage actively, and which is guided by the dynamics of the reflections and speech acts of the participants. The dialogue has been described as a process of open reflection, where participants exchange perspectives in order to develop their own insight (Nørreklit et al., 1987).

Through the dialogue, the researcher gradually gains an understanding of the phenomenon being studied. It is through this process that social actors become aware of the tacit aspects of a specific social practice. The dialogue can take place over one or several sessions, in which the researcher interprets new insights and uses this interpretation in opening a new discussion. A such, the dialogue consists of a series of face-to-face dialogues and reflections, as illustrated in figure 2.2, below (adopted from Andersen 1992).

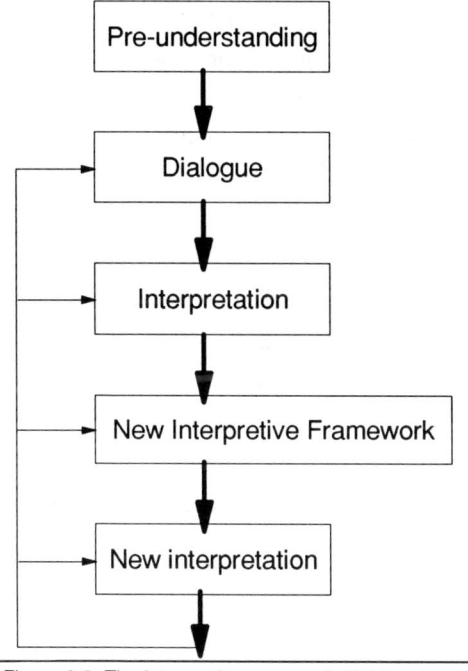

Figure 2.2: The interpretive process in field work

In the reflection phases, the researcher uses imagination, theory and other "ingredients" to generate relevant questions. In this phase, the researcher seeks to distance himself from the context and view the sensory data from an outsider's perspective. Theoretical models can be used here to read and understand the phenomenon. This process has been called "imaginization" (see Morgan, 1986). Reflections serve as entry codes for dialogues with actors in the field. This accords with Morgan (op. cit.), who argues for using metaphors in organizational inquiry to produce a diagnostic reading of the phenomenon being investigated.

However, only by provoking relevant debate is the theoretical predisposition justifiable. The researcher must therefore be able to distance himself from his theoretical perspective in order to understand the social act, this being a prerequisite for interpretation. However, he must also be able to relate to it and develop it on its own premises.

The process of dialogue and reflection continues until the researcher understands all the relevant social and individual logics concerned. As indicated by the "feedback" arrows in figure 2.2, the process is not necessarily logical or linear. It develops, similar to models of experiential learning in cognitive psychology, in iterative loops, where the discrete phases are repeated until a coherent understanding is achieved.

2.2.2.2 Attitudes to the field: The role of the researcher

One important consideration, present in all textbooks on field studies, is the attitude of the researcher to the field. This refers to the degree of involvement of the researcher. Often (though not always), the researcher can choose between several stances. Burgess (Henriksen, 1992) has developed a taxonomy in which he classifies qualitatively-oriented research strategies. These include: a) the complete observer, b) observer as participant, c) participant as observer, and d) the complete participant.

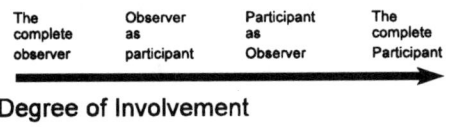

Degree of Involvement

Figure 2.3: Involvement attitudes in Field Research

From left to right in figure 2.3, the researcher increasingly participates in the social processes. The choice of involvement strategy is essentially a trade-off between access to data and isomorphism to specific interests within the social setting.

Researchers following strategy d) may be rewarded with privileged access to data and viewpoints concealed from other persons. A convincing example of the merits of this strategy can be found in studies of the working conditions of immigrant workers in German nuclear power plants, or of German right-wing nationalist parties (Gynther Wallraff, 1987). However, full observance of the complete participant role also includes being identified with a particular social group (and thus being alienated from other groups). This has clear disadvantages. For example, if the researcher becomes identifed too closely with the management of an SME, he risks being accused of representing its interests. Moreover, closeness to social phenomena can make objective analysis difficult, if not impossible.

On the other hand, the researcher who adopts strategy a) is not likely to get a similar "carte blanche" to company information, though he may be able to mingle more freely among different interest groups and to a larger extent form his own opinion, and perhaps be in a better position to challenge the conventional wisdom of the actors in the organization. By adopting this strategy, actors may be provoked into clarifying and arguing for their viewpoints, which in turn can give the researcher considerable knowledge about individual and collective logics in the organization.

In strategy c), the researcher is a member of the site he is investigating. The problem here is to convince the actors that the researcher is not promoting his own interests or the interests of a specific group. If a management trainee tries to reveal informal procedures of organizing work on the factory floor, he will most likely be met by resentment, if not hostility, because he will be seen as furthering his own career prospects or representing the interests of a management group wanting to increase efficiency at the expense of the working conditions of the workers. In other contexts, however, where research efforts do not collide with key interets, this research strategy can be successfully followed. In universities, for example, the teaching staff sometimes succeeds in developing mutual evaluation programmes.

Strategy b), the role of the "observer as participant", has been chosen for the present study. In this role, the position as a visitor to the social setting is preserved, and the researcher is therefore not associated with the interests of a specific group within the organization. In following this strategy, however, the researcher risks obtaining information that is either fabricated or falsified in other ways, as the actor wants to protect himself from being publicly exposed. However, since the actor has agreed to participate in the study in the first place, this also suggests that he has some degree of openness towards the investigation. Moreover, within the "observer as participant" strategy (see figure 2.3), the researcher has the possibility of selecting several different actors and cross-checking their statements, and, from this, ask additional questions, until he reaches a coherent understanding (Nørreklit et al., 1987).

2.2.3 Solving the puzzle: Analysing field data

The analysis of data already starts in the field, as patterns begin to emerge and are pursued and tested against further dialogue. In the collecting and writing of field notes, analytical considerations constantly emerge and are dealt with as they crop up. In addition, the researcher is influenced by the impressions he receives during the field research, which is in itself an analytical activity, although often subconscious. It is therefore somewhat misleading to describe data analysis as an activity which takes place after field studies have been carried out. Nevertheless, an important part of the analysis does in fact takes place after data collection. At least two analytical activities are carried out in this phase of the research: "Post-field" data analysis and report writing.

In the literature, the analysis of field material has, until recently, been an underdeveloped area, as most textbooks on qualitative research strategies focus on the problems of obtaining information and avoiding bias during data collection. Data analysis has been called a *"mysterious, half-formulated art"* (Miles, 1979). A survey of the seven most cited textbooks on qualitative research strategies revealed that less than 5-10% of their content was devoted to data analysis (Sieber, 1976). This imbalance has been corrected somewhat recently, with the appearance of new literature on analytical techniques (Miles & Huberman, 1984; Yin, 1991; Strauss & Corbrin, 1990), while the spread of electronic word processing has led to the emergence of various new instruments and techniques for analysing field data.

The analysis of field data is the process of abstracting insights of a more formal nature, such as ideal types (Mintzberg, 1987) or theory construction (Glaser & Strauss, 1967), from the raw data collected through field studies. This can be done with various degrees of formality, ranging from the completely unstructured analysis, where patterns are expected to "emerge" from the collected material, to formal analysis of language, where the semantic content of dialogues is classified into formal categories. Both extremes create problems. Unstructured data analysis, in the form of creative thinking, hunches, metaphor-building, etc., is a vital part of any analytical work. Relying on this alone demands an extremely large information-handling capacity, however, since field data tends to be voluminous[4] (Miles, 1979; Miles & Huberman, 1984). At the other extreme is computer analysis of semantics. But the rigorous use of computers in qualitative analysis tends to distance the researcher from his field data, because, although acquiring a tool for data processing, the field worker is confined within working environment controlled by binary arithemtics (Lyman 1984).

The aim of any data handling technique is to assist in analytical activity. Field notes represent the various impressions that the researcher has formed during fieldwork, and, at this stage, are present in memory as a complex "whole". The task of data analysis techniques is to help the researcher organize the cognitive process by untangling the various impressions and their relations. One helpful technique in this respect is grounded theory, which is the method chosen for the present research. In the following, the main ideas of grounded theory are briefly described.

The concept of Grounded Theory was originally formulated by Glaser & Strauss (1967), who developed a process for generating sociological theory from collected field data, rather than basing research on testing hypotheses developed from established "grand theories". The main objective was to abstract new theory. Although Glaser & Strauss make recommendations about the collection of field data, the main contribution of grounded theory is a technique for analysing data through categorizations.

The first task is to separate field notes into discrete chunks of observations - usually one or several paragraphs which represent a whole "meaning block". By this means, categories are developed. A category is a concept, a metaphor, or a label, which seems to capture the distinct observation most adequately (Turner, 1981). Additional "meaning blocks" are categorized using this principle on a case-by-case basis. A category can contain more than one meaning block; otherwise, new categories are developed as needed until the site is fully covered. This leads to further elaboration,

---

[4]   In the present study, the raw data (primarily field notes, correspondence, financial statements and brochures) amounted to approximately 700 pages.

and furthers the abstraction of more formal definitions of categories. The set of categories are used in subsequent sites, and new labels are developed to the extent that the original set of "meaning blocks" do not fit into these.

The next step in the grounded theory procedure is to spot links and develop hypothetical relations between categories. However, this part of the analysis can just as well be dealt with in the second analytical activity associated with "puzzle-solving" - the writing process.

The writing process is itself an analysis, where further elaborations and refinements of perceived relationships are made. The argumentation for a specific category is made explicit through the process of writing, and the complex patterns of interrelationships between observations can be further refined, which can in turn lead to additional interpretations. In this process, gerunds, or metaphors, play an important role (Glaser, 1978) as data-reducing devices, by condensing a mass of facts to a single generality. In addition, they serve as pattern-making devices, since they attempt to extract and capture the conceptual significance of findings (Miles & Huberman, 1984).

3. The credibility of field studies: How is validity ensured?

In business research, validity is often interpreted in a positivistic tradition, which assumes a 1:1 relationship between the language or symbols describing reality as an independent objective reality. However, as argued in the first part of this chapter, there is no distinction between a social reality and a language in which this reality can be described in the interpretive approach to social science. This tradition sees language as actively influencing the way in which reality is recognized and acknowledged. Notwithstanding, unless the interpretive researcher bases his study on totally relativistic or post-modernistic assumptions, then the connection to the subject of the study will have to be made explicit in some other way.

The quest for validation (or truth) in the interpretive approach differs from the positivist approach, however, which is seen as unrealistic, if not misplaced, in a social science context. Thus, the emphasis is changed from verification to falsification. The quest for universal truths is abandoned in favour of a conception of defensible knowledge claims (Kvale, 1990). Validation becomes an issue of choosing among competing and falsifiable knowledge claims. This definition of validity emphasizes the communicative and pragmatic aspects of validity. The conception of truth becomes inseperable from a conception of subjective reality.

This definition of validity has influenced the effort to ensure validity in the present study. As discussed earlier, truth is not independent of the obseerver. Knowledge and interests actively define reality rather than passively adopt it. The researcher must overcome his surprise at the difference between the statements of various actors about the same social construction and attempt instead to find out what is producing these statements (Andersen, 1992). As mentioned earlier, it is essential for the validity of field studies that the researcher stays as independent as possible, otherwise actors may use the field researcher in promoting their own interests (Nørreklit et al., 1987).

In the present study, the correspondance with reality is assured through several means. These are outlined below.

1) Interviews have been recorded, so that statements appearing in the case presentations can be verified and assessed. The use of taped interviews in field research is still subject to some suspicion, however. Against their use is the argument that the dialouge situation becomes interrupted and, it is claimed, impossible. An important argument in favour of taped interviewing is that it enables the researcher to participate more freely in the discussion, without worrying whether he will be able to remember all the details afterwards. This argument gains in strength the greater the number of interviews that have to be carried out in a relatively short period of time.

In addition, by taping interviews, the researcher is able to relisten at leisure in search of clues, underlying tones and hunches overheard in the interview situation.

2) Another way to ensure validity is to return interview drafts and case descriptions to the interviewed persons. In this way, misunderstandings can be minimized, and diverging opinions between the researcher and the interviewed person may open up the possibility for future discussions. Once interviewees realize that the researcher is genuinely interested in their professional life, they are often eager to discuss details and explain small misunderstandings.

3) Finally, correspondance of reality is ascertained through testing the assumptions and statements of different actors against each other. Through this process, discrepancies and diverging understandings can often lead to fruitful debates and deeper insights.

In the final analysis, of course, interpretation is based on the choices of the researcher. However, the above-mentioned precautions at least makes it possible to ensure that these choices are influenced by the field studied, and therefore also mirrors the concerns of the actors involved.

CHAPTER 3

In search of an Organizational Perspective

The purpose of this chapter is to develop a conceptual framework for the organization of international economic activity between SMEs and their foreign intermediaries. The framework serves as a set of internally coherent concepts, or *theoretical language,* which can help in formulating theoretical expectations and against which empirical findings can be compared. It can be seen as a metaphorical device for framing and interpreting specific aspects of the raw data. Finally, it serves as a tool for establishing a relationship with existing research on the subject.

The theoretical framework of the present investigation originates from organization theory. This alone represents a choice of theoretical perspective, albeit a broad one. Alternatively, the framework could have been borrowed from the theory of distribution channels, aspects of game theory, or political economy, any of which could no doubt be used to shed light on specific aspects of the present topic, and which also to some extent merge into it. However, more than any of the other perspectives, organization theory lends itself to a broad focus on the forms which the organization of international business takes.

Organizational sociology does not form a coherent body of knowledge. Rather, it can be described as several alternative perspectives, or images, of what an organization is and what it does (Morgan, 1986). As will be seen in the following, organizational thinking has been, and is still, influenced by a broad field of theory and modelling, largely based on the principles of scientific management and its successor, contingency theory. Both see organizational structure as designed to reduce human variation, and subsume their actions into a larger framework of rational conduct[5]. This view of organizations has prevailed for a long time, and, though seldom explicitly stated, is clearly the dominant view in the international business literature (see Bradley, 1991; Root, 1987; Dunning, 1991). In relation to the present study, it is therefore relevant to discuss the ideas of conventional organization theory, since these also underlie the assumptions regarding the present status and future prospects of SMEs in the international economy.

The chapter starts with an outline of conventional organization theory. It will be argued that this applies mainly to the large, integrated, mass-producing firm, and that, in several respects, the concepts of this theoretical framework are inadequate for describing the processes of small companies, which are fundamentally based on different principles of production and organization. The discussion of conventional organization theory will therefore lead to the inclusion of two alternative views of organizations: The network approach and institutional theory, which offer different but (as is argued in the following sections) complementary views on the forces which shape the organization of activity between decision units such as SMEs and foreign intermediaries.

1. Conventional organization theory - background, viewpoints and limitations

Although social life in all cultures has been subject to organizational forces from a very early date, theoretical interest is very much related to the early epoch of industrialization. The technological breakthrough of power-based machinery fuelled an interest in developing practices for solving problems related to the efficient use of this machinery in factory systems. The initial problem was how machines could complement - and perhaps even replace - labour. In the 1770s, Adam Smith made a major contribution towards solving this problem through his analysis of a pin factory. Here, he saw the source of increased productivity as stemming from the

[5]   Scott & Meyer explain this in the following way: [In contingency models] *"The prime business of an organization was to perform work as a technical system; managers were seen as ensuring adequate supplies of resources and markets, designing efficient work arrangements, and coordinating and controlling technical activities."* (Scott & Meyer, 1983, p. 156)

minute division of labour and task specialization[6]. This and other similar contributions have become known as the classical school of organization and management (Ford et al., 1988; Woodward, 1966; Lawrence & Lorsch, 1967).

Smith's study pointed to two fundamental principles for organizing activity into a coherent body of organization, capable of repeating single acts on a mass scale: specialization through the division of labour in discrete tasks, and the coordination of these tasks into a continuous flow of activity. The specialization of assets, which is a prerequisite for efficiency analogous to Smith's division of labour, lies at the heart of the classical school. The core of the classical theory behind industrial development is the idea that increases in productivity can be achieved through an increasingly specialized use of resources.

Specialization through the division of labour produces a need for the coordination of unregulated activities into concerted action. There are numerous ways of doing this. The specialization of resources thus also has an influence on the means of coordination and the structure of the coordinating body of the organization, since work can be divided and activities coordinated more or less efficiently. Traditional microeconomic thinking sees the market as the most efficient way of achieving this - resources are allocated instantly through the mechanism of price or the help of an "invisible hand". In an organizational context, however, the addition of asset specifity is introduced. The firm is dependent on specific resources and becomes a potential victim of malfeasance, as the number of potential exchange actors is reduced, and the amount of information needed to coordinate is increased. This has led Williamson (1975, 1981) to reassert Coases' (1937) original theory of administrative hierarchies by seeing these as the most efficient way of reducing information costs. In a similar vein, Chandler (1977) describes the rise of the modern enterprise as an institution founded on the internalization of previously market-based exchange activities. This enables the firm to exploit advantages of

---

[6] "A workman not eductated to this business... could scarce, perhaps, make one pin in a day, and certainly not twenty. But in the way in which this business is now carried on, not only the whole work is a peculiar trade, but it is divided into a number of branches... One man draws out the wire, another straightens it, a third cuts it, a fourth points it, a fifth grinds it at the top for reciving the head ... Ten persons, could make among them upwards of forty-eight thousand pins in a day." (Smith 1776 [1937])

administrative coordination as production is stabilized through the scheduling of activity flows. Thus, administration or control are closely related to specialization and coordination. Following these ideas, a formal organization presupposes the efficiency of scale-intensive production in order to *"specify a detailed program of behaviour, transforming the labour force from being a general purpose mechanism into a more efficient special-purpose mechanism"* (March & Simon, 1958, pp. 31-32). Organizational efficiency is therefore equated with regarding organizations as machines, in which workers are seen as adjuncts to machines in the performance of management-regulated tasks (Burrell & Morgan, 1979; Piore & Sabel, 1984; March & Simon, 1958).

Resource specialization also means the introduction of long-term planning in organizations. Resources are allocated through investments in machinery and other means of capital-intensive production, which increases the proportion of sunk costs vis-à-vis variable costs. The specialization of resources is an investment. Resource fixation hinders reallocation, and thus makes firms more dependent on the stability of demand and supply over the payoff period of the investment. Moreover, the specialization of resources increases dependency on other firms, since input and output stability depends on the collaboration of other firms adapting to the specialized needs of the mass-producer. Fixed costs thus introduce a rigidity into the system of production (Piore & Sabel, 1984). Resource allocation through investments in specialized assets make manufacturers dependent on the stability of demand and supply, which is necessary to ensure a satisfactory outcome to meet the demands of capital renting. The stability of demand and supply depends on factors outside the administrative control of organizations, however. This was recognized by the contingency school of organization theory, which criticized the classical view for omitting any reference to the task environment when debating efficiency in relation to organizations (Lawrence & Lorsch, 1967). This critique was emphasized by the succession of economic crises which began in the 1970s. From being coddled in a fairly stable economic environment, underpinned by international agreements, e.g. Bretton Woods, and a growing world economy, firms suddenly found themselves cast adrift in unstable and turbulent surroundings (Ansoff, 1986; Kotler, 1984). Practitioners began to look for administrative methods which could take the instability of environmental conditions into consideration. This eventually resulted in the contingency view of organizations (Thompson, 1967; Lawrence & Lorsch, 1967; Burns & Stalker, 1961; Woodward, 1966). This view contends that the prime factors of organizational success are to be found outside rather than inside the organization. According to this view, the crucial task of management is to ensure a fit between the capabilities of the internal structure and the demands of the external environment.

As a result of this development, long-range or strategic planning has established itself as a viable management tool in mass-producing firms, where it is used to achieve a fit between organizational structure and constantly changing environments (see Ansoff, 1966; Katz & Kahn, 1967; Chandler, 1977; Porter, 1980; Rasmussen, 1988). At the same time, many large firms have failed to adjust to abrupt changes in demand and relative costs, inflation and unemployment (UN, 1993; Piore & Sabel, 1984; Bannock, 1981).

These viewpoints have become increasingly important in view of the volatile nature of the world economy, which became even more turbulent and unpredictable during the 1970s and 1980s, requiring a constant effort of strategic monitoring and planning.

A related aspect of the rigidity of mass-producing firms is the structural imperative. Once resources are committed, the role and responsibilities of the human actors are also more or less defined within the realms of this structure. In formally structured and integrated firms, for example, the role of top management is mainly regulative (Astley & Van de Ven, 1983; Scott, 1989; Morgan, 1986; Bruzelius & Skärvad, 1983).

In summary, conventional organization theory focuses on the establishment of an administrative structure for exploiting the scale advantages of mass-production. Consequently, most theorizing within this field considers organizational issues from a structural functionalistic viewpoint, based on the characteristics of large enterprises. Here, the allocation and coordination of resources are under administrative, or ownership control. The role of administration theory is to outline the structure of such a system and the means of operating it. Together, these form the core means of running the firm.

In relation to the organization of international activity, the demand for stabilization of input and output conditions is also reflected in the literature, inspired by transaction cost theory. In the literature, internationalization is viewed as being based on a specialized firm-specific advantage (Dunning, 1991). In international exchange, the special character of this advantage results in market failure, since it can only be exchanged in a "small-numbers-bargain" situation, in which it is difficult to price the advantage, and where opportunistic behaviour is possible as the firm becomes dependent on a small exchange party (Rugman et al., 1981). Due to the specialized nature of firms' specific advantages, their international *raison d'etre* can be said to constitute their control of the supply of market outlets, input sources, or even both (Rugman et al., 1981).

For these and other reasons, international market expansion is characterized by uncertainty and dependence on others. Transaction cost theorists thus stress hierarchical control as the most important feature of a sustainable international engagement (Root, 1987; Young et al., 1989; Rugman et al., 1981). Firm-specific advantage is again based on economies of scale and/or scope, which incur fixed costs and involve the allocation of resources through ownership control. Thus, it is through the specialization of firm-specific advantages that some modes of international engagement are argued to be superior to others.

Since the transaction cost argument of hierarchical control is closely connected with the reasoning behind capital-intensive operations, its validity is also somewhat limited to this type of organization. In an organizational setup where international activities are not a result of resource dedication, the argumentation put forward by transaction cost theory is not as obvious. Thus, an argument that is valid in one production system might prove inadequate in other systems of production not based on a division of labour managed through a linear chain of command. This will become clearer in the following discussion of the competitiveness of SMEs versus large, integrated firms.

1.1 SMEs in classical organization theory

The SME literature has generally criticized conventional organizational literature for treating SMEs as embryonic versions of large firms (Dandridge, 1979). Scholars in the classical tradition tend more to stress the absence of certain organizational characteristics of large enterprises (e.g. a high degree of specialization and a regulative structure) than to deal with the SME on its own terms. SMEs have been seen as a transitional stage in the life cycle of organizations (Mintzberg, 1983; Whetten, 1987; Greiner, 1972). Small firms are either expected to prosper or to fail, in line with the general principles of capitalism. Since they are unable to compete with larger firms by staying small, and as growth involves generic problems of organization and information processing, this development is inevitable (Greiner, 1972; Gailbraith, 1976; Mintzberg, 1983).

Another viewpoint has been presented by the so-called "dualist" perspective of industrial economics (Biggart, 1992; Weiss, 1992; Piore & Sabel, 1984). According to this view, SMEs exist in tandem with larger firms, serving as a kind of shock absorber for them. Furthermore, it is claimed, the main rationale behind the continued existence of SMEs is that the increasing specialization of LEs encourages the development of a market for intermediate goods so specialized that it cannot be satisfied by mass production. This leaves a gap in the market which is subsequently filled by niche producers (read: SMEs) serving the demands of the LEs. Weiss summarizes the different viewpoints on small firms in the following way:

> *"Shock absorbers of the business cycle, outlets for the displacement of risk, a vast sponge for the unemployed labour of large enterprise, a form of exploitation practised by larger firms, such are the prevailing images projected of small firms."* (Weiss, 1992, p. 100-101)

The size of SMEs has been used as an approximation to describe the resources which can be marshalled for international activity. Several authors have linked international performance with company size, and have suggested a positive relation between this and export intensity (Cavusgil, 1984; Czinkota & Johnston, 1983; Bilkey & Tesar, 1977). Others have equated the development of an international engagement with the a firm's growth (Johanson & Vahlne, 1977 & 1990; Loustari-nen, 1992).

These viewpoints have been neatly summed up by Aaby & Slater (1989), who conclude: *"The most common hypothesis is that larger companies have size-related advantages that enable them more efficiently to engage in export"* (Aaby & Slater, 1989, p. 17). Size disadvantages are generally connected with the limited number of resources controlled through ownership, combined with high risk and the lack of scale advantages (see also chapter 1). Mostly, the assumptions behind these arguments lack credibility, and empirical findings seldom back them up. A growing number of studies question these doctrinaire statements about small firms' ability to achieve competitive strength as compared with the advantages of mass production.

Several studies in Europe and the USA show that there is a definite shift towards smaller units of production in terms of employment (Sengenberger et al., 1990; Evans, 1991; Sabel, 1990; Perrow, 1992; UN, 1993). Several explanations for this radical change have been put forward, some of which are rooted in the so-called school of flexible production, in which technological change, together with a more unstable economy, has biased business conditions in favour of smaller enterprises (Perrow, 1992; Smith et al., 1991; Drucker, 1991; Brusco, 1982). Some of these arguments are given below:

* SMEs are claimed to be more flexible in the face of changing and fragmented markets, because small suppliers have more direct information and have it more quickly than the specialized units of large bureaucracies (Evans, 1991).

* Labour economists stress that small firms have more widely skilled personnel who can be redeployed more quickly, and that large firms can neither recognize nor reward superior performance on the shop floor, due to the deallocation problems of the large enterprise (Stymne, 1989).

* The impact of new technology has biased business conditions in favour of small enterprises. Information technology reduces transaction delays and

costs, e.g. when firm A searches for the best supplier among firms B, C and D, thus offsetting the advantage large firms have of centralized purchasing or in-house suppliers (Perrow, 1992).

* Complementary developments in production technology make decentralized production and the production of small runs and changes in products more feasible, which in turn facilitates tailor-made production on a mass scale (Toffler, 1981; Piore & Sabel, 1984).

* Effort is more directly related to reward in the small firm, and the chances of achieving ownership status are bigger, suggesting the existence of a more self-driving and meaningful work orientation than in large enterprises (Alvesson & Wilmott, 1989; Piore & Sabel, 1984; Kristensen, 1986).

Although it could be argued that many of the developments in technology and administrative insights could be exploited by or designed into large enterprises (and are, in fact, judging by the huge amount of anecdotal evidence on downsizing and restructuring in large enterprises[7] (see also Miles & Snow, 1992)), most of the possibilities of this social and technological change may be better utilized by small firms (Perrow, 1992). One reason is that the restructuring of large enterprises to resemble the networks of small firms would lead to an increase in overhead costs (due to many functional units) and a decrease in the premium paid to resource holders. These resources may be better used by contracting activities out, thereby shrinking the firm. Secondly, a highly decentralized, divisionalized firm may be disadvantaged by belonging to a larger group which may be suspected of taking control. It may therefore lack some of the abilities to interact and build up relations to customers and suppliers which SMEs have (Perrow, 1992; Lundvall, 1993).

From seeing small firms as miniature versions of large ones and addressing their characteristics accordingly, scholars have begun to see them as nodes in an essentially different form of industrial organization, characterized by systemic interdependence (Lundvall, 1988). From this point of view, a set of interrelated

[7] Managing Director Percy Barnevik has turned ABB into 5,000 profit centres, each with their own balance sheet, and reduced headquarters staff in Zurich from 4,000 to 200. (Hofheinz, 1993)

firms may be seen as a loosely coupled system (Weick, 1976; Glassman, 1973; Aldrich & Whetten, 1981; Smith et al., 1981). A loosely coupled system consists of entities which can fulfil a task collectively, but which also preserve their identity and physical and logical separateness as individual decision-making units (cf. Weick, 1976). Compared with the large, integrated *or* restructured firm, this alternative production system has several advantages: Loosely coupled systems contain a smaller degree of interdependency and internal constraints. Members of loosely coupled systems act more independently than tightly coupled ones, and therefore contain many sensory elements. They "know" their environments better than more tightly coupled systems with fewer external components (Weick, 1976), and they can adapt to local circumstances without having to change the complete organizatio-nal setup. Finally, loosely coupled systems incur smaller coordinating costs. Jarillio (1988) argues that firms internalize to avoid higher transaction costs, since price signals from the market become inadequate for transferring information about the coordination of exchange. According to Jarillio (op. cit.), however, the costs associated with the internal governance of transactions are greater than those of a system such as that discussed above, since this system allows for the exchange of information without incurring administrative costs.

1.2   The application of organization theory to international activity from a Danish perspective

The view of organizations as vertically integrated mass-producing firms striving to achieve stable patterns of demand and supply fits badly with the picture of Danish Industry presented in chapter 1. This is supported by a number of investigations, which show that Danish SMEs depend to a large degree on externalized activities in cooperation with other firms (Christensen, 1988; Grøn, 1985; Henriksen, 1992; Karnøe, 1991; Kristensen, 1992; Mønsted; 1985; Nielsen, 1991; Norus, 1993). Danish SMEs resemble not so much integrated production units, or the tier system of Japanese industry, in which a few large firms control a hierarchy of suppliers and subcontractors, as loosely coupled business systems (Andersen & Christensen, 1993), or industrial districts, in which competencies are connected with specific activities. Surveys in Italian industrial districts have demonstrated that SMEs are major initiators of subcontracting relations. A study of the metallurgy industry in the

Bologna province revealed that, on average, the smallest firms (20-49 employees) subcontracted 30 per cent of their total production output, whereas firms with more than 1,000 employees subcontracted only an average of 17 per cent (Weiss, 1992).

SMEs can more properly be described as actors in a network of activities and resources. Consequently, their organization task can be related to the specific problems associated with organizing activity in this context.

SMEs practices have important implications for the transaction cost arguments relating to international organization. As discussed earlier, the specialized asset argument assumes mass production. In alternative production systems, the transaction cost arguments for extending hierarchical control in order to achieve stabilization are no longer valid. In the vertically integrated firm, efficiency depends on stabilization. This is achieved by limiting the amount of specialized assets controlled by market actors. In the international market entry situation, the knowledge of a foreign market intermediary may represent such a type of specialized asset (Hymer, 1976; Pedersen & Petersen, 1993). However, in systemic production, the ability to participate in several activities is contingent on flexibility. Flexibility is again only possible if the rigidity of resource dedication is avoided. In relation to international activity, Bonaccorsi (1992) has pointed this out by stating that small firms tend to internationalize in a reversible way. It could be argued that, because of their participation in low- or non-investment modes of international activity, SMEs have the advantage of exit mobility, able to exploit business opportunities as they arise and exit quickly from foreign markets when they peter out.

Compared with the internationalization potential of larger firms, this indicates an alternative way of organizing international activity. Larger firms, whose decisions have strategic impact and are therefore only flexible within the limits of their present production setup, maintain their international participation through direct investment. This can be problematical for SMEs, however. Rather than seeing one type of international activity as being superior to another, however, the view of this study is that forms of international organization must be seen as alternative paths of international activity, in which decision makers make individual strategic choices

71

based on the structural constraints of their situation. Thus, the purpose of the following sections is to develop a theoretical framework in which the relational nature of international activity between SMEs and their exchange parties can be understood. In the following, therefore, we will draw on theoretical contributions of organizational theory to the extent that they shed light on the ways and means of organizing activity, and coordinating, specializing and dividing labour in SMEs. This theoretical basis is primarily built on theories of interorganizational relations, more specifically the "network approach". This approach also has weaknesses and shortcomings in relation to understanding how SMEs organize and develop international activity, however. It is therefore suggested that the network approach be supplemented by an institutional approach to the sociology of knowledge, and that these can be combined in a conceptual framework for the present study.

2. Interorganizational relations: The network approach

The phrase "No business is an island" (Snehota & Håkansson, 1992) aptly describes the basic insight of interorganizational theory. From seeing firms as *"lumps of butter in a sea of milk"* (cf. Coase, 1937) adapting to environmental constraints, a number of studies over the past two decades have started to focus on interorganizational issues (Pfeffer & Salancick, 1978; Astley & Van de Ven, 1983; Scott & Meyer, 1983; Perrow, 1986; Weick, 1976; Håkansson, 1982; Snehota, 1990). What these approaches have in common is the idea that, for most firms, business contexts consist of few and identifiable exchange actors, between which there is continuous interaction, and in which there is some degree of mutual adaption. Consequently, the allocation of resources internally reflects an adaptation to external relationships, including patterns of organization of the environment. As such, the traditional view of organizations as a collection of resources within administrative control is substituted by a view of firms as *"actors which are symbiotically interdependent, yet semiautonomous and which interact to construct or modify their collective rules and environment"* (cf. Astley & Van de Ven, 1983).

The following is based primarily on the Scandinavian tradition in the field, also known as the network approach. The network approach does not have the status of a theory, however. Rather, it consists of many autonomous, yet interdependent, contributions (and in this sense reflects several qualities of the studied field), which share the conception of the business context of a firm as a frame, or environmental texture (Lorenzioni & Ornati, 1988), in which the firm can be seen as member, and upon which its business opportunities depend. Although the starting point of the discussion is the Scandinavian network approach, various related theoretical contributions will be included where they can shed light on specific aspects of the argumentation.

According to the network view, firms participate in an interorganizational division of labour, in which they specialize in certain activities and leave other activities to suppliers, customers and various types of intermediaries. Consequently, no individual firm controls all the inputs necessary for its activities, and thus depends on the resources and activities of other organizations. Firms are interdependent rather than independent members of a larger, value-adding activity structure. Interdependence is further strengthened by the firm's propensity for developing long-term relationships which foster a considerable degree of mutual adaption. This has been underlined by empirical studies in industrial marketing and purchasing (Johanson & Hallén, 1989). These findings support the assumed importance of lasting business relationships, and have influenced business research in general. Although the network perspective was originally developed in connection with conventional marketing theory, the important role that customer and supplier relationships play in the organization of firms' business activities transcends the network approach, embracing many aspects and contributions of organization and management theory (Gummesson, 1987). These broader aspects of the network approach are the subject of the following section.

2.1 The composition of networks

One way of understanding networks is to view them as three interrelated dimensions: Actors, activities and resources (Håkansson, 1982; Johanson & Mattson, 1992). Actors are individuals or business entities who control resources and perform activities by linking, changing and exchanging resources with other actors. They have two distinctive characteristics: 1) they influence network processes through their control over resources, and 2) they initiate activities by applying knowledge to resource use.

Activities are processes which involve the transaction or transformation of resources in order to initiate, process or conclude activity cycles. Activities therefore link resources to each other to such an extent that resource use becomes interdependent.

Resources are production factors controlled by actors. They can be tangible, e.g. production facilities, or intangible or "invisible", e.g. competencies or core knowledge (Imai, 1987). This is illustrated below in figure 3.1.

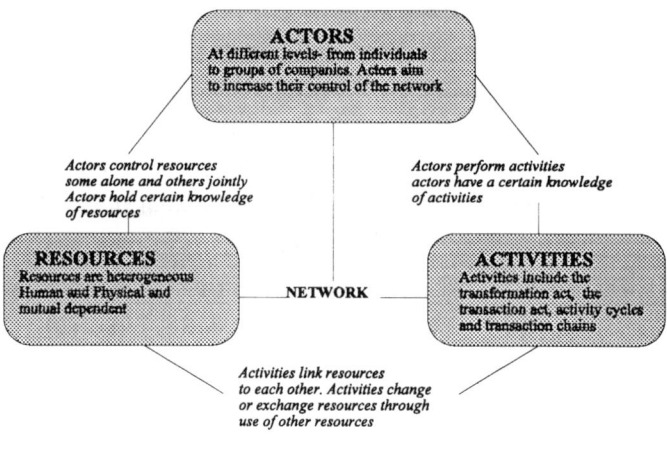

Figure 3.1: A network Model

Actors form a unique constellation of activities and resources, on which their market differential is based (Snehota, 1990). Elsewhere, it has been argued that this resource heterogeneity constitutes the *raison d'etre* of the individual firm (Alchain & Demsetz, 1972). The argument can be further developed to include business relationships, since it expresses some form of specialization and mutual interdependence in an exchange relationship (Håkansson & Johanson, 1993). Through relationships characterized by resource heterogeneity, in which each actor has competence in one area, specific activities can be externalized, allowing for a focus on the remaining resources. Although specialization through heterogeneity is an

74

aspect of networks, it does not imply that networks are characterized by rigidity in terms of the invariability of activity. Because of the indeterminate nature of regulation in networks, actors necessarily have more than one role towards each other. They cannot solely be characterized as buyers, sellers or intermediaries, because the lack of an overall plan would leave the actor too dependent on the exchange acts of other actors. As such, they are the expression of a stable (but not necessarily static) exchange pattern, where relations are developed between exchange partners.

Because of the heterogeneity of supply in any exchange situation, exchange involves the use of various resource elements. An exchange act in one relation is also connected to a number of other relations. In all exchange acts, therefore, actors are simultaneously buyers, sellers and intermediaries. Thus, relations between actors can consist of several role sets, corresponding with the relational nature of network positions. Exchange networks link actors with specific role sets, and activity carried out in any one network is only one of several possible combinations of actors fulfiling value-adding activity. Rather than representing a well-defined organization, they represent an interpretive field, in which an actor can define and configure a selection of actors into a task-fulfilment activity. Individual actors thus only play a transitory role in the activity of the network. If an actor stops participating, the activities he controls can immediately and automatically be distributed to the remaining exchange actors in the network.

In this sense, therefore, the firm can be thought of as a pattern of internal and external relations, in which the ownership-controlled resources of the firm have contextual rather than absolute value. It is through the market-bound configuration of external and internal resources that the firm gains its ability. A firm maintains its existence as a legal entity as a point of tension between internal interests and external resources, and in this respect, it is a truce (Nelson & Winther, 1982; Cyert & March, 1963). This, however, also furthers the development of a structuralized context in which the dependency on and persistence of one relationship are ingrained with the pattern and coherence of other resources. Relations increase the interdependency of the organization of activity, and can be economical, social, technical, legal, etc., in nature (Håkansson, 1982). Thus, the discrete actions of any actor must be seen in relation to the activities to which they relate and the extent to which they are mutually interdependent. For example, it can be claimed that, on the macro level, dependency on oil is built into the physical design of cars, homes and industry (Zeits, 1980). On the level of the firm, the development of Just-In-Time delivery systems reflects a situation in which activity in one relationship depends on the timing in another, etc.

In sum, the network approach proposes that business activity, rather than being understood as the decisions of discrete economic actors exchanging goods in anonymous markets and directed by price, must be seen as interdependent acts of organized business activities. Networks therefore do not conform to the traditional view of economic organization. They are not something between a market or a hierarchy, as some authors have suggested (Williamson, 1985), but, as regards aspects of specialization, coordination and authority, can be clearly distinguished from both of these ideal types.

In addition, network organizations are characterized by undeterminedness (Snehota, 1990), multiple ties between actors, and, far from being a static exchange structure, networks constitute a dynamic form of structure characterized by antagonistic forces of collaboration and competition, and stabilization and change.

The following deals with networks as a specific organizational form. The discussion starts with the forces behind the emergence of these kinds of social structure and how they function. This will then be used to try to achieve an understanding of the organization and the development of international business activity.

2.2 The emergence of business relationships

If networks are not the product of any grand plan or brought about by a set of unique conditions, how do they emerge? The key word for the development of structured exchange relationships in the network approach is interaction. The specialized nature of business actors in industrial markets endows them with specific needs, the fulfilment of which involves a search routine, which in turn takes time and effort. It is therefore economically rational to keep the partner you know rather than search for a new one for each exchange act (Jarillio, 1988; Snehota, 1990). This also makes for more stable patterns of exchange. Over time, exchange actors engage in a process of mutual adaptation (Ford, 1979). Relationships mark a commitment of resources to specialized assets, which also rationalizes business exchange and increases dependency on exchange parties.

Commitment can be risky, however, since resource dedication means specialization, which in turn is pursued at the expense of flexibility. Decisions concerning relations are therefore not sudden, but develop over time. They are the product of a gradual, or incremental, adaption to the needs of other exchange parties, in which mutual commitment and the proven ability not to renege on promises gradually builds up trust (Blau, 1964). Trust is therefore analogous to the ability to meet expectations of specific demand. Sabel (1991) points out that trust is never intentionally created but hinges on the existence of trust-sustaining criteria. In turn, trust intensifies adaption, including the interconnection of activities (Håkansson & Johanson, 1988). As such, the relation is the outcome of an incremental process, in which each transaction builds on the previous transaction and adds to the constitution of new transactions. Previous transaction episodes build on a pattern of rules, which are formed, reinforced and modified through the exchange acts (Hallén & Sandström, 1991). Thus the areas and ways in which trust binds actors together constitutes a social construction. In some relations, or regimes, trust is capable of replacing formal contracts, while in others it is not. This does not so much reflect a lack of trust, however, as the fact that the definition of trust differs in different contexts.

Several models have been developed to describe this gradual development of relationships (Ford, 1979; Dwyer, Schurr & Oh, 1987; Hedaa, 1991). According to these models, relations can (ex post) be described in several stages, analogous to life cycle theory, including initiation, expansion, commitment, and (in some versions) dissolution. Though some empirical research has been conducted on this matter, it has produced somewhat ambiguous results (Hallén et al., 1991; Hedaa, 1991). As will be argued later, the notion of a relationship life cycle seems incompatible with the idea of networks as interconnected relationships, and one major weakness of the network approach may be the close relation to the dyadic universe of social exchange theory, which does little to explain the complexity of the social organization of a large number of exchange actors (Zeits, 1980).

2.3 Networks as organizations

Some aspects of network organization, including coordination, control and management, differ in many respects from those of traditional organizations. Unlike the latter, networks are not social groupings designed to serve the purpose of some authority. On the other hand, networks bear little resemblance to the market ideal type found in economic literature, as exchange is not organized randomly through the price mechanism. Imai & Baba (1989) see an important difference in the way activities are organized in networks as compared with market and hierarchies, which stem from their abilities to receive and condense information. According to these authors, information condensed through the network is richer than information derived from random market exchange, and more free than that of the hierarchy.

Another crucial difference is that networks are not organized by a single body of authority. Networks have no identifiable centre from which authority emanates, as in the traditional organizational type. In the network organization, decisions are made by several independent, yet interdependent, decision units. Each actor has control over a range of activities and resources, but because the use of these is dependent on access to complementary resources and activities, the actor posseses some control over other actors, and is also controlled by them. This means that power is distributed throughout the network rather than being held by only one actor. Thus, the power which drives the complex patterns of coordination found in the network are vested in individual exchange relationships. According to Weick (1993), if actors know how to coordinate their activities with the technologies at hand and the actors with whom they interact, the global structure of the task performance will emerge from local interaction.

The authoritarian nature of coordination and direction of hierarchies is therefore absent in networks. Rather than being based on an administrative frame of rules and procedures controlled by a central management function, coordination and direction suggest a negotiating frame of dialogue, in which decisions result from multiple interaction in an elaborate network structure. Direction is thus not based on the legitimate rule of authority, but on activity. It is the provision of specific activities which legitimizes authority in networks and enables actors to direct activities.

Exchange takes place, over time, between a few exchange actors with interrelated interests. As exchange acts become contingent on each other, heterogeneity and mutual adaption develops. Coordination is thus not imposed exogenously, based on a specific overriding purpose, but emerges morphogenetically in the network. Thus networks are self-organizing, evolving structures of single exchange acts which emerge into a larger frame of activity (Snehota, 1993).

In economic theory, the ability to both pursue self-interest and act for the benefit of the larger society may be seen as an (unrealistic) expression of altruism, but it can also just be the product of self-interest, restrained by the impediments of the network. Networks contain several sanction mechanisms for discouraging malfeasance. These can be seen in the dyadic exchange relationship, but also in relation to the broader context of network relationships. Scott (1983) explains these as follows:

> *"Relevant to the operation of interorganizational fields are normative systems that attempt to define rights and relations of the organizational members and the meaning systems that are employed to define and interpret actions within this field [of exchange] (my addition, author)."* (Scott, 1983, p. 166)

First, as suggested by game theory, the network appears as a "continuous game" situation in which players repeatedly confront each other, and reputation becomes a viable asset for the business actor. The most successful strategy in reputational systems is one of trust and cooperation, as shown by Jarillio (1988). This is also mirrored in discrete relationships, since any one event has a direct bearing on subsequent exchange episodes. This has been discussed elsewhere as relationship atmosphere (Hallén & Sandström, 1991). In broader network situations, sanctional mechanisms are institutionalized through reputational mechanisms.

Secondly, the trust developed by exchange partners, in terms of role expectations, is an asset which the individual firm regards as worth protecting, since it gives the firm access to resources outside its administrative control, without its having to internalize them. Opportunistic behaviour is punished through the loss of credibility within the network, and may lead to further access to exchange partners being denied.

The existence of a broader set of internalized values which exchange partners conform to does not mean that that there is no competition within networks. Pfeffer & Salancick (1978) have shown that dependence on other firms is a mediator of uncertainty, which management attempts to reduce either by 1) weakening the dependence on other firms, or 2) strengthening the dependence of other firms to their firm. Each relation may therefore be seen in terms of collaboration and competition. For exchange to occur, both parties must possess something that the other party wants, whether ownership over resources or access to other relations. On the other hand, the basic value of these resources lies in their exchange potency, which is a product of collaboration and adaption through the specialization and division of labour between exchange parties. Departmentalization eventually leads to differences in interests and in perceptions of these interests. Both these factors are a source of conflict and competition. Both competition and collaboration are therefore individually determined by each relationship, as they mark the connection of two unique positions in any network. Consequently, competition must be understood from a relationship level rather than from an overall industrial level, as suggested by industrial economists (see Bain, 1958; Porter, 1980, 1985).

Håkansson has called these processes structurizing and heterogenizing processes (Håkansson, 1992). By structurizing is meant the attempt to strengthen one pattern of collaboration vis-à-vis other patterns, by increasing the interconnectedness and linkage of activities and resources, and with this increasing switching costs (Porter, 1980). The process of structurizing is the cornerstone of relationship interconnectedness, since it transcends the influence of dyadic exchange to the network structure. According to the interconnectedness argument, relations are connected to the extent that exchange in one relation is contingent on exchange (or non-exchange) in another (Cook & Emerson, 1978). It is possible to discern two distinct types of network connections: Positive connections, where exchange in one relation is contingent on exchange in another (such as in distribution chains), and negative connections, where exchange in one relationship is contingent on non-exchange in another relationship (e.g. single-sourcing business arrangements).

The above discussion can be seen as a criticism of earlier comments on the relationship life cycle, because this attempts to extrapolate a pattern of development with an independent momentum from the remaining exchange relationships of the exchange actor. However, if networks are characterized by interconnectedness, it is only to be expected that events in one relationship would effect the other relationships. As such, discussing relationship development models on a dyadic level is problematic, and runs counter to the general idea of interconnectedness. This has been recognized by Mattson & Johanson (1992), who claim that:

> *Through the exchange relation the actors ... develop some trust in each other. On that basis they adopt and develop their resource use ... which also leads to increased resource interdependence between them. At the same time as a result of interdependence, the actors develop their relationships thus linking them to each other. Consequently unless no other factor intervene, ... the specific dependencies will become gradually stronger and closer. However, as the specific relationship is embedded in a network of such relationships, and since this focal dependence is only one in a fabric of such dependencies there are always such intervening factors affecting the casual circle.* (Mattson & Johanson, 1992, p.9)

Heterogenizing relates to the entrepreneurial function of actors in networks, which is conducted through connecting activities and resources in new ways, and as such 'destroys' established exchange structures. In a sense, an exchange structure also expresses a power system with distributive differences, in which forces for change are working.

2.4 Strengths and weaknesses of the network perspective: Processes of organization explained

The previous section discussed the way in which the organization of activity is established and maintained among organizations, and the extent to which organizing activities stretch over organizational boundaries and combine the resources, activities and actors of separate organizations. A framework for understanding both the embryonic and interconnected nature of organization and decision-making in networks and the forces affecting this was also presented. Since a network consists of self-serving actors interconnected in exchange relationships, processes of organizing follow a different path from that found within traditional organizations. In networks, coordination is carried out through exchange acts in discrete relations among actors, not through a regulating authority such as the administrative hierarchy of traditional organizations. Discrete activities between exchange partners lead to the strengthening and weakening of ties in the network, which, due to the interconnectedness of relations, make networks continuously changing structures. The distribution of influence and knowledge among the exchange actors is constantly changing, which again changes the pattern of competition and cooperation.

The network structure is always in a state of being. Networks are stable, but not static (Easton, 1992). They have the ability to self-organize, which implies that organizing processes are based on other governance mechanisms than those found in the market ideal and the concept of the firm. Moreover, exchange, as in markets, is based on the desire to be better off after the exchange than before it. In other words, any engagement in exchange is an attempt by the actor to increase the value of the resources he controls. Value, again, is based on the set of ends and means held by the exchange party (Snehota, 1990). Network actors carry out exchange for diverse reasons, and pursue individual ends. Like organizations, however, networks also form an interlocked exchange arena with few potential exchange actors, due to the specialization and heterogeneity of demand and supply. Thus, network theorists mainly explain the emergence of relationships through structural contingencies. The development of relations is, analogous to social exchange theory (Blau, 1964; Emerson, 1976), an expression of inevitable economic logic: As supply becomes increasingly sophisticated, so does specialization, which again increases mutual dependency. The most economically rational reaction to this is to commit oneself to long-term relationships, since these both allow specialization and stabilize demand and supply (Lundvall, 1993; Smith et al., 1993). The structural viewpoint is problematic, however. First, interaction and exchange do not necessarily coincide, because actors in different organizations may choose to interact for other reasons than strictly economic ones. Second, exchange does not necessarily lead to increasing interconnectedness, introducing patterns of heterogeneity and structuralization. Activities may be logically separate and resources may remain flexible, despite close interaction. This has, among others, been emphasized by Miles & Snow (1992), who have developed a typology of networks, including networks characterized by both stability and temporability in exchange. Temporability in network interaction can be seen in project-like organizational forms, such as construction consortia, as well as in SMEs attempting to preserve flexibility. As pointed out by Kallinikos (1989), although cooperation in construction consortia is organized around projects, where actors participate for a limited time and where there is a substantial turnover of actors and constellations, they are still able to capitalize on shared experiences, using these to rationalize coordination. Thus, the major problem of the network approach is whether the strength and interconnectedness of relations can be measured from structural contingencies and be used to predict and/or explain the nature of network formation, organization and development.

From an interpretive point of view, any social order must be seen as organized by actors in ways that are meaningful to them. The relationship content is therefore not given in advance, but hinges on the actors' interpretation. Knowledge is not merely formed by structural contingencies of networks, but actively shapes them. Johanson & Mattson (1992) partly acknowledge the importance of the interpretations of network actors by stating that:

> "... connections between networks may also take place exclusively via the actors at the network level. In this case they are of a subjective nature and are a matter of intensions, strategies, views and network theories of the actors." (Johanson & Mattson, 1992, p. 209)

Whether the actor's "theory" is that the industrial system in which he operates is governed by collaborative relations between actors or by market fiat, it is obviously relevant to his reflections and his actions towards and interaction with others. Thus, a market theory represents a theoretical choice concerning the way in which markets are seen, or "enacted" (Weick, 1979), from the perspective of the firm. In this sense, network structures, like any other form of social structure, are not actor-external objects. Networks exist in the minds of actors and are continually reconstructed by the meaning-shaping acts of these. Christensen (1992) has illustrated this by means of two theories of strategic conduct in international situations: A collaborative-minded firm may search for potential business partners, while a firm with a more competitive outlook may search for market positions from which it can build a strong competitive base.

The main criticism of the network approach is therefore its lack of ability to take the knowledge and meaning-generating activities of actors seriously. Although the organization of activities depends to a large degree on structural contingencies, it is actors who interpret network possibilities, form relations, and eventually transform network structures. The neglect of the cognitive aspects of actors' decision-making in the network perspective, in spite of the focus on structural elements, leaves some unanswered questions about the role of knowledge and action. Organizations consist of actors, whose activities are coordinated. Organized activity, whether it takes place under the auspices of the organization or between organizations, is an act of applying meaning to reality, analogous to Smith's study on the division of labour in a pin factory mentioned above. Apart from pointing to historical interaction as the basis for shaping shared experiences and learning among interacting organizations, the network perspective has not offered any convincing or integrated explanations for how specific meanings emerge and become shared in a larger community of actors. However, this question has been thoroughly discussed in institutional sociology, and the recent interest in this field among network scholars suggests that it may strengthen the propositions and analytical tools of the network approach. The following section briefly discusses institutional theory, and it will be argued that this branch of theory can enrich the network position and lead to a more in-depth understanding of how organizing efforts take place in organizations.

3. The social construction of networks: An institutional perspective

Networks are not developed in a vacuum, but build on the world views and traditions of the involved actors. Therefore, firms and networks do not represent universal concepts of governance. As several studies have shown (Imai & Itami, 1984; Whitley, 1993), patterns of interaction and the construction of networks can vary considerably in different contexts. Industrial organization reflects the path of organized behaviour which, in a given context, has become internalized, and which is transferred from one context to another. The nature and degree to which economic activity is shaped by particular forms of economic organization transcends the single network, which can be seen as a manifestation of these forms.

The organization of economic activity must therefore be seen in a broader perspective, in which particular forms of organization express the underlying cognitions and rationalities of a given context. The network view has been criticised for being weak in this respect, since little beyond the focal network of a firm is considered. A more holistic and less functionalistic approach has been called for, one which includes the peculiarities of the business context rather than addressing networks as expressions of universal mechanisms of organizational conduct (Hellgren, Melin & Petterson, 1992).

This has also been emphasized in a new academic debate on the social nature of economic activity, which criticizes traditional thinking (Granovetter, 1985) and challenges the demarcation line between formal economics and sociology (Swedberg & Granovetter, 1992). Other scholars have addressed the socially constructed nature of markets and business enterprises (Dimaggio & Powell, 1991; Whitley, 1992; Grabher, 1993). Pettigrew (1990) calls for a contextual approach, in which "embeddedness is a principle of method". By this he means that processes of organization must be understood on a multiple level of analysis, and incorporate the time for capturing the sequential interconnectedness between phenomena. In other words, the processes through which networks are formed and change over time should be the focus of analysis rather than the concept of the network itself.

One theoretical approach which supports this, by emphasizing the interdependency of economic activity and social institutions, is known as institutionalism. The term "institutionalism" is used rather ambiguously to denote a number of heterogeneous approaches within economic theory, politics, sociology and organization theory (Williamson, 1975; Zucker, 1987; DiMaggio & Powell, 1983; Johnson, 1992). While these approaches are interconnected, and share a common ambition to merge human and structural aspects into a more holistic understanding of social affairs, they disagree in several respects. In the following, the interpretive view of institutions is adopted. This tradition has been most fully developed in sociological theory, but is having an increasing influence on organization theory. Some central differences between this and other approaches will be mentioned later (for a more detailed discussion of the institutional approach, see DiMaggio & Powell, 1991, and Swedberg & Grannovetter, 1992).

Institutions play an important role in the organization of economic activity. They provide actors with the means for retaining patterns of interaction, and, by assigning symbols to these patterns, enable them to be transferred between different situations. In this sense, raw data are "bracketed" and given a meaning which is shared by a larger group of persons. This bracketing includes a script, in the sense of a role system with which the actor can identify and expect a pattern of acts from other actors (Goffman, 1959). Through a shared grammar of symbols, actors can reduce interaction complexity, and thus conduct several interacts without having to engage in global rational calculation each time a new situation occurs. When interacts are assigned symbols, they cause social regularities in behaviour, which become ingrained in interaction and to which actors are socialized (Berger & Luckman, 1966). Gradually, organizational and ideological arrangements are worked out by actors. Economic actors, such as banks and equity markets, are routinized means of raising capital (Biggart, 1992).

The interdependece of actors underpins and promotes the institutionalization of reality. It is difficult to disregard the institutionalized patterns of behaviour of other actors if one's own actions are contingent on an understanding of these actors. Institutions can therefore be defined as the collective interpretations of classifica-tions and typifications built into society and enforced and reproduced by public opinion or the force of law.

What social regularities such as norms, customs, traditions, rules and laws have in common is the fact that they relate to how individuals interact and that they can be transferred to new individuals. In business exchange, rules give collective meaning to interaction. Johnson (1992) puts it thus:

> *"An important quality common to different kinds of regularities in behaviour is that they function as informational devices, which reduce uncertainties. They make it unnecessary to start life from scratch every day... They are the signposts for the relationship between people and people."* (Johnson, 1992, p.25)

The function of institutions is thus to stabilize specific patterns of behaviour. They form an institutional matrix, which anchors specific behavioural patterns and is relatively stable over time. Thus, institutions are seen here not just as a product of rational design, as proposed by the structural functionalist (Selznick, 1958; March & Simon, 1958) and economic rationalist (Williamson 1985, Demsetz, 1992) approach to institutions and their role in the organization of activity. Rather, the institutionalizations themselves form the process by which social relationships and actions become objective and external to the actors (Zucker, 1983; Berger & Luckman, 1966). Institutions thus cognitively define what has meaning and which acts are possible (Powell & Dimaggio, 1991).

This leads to the important quality of institutions as a collective memory, influencing the way new learning is acquired and the cognitive processes of actors in general. Institutions are a pattern of thinking ingrained in a group of actors, and may therefore be seen as an encultured programme (Hofsteede 1981) which shapes individual world views. Economists are no exception in this respect:

> *"Like other men the economist is an individual with but one intelligence. He is a creature of habits and propensities given through the antecedents hereditary and cultural, of which he is an outcome; and the basis of thought*

formed in any one line of experience affects his thinking in any other."
(Veblen, 1898, p. xxiv-xxv)

Institutionalization takes place through various processes of socialization. DiMaggio & Powell (1983) identify three channels for the transformation of institutions: a) imitative or mimetic, adopting others' successful elements when uncertain about the alternatives; b) normative transmission of social facts through disciplinary sources, such as social and educational institutions and professions; and c) coercive, through legislation.

Thus, economic behaviour does not reflect universal human characteristics, as generally believed by economic rationalists, but is rather a process of enculturation (Mayhew, 1987). Information is therefore never transmitted as raw data, but is selected, arranged and perceived through institutions. Groups which share institutions tend to be dominated by particular ideas and ideals. These come to serve as group-think (Grahber, 1993), as in the German Ruhr district, where the general recession in demand for steel in the 1970s was collectively interpreted as a sign of coming market expansion by producers as well as local authorities, or industrial wisdom (Hellgren, Melin & Petterson, 1992), as in the case of the newsprint industry, where the attitude of producers shifted from seeing recycled paper as a marginal business area to seeing large cities as major reservoirs of raw material.

From an institutionalist point of view, the organization of economic activity takes place in the highly institutionalized context of modern society to which organizations must respond (Meyer & Rowan, 1977). Organizations are therefore *"driven to incorporate the practices and procedures defined by prevailing rationalized concepts of organizational work and institutionalized in society"* (Meyer & Rowan, op. cit., p. 304). Institutions influence the conduct of individual firms in many ways. One way is through legislation, which makes specific demands on organizations. Other institutions include activities which may be externalized or internalized from the labour force, and the industrial structure in which the firm is situated. In addition, institutions define the "rules of the game" in the factor markets where the firm obtains its resources.

3.1 The Business System Concept

Clearly, the institutional context of firms differs, both in relation to industries, professions, regions and nations. National institutions have a particularly strong influence on business conduct, since several of the institutions which the firm is subject to are organized around the nation state. This has been addressed by Whitley (1992, 1993) through the concept of business systems. According to Whitley (op. cit.), business systems are

> *"Particular arrangements of hierarchy-market relations, which become institutionalized and relatively successful in particular contexts."* (Whitley, 1993, p.6)

Economic activity is thus socially constructed and varies across significantly different social contexts. Business systems include specific ways or rules for dividing, coordinating and controlling activities and resources within and between separate decision-making units. Particular patterns of business interact with social institutions, and together they create a transformation field in which specific forms of economic organization can emerge, prosper and disappear. Imai & Itami (1984) have studied the considerable disparity between the organization of economic activity in Japan and the USA in terms of the differences in resource allocation in markets and firms, and their interconnectedness in various organized markets. In a similar vein, Ouchi (1982) has stressed the difference between American and Japanese employer-employee relations and the importance these differences have for the organization of economic activity.

A business system can be seen as a response to three fundamental issues of economic organization: First, the principles by which economic activities and resources are coordinated and controlled; second, the principles by which connections between authority-coordinated economic activities are organized; and third, how skills within firms are organized and directed. Whitley (op. cit.) describes business systems through three analytical dimensions, which are illustrated in figure 3.2 below:

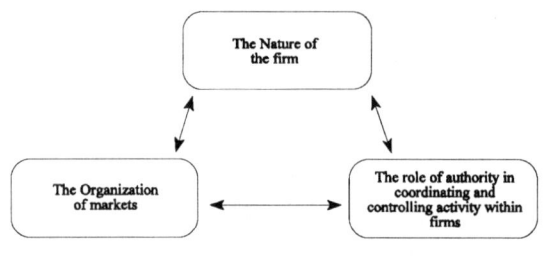

Figure 3.2: The Basic elements of the Business System

The first dimension concerns the nature and role of the firm and the main ways in which firms develop and compete in a particular economy. The nature of the firm as the unit through which input is transformed into output has received considerable attention in the literature. However, this process demands knowledge in terms of skills and practices, which reflects the traditional role and discretion of firms as coordinators and directors in economic organization.

A second, but related, dimension is the organization of markets. These may vary in degree and type, both across industries and across societies (Imai & Itami, 1984). Thus, firms may be more or less interconnected, and their interconnectedness may stretch and vary across both industrial and national contexts.

The third component in the figure relates to how authority is legitimized in a business system. This is reflected in control and coordination systems for the allocation and direction of resources, and in activities in and between firms.

These components are interconnected and mutually form and affect each other. First, the nature of the firm depends on the degree of specialization and interdependency on quasi-market relationships, or the variety of skills they possess. Thus, this factor also has a bearing on the discretion of decision-making in economic units such as firms.

Second, the number and type of relations which firms develop are clearly related to the degree of specialization and the distribution of skills among firms. How and how

90

far activities are interconnected thus affects the development of relationships between decision-making economic units.

Third, the way in which activities are directed within firms is a question of the role of managerial authority and resource allocation. While this dimension also reflects the peculiarities of the other components, it is in itself an important institution, which both defines the role of the firm and the importance of inter-firm relations. The efficiency of managerial practices can therefore also be expected to differ in various contexts. Practices which have proven successful in one context can, and often will, produce different outcomes in other contexts, where expectations and rationalities vary. Thus, the more institutionalized meaning systems differ from context to context, the less transferable any particular practice will be.

3.2 Open and closed business systems

So far, business systems have been defined by and separated from each other through the national boundaries. This is due to the central role of the state in defining and reproducing institutions which affect the organization of economic activity. However, there are clear differences in the national specificity of business systems. The increasing internationalization of business activity has led to the spread of institutionalized practices beyond the boundaries of the single nation-state. This is reflected in both technology and business practices in general. Moreover, as mentioned briefly in chapter 1, factor and product markets are becoming increasingly interrelated across national boundaries, and the development of global industries has meant that firms in national markets are interrelated (Porter, 1986; Holm, Forsgren & Johanson, 1991; Kristensen, 1992). By transforming practices learnt in one context to other areas, multinational firms are important actors in this process (Dunning, 1991). Business systems can therefore be seen as open, to the extent that the generation and reproduction of business practices takes place outside the confines of the national business system.

While business practices are developed and adapted to different situations across national borders, they cannot be seen separately from national institutional contexts. In other words, they must always interrelate with these, which limits the transferability of business practices developed in a national context to a global context. This can be clearly seen in research on international management practices, as well as in studies of the practices of multinational organizations, which, as a result of their cultural or administrative heritage, reveal considerable differences in organizational structure and managerial career routes (Bartlett & Ghosal, 1982; Hofsteede, 1981). The development of international firms and markets thus reflects the struggle between different business practices, rather than the emergence of some overriding business logic, as implied by some marketing and organizational authors (Leavitt, 1983; Dunning, 1991).

3.3 Business systems and entrepreneurial logics

As demonstrated by the business system concept, institutional contexts gradually form a system of business practices. As practices emerge and are reproduced, they express a structure of interdependencies to which new actors and activities must conform. A practice simultaneously expresses a choice of means and ends and a subordination of alternative practices, and therefore restricts the development of these. This has been discussed in innovation literature as development trajectories (Imai & Baba, 1989), or development corridors (Nelson & Winther, 1982). For example, the development and general acceptance of one technology makes it harder for alternative technologies to become established and accepted, because activities and interests become dependent on this technology. In this sense, technical solutions express regimes (Imai & Baba, 1989; Teece, 1986). The systemic nature of practices is not confined to the development of technical solutions, however. Toffler (1981) has convincingly argued that the development of mass industrialization throughout the 19th century and most of the 20th century has depended, on and mutually reinforced, the internalization of a number of socially constructed codes for the disciplining of the workforce and the organization of firms and markets. [8]

Although institutional contexts form a commercial field in which business activity can take place, development paths do not decide the individual acts of economic decision-makers. Rather, they define the rules of the game, and the actor attempts

---

[8] These codes include: Standardization, Optimization, Centralization, Synchronization and Specialization

to allocate resources and relate his own capabilities to this configuration, more or less following existing possibilities. Håkansson (1992) compares the process of networking with a game of chess, in which players must follow certain rules and make their moves according to a complex of interdependencies. From the perspective of the individual actor, the institutional context does not decide his actions, but is recognized as a frame in which activities can be arranged. An individual chess player follows his interpretation of the game and his way of formulating the logic of his position on the chess board (or in the network). His possibilities in the game are thus a product of this interpretation, which is unique. These possibilities are dependent on his idiosyncrasies, and the way in which he combines means and ends. However, unlike the game of chess, network rules are not fixed, but are changed during the game, partly as a result of the activities of the actor.

Thus, the actor can be said to serve an entrepreneurial function in the network (Johannison, 1988; Snehota, 1992), by combining resources, actors and activities in various ways in the pursuit of added value. In a similar vein, Kirzner (1973) has described the entrepreneur as a person who assiduously exploits opportunities by organizing those in control of resources.[9]

In the same way, Imai & Baba (1989) emphasize that entrepreneurs are key actors in networks, where they configure and coordinate activities. However, in contrast to the traditional definition of entreprenurship, they also stress the role of the network in which the actor is situated: *"Entrepreneurs, like everyone else, obtain information in a social context and make judgements, based on their interaction with others."* (cf. Imai & Baba, 1989, p. 28)

The above points to the actor's knowledge as being central to an understanding of how institutions are transformed into networks. Actors are not passive recipients of information, however. Any actor possesses a unique knowledge and a unique assortment of relations, on which the configuration and coordination of resources

---

[9]   Opportunity has been defined as unmet market needs (Kamm & Nurick 1993)

and activities can be based and value-adding pursued. This was also pointed out by Hayek (1945):

> *"It is with respect to this [knowledge of circumstance of the fleeting moment] that practically every individual has some advantage over all others in that he possesses unique information of which beneficial use might be made, but of which use can be made only if the decisions depending on it are left to him or are made with his active cooperation."* (Hayek, 1945, p. 521-522)

Thus, any actor interprets possibilities and acts accordingly, based on previous knowledge. This is analogous to what Weick (1979) has described as processes of enactment. By this he means that knowledge is a set of rules to enact meaning from sensory data through processes of framing. Rules produce a definition of a situation, which *"transform events scattered in chronological time into events cohesive in social time and [...] glue events separated in physical space into units in social space"* (Hedberg, 1981, p.6). A frame is a specific principle for classifying data and relating these to outcomes and actions. According to Weick, frames are imposed on reality by actors, and through these frames actors enact meaning to situations and arrive at an appropriate action based on the existing means-ends framework.

Frames are developed by trial and error, through which actors gradually extend and change their classificatory schemes. Actors' knowledge is thus combined with their actions through a process of reflection, in which existing frames are used and challenged in attempts to generate meaning out of the sensory data received by the network actor. Learning depends on existing schemes, however, and is thus mostly takes the form of error-correction of existing understandings, or what has been labelled "single-loop learning" (Argyris & Schön, 1978). A radical departure from existing interpretive frameworks seldom occurs, since challenges to the present order are alien to the definitional character of frames. The replacement of frames means a challenge to the existing order of knowledge and is therefore also a process of unlearning. Argyris & Schön (op.cit.) have called this double-loop learning.

Due to the interdependency of activities in networks, actors must draw in other actors in order to combine their resources. It is therefore crucial for the network actor to be able to legitimize his actions to other actors. To a large degree, this legitimization depends on the establishment of an interpretive frame, including a reciprocal understanding. However, unlike organizations, shared interpretive frames do not necessarily mean shared values and belief systems. As with institutions, the crucial task is to develop a web of significations through which situations can be defined, and which enables actors to act in a concerted way. In Weick's (1979) terms, organizing depends on:

> *"The validated grammar for reducing equivocality by means of sensible interlocked behaviours. To organize is to assemble interdependent actions into sensible sequences that generate sensible outcomes."* (Weick, 1979, p.3)

Thus, the crux of organization is the development of a grammar which ensures interlocked patterns of behaviour. Individual actors are motivated into pursuing collective acts by means of a shared grammar which encodes different meanings. It is through such a grammar that specific procedures are elicited without the costs and delay of expensive explanations. As expressed by Nelson & Winther (1982):

> *"What is central to productive organizational performance is coordination; what is central to coordination is that individual members, knowing their jobs, correctly interpret and respond to the messages they receive. The interpretations that members give to messages are the mechanism that picks out, from a vast array of possibilities consistent with the roster of member repertoires, a collection of individual performances that actually constitute a productive performance of the organization as a whole."* (Nelson & Winther, 1982, p. 104)

Similar ideas have been expressed by Arrow, in the form of information codes (Arrow, 1974, p. 56-57). Language offers a structure in which phenomena can be categorized and activities ascribed. In other words, it is an instrument which enables definitions of a particular situation to be shared, and, through this, allows for the rationalization of interpersonal interaction.

The grammar of an organization consists of an organizational dialect which is used and elaborated in everyday interaction. Other forms of illocutionary acts than the spoken word also exist, however. For example, a signal lamp on the factory floor can communicate a flow of information to individual actors. The same could be said about a formula faxed to an intermediary. In both cases, the message is encoded and decoded from previous interactions, which represent tacit knowledge in the organizational act.

Thus, organizing does not need a set of shared means and ends, but is based on the principle of reciprocity of benefits - although the returned favour does not require equality in any objective sense of the word (Gouldner, 1960; Singleman, 1972). According to Weick, sensible interlocked behaviour can develop if the following three conditions are met: 1) the actor must perceive that, within the limits of the context, the ability to perform a consummatory act depends on other actors performing instrumental acts. 2) The actor must understand that the performance of an instrumental act serves to elicit an instrumental act from his exchange partner, and 3) The actor must believe that the pattern of consumatory and instrumental acts is likely to be repeated.

These premises for the development of organized activity are clearly met by networks. Network actors can therefore develop interlocked grammars based on mutual prediction rather than mutual values.

The network can be seen as a number of capabilities or skills, vested in the knowledge of actors, organizations and relations. These capabilities comprise the resource base of value-adding activity. A crucial task for the manager in configuring activity is therefore to draw on the resources of other actors. In the following section, this is further discussed as the configuration of resource chains.

3.4 Resource Chains: A conceptualization

The terms of strategic networks, production sets, networks, networks, chains of value-added, focal networks, etc.. are inconsistently used in literature, and may therefore cause some confusion concerning the phenomena addressed. Some clarification of the theoretical language used, including concepts and their definitions therefore seems in its place (Storper & Harrison 1991, Håkansson & Snehota 1994).

The activities of any system of production consists of interrelated tasks which bridges the activities of the producers with the wants of the end-users. At the core of production organization is therefore the physically integrated, inseparable task. How the inseparability of task is to be defined is an issue which is not debated here (See Demsetz 1992). In the present context, tasks are as much socially constructed as technology, and they may therefore be viewed upon as conventional ways of partitioning task complexities into separated tasks.

A firm may conduct one or more task, or these may be conducted collaboratively by firms. Thus in some cases, tasks are not separated by legal boundaries of the firm. On the other hand, a firm may be involved in conducting more than one task. From a task viewpoint a firm may consist of one or more tasks, which can (but need not to be) technologically interrelated. A resource chain is then a collection of tasks which are activated into the production of a specific marketable output. Resource chains thus are the functional core of the economy, as they are the patterns in which outputs in fact are manufactured ((Storper & Harrison 1991) They are characterized by an interfirm division of labor, where each takes on specialized roles and where some sort of coordination is needed. Resource chains are normally characterized by one lead firm and a set of external resource controllers, but the constellation of resource chains may very considerably.

Finally, resource chains form a branch of production delivering a specific type of output, with a large degree of interchangeability in technology used and/or customers served. This level considers an array of tasks which can be combined in numerous ways in configuring specific resource chains.

The process of combining the activities and resources of other actors with those of the focal firm can be described through the concept of resource chains. A resource chain is defined as the set of organizations involved in a particular task. A conceptual model of a resource chain is shown in figure 3.3 (from Christensen, 1987).

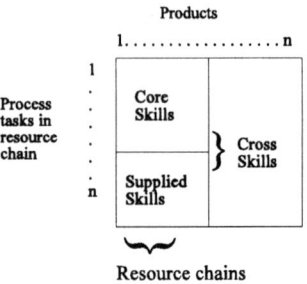

Figure 3.3: The Resource chain: A Conceptual Model

The resource chain displays the activities and the division of labour within the organization of international activity, and is therefore also closely related to the value-added chain, which has been the focus of a number of authors, including Porter (1985). The value chain sees the firm as a collection of activities performed in a particular industry. In this sense, it is a tool for disintegrating firms' performance into discrete activities, for the purpose of comparative analysis.

The resource chain concept differs from the value-added chain in several respects. It does not depict activities in an authoritarian frame. Instead, it reflects a knowledge-based division of labour among a more or less loosely configured collection of firms. While the principle of organization in the value-added chain is the status of activities, i.e. whether they are found inside or outside the authoritarian frame, the organizing principle underlying the resource chain is the actual activity carried out. The activities performed in the resource chain can thus be represented in multiple resource chains and play different roles, depending on the context in which they are connected (Aldrich & Whetten, 1981).

According to Christensen (op. cit), the firm depends on the combined efforts of a number of specific skills in order to extract value from its core skills. Through the process of combination, patterns of interlocked behaviour become ingrained, leading to the development of cross-skills. A resource chain thus represents an activity which combines several actors and resources into value-adding activity. A firm can participate in several activities which together add up to its relationship profile.

Analogous to this, cross-skills can be seen as a gradually emerging grammar which is shared among business actors. A grammar represents the shared code that makes organized action possible, and is thus an enactment of the market to routinized processes of interaction. In this sense, the resource chain generates new knowledge which can eventually lead to the development and institutionalization of new practices, shared in a wider community, through the mimetic processes described earlier.

3.4.1 Relationship dialogues: The social construction of organizing grammars
A resource chain can be seen as the joining of several shared routines into a pattern of value-adding activities in a vertical production-consumption sequence. Networks of SMEs do not represent hierarchies, but heterarchies, in which the distribution of power tends to be symmetrical rather than asymmetrical, and in which structure is undetermined (Hedlund, 1981). Actor structures are not interlocked, but organized around projects or activities, which in turn are not static patterns of production, but constantly changing arrangements.

The dialogue thus plays a central role in the organization of resource chains, allowing SMEs and foreign intermediaries to establish and develop a basis for integrating core and supplied skills through a shared grammar. The dialogue enables activities and roles to be decided and a mutual understanding to be reached. Dialogue partners can be more or less distant, depending on the degree to which cognitions are shared. The process of creating a shared grammar through which the organization of activity can be rationalized can therefore be more or less complex. The internalization of the organization task is expected to strengthen the process of establishing and developing a relationship dialogue, as cultural differences are often found between actors from different countries, distorting the transfer and development of shared meaning systems. This has been noted both in comparative studies of management practices (Hofsteede, 1981) and marketing communication (Niss, 1993).

The dialogue serves different functions throughout the development of a shared grammar in a resource chain (Freytag & Nørreklit, 1993). It is possible to speak of three different dialogue types: A) configuring dialogues; B) developing dialogues, and C) calibrating dialogues. These are explained in the following.

The configuring dialogue serves to reduce experienced uncertainty and facilitate mutual comprehension. The function of this dialogue type is to establish mutual identities. As pointed out by Webster (1975), distributors and producers often have stereotyped ideas of their own role and the role of counterparts in the organization of marketing. In order to address the peculiarities of each others' resource profile, the configuration dialogue must go beyond these stereotypes.

The function of the second dialogue type is to routinize exchange by rationalizing the information exchanged in the resource chain. As mutual understanding gradually develops, the number of interlocked behaviour patterns increases. Weick (1991) has described this as a sequential process, in which the reduction of equivocality gradually expands the number of rules related to exchange, which again reduces the number of activity cycles that can be based on these rules. This process represents a rationalization of interaction. The process is shown in figure 3.4 below:

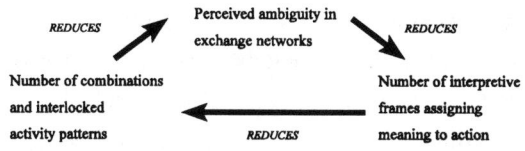

Figure 3.4: The development of Shared Routines

The function of the third dialogue type is to calibrate activities through the development of shared knowledge, as well as developing the knowledge base of each partner. As a shared grammar emerges, solutions to individual problems and challenges can be dealt with in a wider community. This can result in quicker solutions, because more information about the problem can be obtained and processed, and it can be treated from many different angles. Moreover, the knowledge obtained in one relationship can be used innovatively, and provide the basis for the creation of value-added activity in other relationships, thus expanding the competence of the individual actor.

The knowledge-development aspect of dialogues also touches on a central problem in the establishment and development of a relationship profile for the single firm. As pointed out by Håkansson earlier, the firm cooperates in multiple networks, each seeking to rationalize the efforts made in any one resource chain.

From the above, it can be seen that network actors become arenas for connecting activity cycles into a larger pattern of concerted action, in which exchange actors need to strike a coherent balance between the ability to absorb new knowledge (and thus participate in concluding activity) and the maintenance of an existing grammar. Other authors have also drawn attention to this tradeoff between rationalization and innovative capacity (Weick, 1991; Håkansson, 1992; Metcalfe, 1981; Håkansson & Axelsson, 1989).

There are two possible ways in which the network actor can retain the balance, and thus reduce complexity: 1) Reduce the number of exchange interfaces, or 2) reduce the depth of the interface. These strategies can also be applied to other observations in the literature regarding the organizing of international activity. The number of exchange interfaces can, analogous to the 'market failure approach' (see chapter 1), be reduced through entry mode investments. Here, the actor internalizes the interface, and thus obtains greater control of the interaction. Secondly, the actor can refrain from participating in further exchange relationships. This strategy has been described as 'stuck in the middle' of a firm's internationalization process (Bohn et al., 1989). The second possible strategy is to reduce the depth of interaction. This can be achieved by means of task partitioning, where the actor clearly refrains from specific activities and strictly divides labour and structure interaction by other means (Von Hippel, 1988).

In a broader perspective, the development of business practices in resource chains may affect the business system, because they add to actors' knowledge. If they constitute valuable insights, they will be used by the actors in subsequent resource chains, and thereby distributed to a broader community of actors. In this sense, the entrepreneurial function of an economy is not restricted to the activities of a single actor, but is rather a product of actions and the ease with which these can be implemented in other activities.

Overall, the processes of institutionalization and resource chain development form two processes which are partly contradictionary: one of reproduction and one of generation. The reproductive element attempts to stabilize the existing order and the interests it supports. This is analogous to what Håkansson (1992) earlier described as structuration on the network level. The generation of activity, on the other hand, attempts to break with existing practices. These actions stem from entrepreneurs with novel interpretations, and who pursue other interests than those of established interest groups - what Håkansson described as heterogenization (Håkansson, op.

cit.). Together, the processes of generation and reproduction form the dynamics of networks. This is illustrated in figure 3.5.

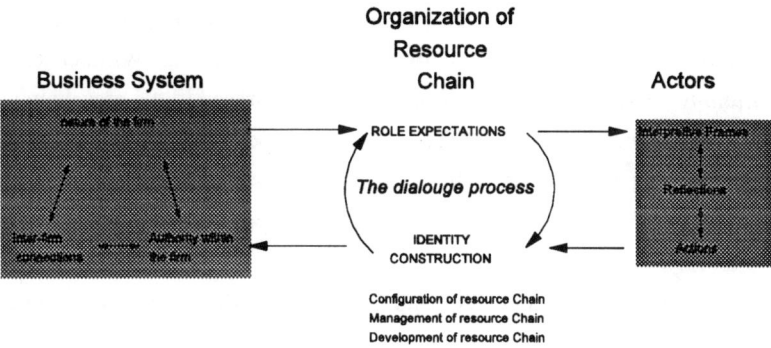

Figure 3.5: The mutual configuration of actors and business systems

The institutional context makes several demands on the actors, which they must meet in order to legitimize their actions. Together, these form a set of role expectations. At the same time, the actor attempts to implement his own interpretations of market opportunities, and gain the acceptance of other resource holders for these in order to acquire/commit the resources necessary for his own activities. This is a process of identity construction. Together, these activities form the basic components of which resource chains are constructed.

The social construction of resource chains can also be seen as a competence-building process, by which, through trial and error, actors acquire new competencies. In addition, as they become shared in a broader community, these processes lead to new practices being acquired from the distribution processes earlier described by Zucker (op. cit.).

In this process, the resource chain gradually acquires an independent status. Actors develop a shared grammar, which allows the configuration, management and development of shared routines. The resource chain, and the institutionalized codes associated with it, becomes a competence in itself, as it retains a constitution of standard operation procedures, which can be elicited and carried out in an economically efficient way. As pointed out by Nelson & Winther (1982), *"organizations remember by doing"*. This can be paraphrased in the present context as *"firms remember by interacting"*. Thus, one firm's performance is dependent on the complementary skills of other firms, and only exists as a distinct competence configuration in connection with other skills than those possessed by the single firm.

In the following, the above model and the network theory together form the background for the formulation of a conceptual framework which can be used to understand how SMEs draw on and organize external resources. By this means, it is hoped to shed some light on the ways in which they establish and develop a position in the international division of labour. The above discussion has outlined a general framework for the analysis of business systems. It has been shown, both by the network approach and the business systems approach, that organization in and among firms must be seen in a broader frame of activity.

In the next section, these more general observations will be used to construct a conceptual framework for the present study. The section starts with an analysis of the Danish business system, and relates this to the organization of SMEs and the development of international activity. This is followed by the development of three analytical phases used in analysing the business practices in the empirical part.

4. A framework for the present study

4.1 The Danish Business System

Analogous to the components depicted in figure 3.2, the Danish business system is characterized by three interdependent factors[10]: (A) The structural and traditional

---

[10]   The following largely builds on Andersen & Christensen (1993, 1994).

foundation of Danish industry, (B) the administrative logic of business managers, and (C) the collaborative orientation of production units. This model is presented in figure 3.6.

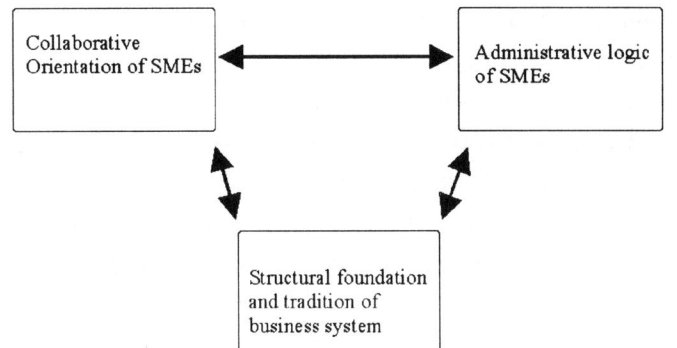

Figure 3.6: Three main factors of the Danish Business System

The structural and traditional foundation of Danish industry is a key factor in explaining the potentials of the Danish business system. The characteristics of Danish industry are to a large extent related to agricultural traditions. Although the direct relation between agriculture and industrial production has been weakened (Hansen & Lunding, 1993), the heritage of the "agro-industrial complex" is still evident in studies of the structure of Danish industry (Møller & Pade, 1988; Lundvall et al., 1984).

Kristensen (1992), has described the emergence of the Danish business structure as the development of small, self-sufficient growth centres in agricultural societies centred around small provincial "railway" towns. In these growth centres, production developed around village philosophies of independence and cooperation, as characterized by, for example, the cooperative movement (Skrubbeltrang, 1948). Another decisive factor was the development of the craft system in Denmark, by which a class of educated craftsmen were able to take advantage of supplying farmers with goods and services to demand labour when this production factor was in seasonal surplus on the farms. At the same time, small producers could act as subcontractors to the modern industry found in the large cities.

This has given rise to a large group of SMEs in the Danish business system, based on the skills of a single craftsman, and characterized by a large degree of both specialization and flexibility. Specialization largely follows the craft of the entrepreneur. However, this specialist knowledge can be implemented in several products, which means that SMEs can have multiple relations, rather than simply being subcontractors for larger firms (Grøn, 1985). SMEs are therefore loosely rather than tightly coupled, and, on an industry level, can organize around patterns of activity rather than around dependency. SMEs support, and receive support, from the "environmental texture" of the firm. By environmental texture is meant a context characterized by infrastructures particular to the input needs of a group of firms (Lorenzioni & Ornati, 1988). According to Lorenzioni & Ornati (op. cit):

> *"The needs of various new firms are met through the availability of suppliers who thereby create an environmental texture of opportunities not fully characterizable by a physical or a geographical boundary."* (Lorenzioni & Ornati, 1988, p. 42)

As such, it is possible for the single firm to retain its identity and simultaneously adapt to changing business conditions without changing the business system as a whole.

Another result of the flexibility and specialization of Danish SMEs is the large degree of externalization. In Denmark, a business venture can be started on the basis of only a few fixed assets, because the environment of the entrepreneur allows the possibility of subcontracting both production and administrative functions (Kristensen, 1994; Larsen, 1990).

The structural foundation of the Danish business system has a decisive influence on both the mutual orientation and administrative logic of the business system. The above-mentioned characteristics both foster and, to a large degree, depend on a collaborative orientation among business enterprises. Lacking control of resources internally, SMEs rely on their capacity to build up long-term relations with external actors (Mønsted, 1985). One major vehicle of support is other SMEs, which offer complementary goods and services or the opportunity for extending production

106

capacity. This has been shown in Karnøe (1992), who has analysed the organizational patterns of the windmill industry, where competition and collaboration go hand in hand. Similar observations have been made in the horticultural industry (Christensen, 1993) and the dairy industry (Andersen, 1993).

The structural foundation and organization of industry has also led to a high degree of interwovenness within industries, where organizational boundaries are crossed by shared skills and mutual knowledge and interaction patterns, and where the competencies of the SME unit are developed in close interaction with other business units. This both supports and is supported by the development of specific administrative logics within business.

Several of the factors which have led to the institutionalization of specific administrative logics in SMEs have their origin in the professions. For example, the guild system can be seen as a socio-cognitive community which evolves around identifiable work domains, and develops specific work methods and standards, as well as social and cultural conventions. The career paths of individuals may be seen as another medium through which shared beliefs and thought structures are developed. They provide a common language for framing and interpreting the flow of raw data which people are confronted by in everyday activity. Interaction and communication are thus to a large degree the result of tacit knowledge and presumptions. They are principles and rules learnt through experience, and are not easily accessible to people outside the social domain. Inside this domain, however, they lead to a high degree of transparency, since members of a profession can easily coordinate and build up shared action patterns across organizational boundaries. Shared knowledge becomes institutionalized and is transformed into a social fact.

4.2 The internationalization of SMEs in open business systems

The internationalization process is often described as one of risk minimization through learning and the stepwise development of international competence internally in the firm (Johanson & Vahlne, 1977 & 1990). The argument for this is that the management decision-making system, which is analogous to the decision-making model outlined by Cyert & March (1963) and March & Simon (1958), is risk-aversive and seeks to avoid uncertainty.[11] International business is considered relatively more risky than doing business in a national context, but these differences in risk perception are gradually reduced through the stepwise accumulation knowledge, which strengthens the perceptions of business opportunities and encourages increasing foreign market commitment, thus supporting the internationalization of the firm.

The model, which is based on the behavioural theory of the firm, has two major weaknesses: First, it leaves very little room for the cognitions and reflections of individuals in actively shaping realities. In the same way as the S-O-R paradigm of behavioural theory, the management decision-making system is seen as a passive recipient of information, which is processed and computed into decision-making in a Bayesian manner. Second, the generality of the model is criticizable, as mentioned earlier in chapter 1.

However, the resource chain perspective outlined above suggests that a) learning can take place and competence generated and maintained in the network of relations of the individual SME actor, and b) the deterministic linking of knowledge and behaviour in the Uppsala model of internationalization is based on a knowledge concept of the rational agent from economic theory rather than on the institutionalist concept of the enacting actor. To paraphrase Veblen, the decision-maker of the internationalization model is not so much a "prime mover" as a hedonistic agent. These issues will be addressed in turn.

First, as pointed out earlier, firms never act in faceless markets. In economic theory, the concept of a faceless market can perhaps serve a purpose in explaining price formation in an ideal market, but it has limited value in explaining what is going on between buyers and sellers in processes of exchange (Snehota, 1992). Firms are not agglomerates of resources allocated independently by management. Rather, a firm's

---

[11]   According to these authors, human decision-making is characterized by limitied mental capability. Thus, we do not engage in global rational calculations, since this is impossible and too costly. Rather, we attempt to *satisfice* by achieving results above a certain standard. March & Simon (1958) describe the difference between the optimal decision model and satisfying behaviour as: *"The difference between searching a haystack to find the sharpest needle in it and searching the haystack to find a needle sharp enough to sew with"* (op. cit., p.162).

resources and activities are interconnected and dependent on other firms. This also means that learning processes which relate to the rationalization and development of the production and distribution of goods are developed in interaction with others, and requires the experiences of multiple actors. Often, the knowledge of the single actor may only relate to part of the process of producing and distributing internationally, which makes him dependent on the knowledge of other actors. The network of actors can therefore be seen as a knowledge network, where thought patterns become institutionalized and have a shared grammar, which makes interlocked activities possible. Thus the network, so to speak, remembers. Information is not transmitted raw, but is processed in the network, where the coupling of information and action is determined by previous interactions, and which in turn influences the likelihood of following these successful interrelations. The patterns of connecting knowledge and action within the network thus tend to repeat themselves over time, and the early experiences of cooperation tend to become routinized and lock in subsequent cooperation. Thus the internationalization of the single firm is not a solo effort, but is also based on collaboration with other firms. Activities, and the knowledge related to these, are not wholly controlled by the individual firm, but have an inertia of their own. This has also been pointed out by other authors, who suggest that any analysis of the processes furthering and/or hindering the internationalization of the firm should take a starting point in the internationalization of the market. Decisions concerning internationalization are not taken on the basis of the individual firm seeking to optimize the allocation of ownership-controlled resources. Rather, the internationalization process is a result of the firm extending and/or integrating different relationships with actors located in other countries. The development of organizational patterns is therefore an alternative way of connecting or strengthening the network position of a firm (Johanson & Mattson, 1988. See also Toyne, 1989, and Bradley, 1991).

Secondly, networks do not determine the knowledge of individual actors. Rather than seeing learning and knowledge as an accumulative process, it should be seen as a process in which the actor constantly interprets and enacts reality according to his frame of mind. This process enables the actor to influence and gradually construct reality, provided his acts are legitimized by the external resource holders on whom his internationalization depends.

This brings us to an alternative model for the internationalization of SMEs, which can explain how SMEs manage to develop an extensive international position, analogous to the research objective outlined in chapter 1.

Central to the picture of the SME outlined above is that SMEs can draw on external resources and organize them in a way which allows mutual adaption, and which avoids the administrative costs typical of larger firms. This suggests that collaboration is a central to understanding the internationalization of SME activity. "Collaboration" is often used as a concept in business studies of strategic alliances, which has resulted in a number of different definitions of the term. Here, collaboration is defined as arrangements whereby partners share skills and personnel, and which, over time, develop shared capabilities (Dogdson, 1993).

Furthermore, it has been suggested that networks act as reputational systems, which discourage malfeasance and strengthen the development of trust, here defined as meeting the expectations of others. It has also been suggested that the development of international resource chains is a process which takes time. In simple terms, it is a development process which can be described by means of three main phases, relating to the organization and development of collaborative internationalization in resource chains. These phases are: Configuration of resource chains, rationalization of resource chains, and development of resource chains. These phases are not sequential - the SME simultaneously configures, manages and develops resource chains with other actors. For purposes of analysis, however, they can be discussed separately.

The collaborative and open environment of Danish SMEs presents both business opportunities and challenges. Generally, the management task consists of three generic tasks: (1) Configuration of international resource chains, (2) management of international resource chain activity, and (3) expansion into international markets.

In line with the theoretical basis of this thesis, the main aspects of the resource chain development process are: 1) The operational logic, or business framework, in which the SME carries out its activities; 2) The characteristics of the dialogue between the SME and external resource controllers; and 3) The characteristics of the activity-coordinating role of the SME in the resource chain throughout the various phases. These phases and their main characteristics are shown in table 3.1 below.

Table 3.1: Phases of international resource chain development

	Configuration	Rationalization	Development
Operating Logic	INDEPENDENCE	STRUCTURATION	HETEROGENIZATION
Dialogue Characteristic	CONFIGURATION	ROUTINIZATION	CALIBRATION
Role of SME	ENTREPRENEUR	PARTNER	BROKER

These phases are described in more detail below.

4.2.1 Configuration of International Resource chains

Broadly speaking, the configuration of the resource chain has three phases: A latent, pre-production phase; a configuration phase, in which the network is formed and routinized; and a change phase, where some basic contingencies of the network are altered.

The business system in which the SME operates is characterized by independent resource controllers, who participate in several activities for a given activity cycle and are then included in new activities. A crucial task in configuring resource chains is finding and committing external resources to support the international ambitions and activities of the firm. Here, two factors can be considered very important: The ability of the entrepreneur to evaluate the "collaborative environment of the firm", and the ability to create external incentives attractive enough to potential partners. Success in finding such resources depends on the resource base of the environmental texture, of course. No matter how favourable this may be, however, it is not automatically activated in support of the firm. The exploitation of supply-side conditions depends on the ability of management to find and commit contacts (Christensen & Lindmark, 1992).

Personal relations are often used as bridges to previously unknown or impersonal resource controllers (Granovetter, 1973). Several studies have pointed to the importance of previous working relationships, kinship and community ties (Kamm & Nurick, 1993; Larson & Starr, 1993). Here, trust is an implicit feature of the overall economic system (Granovetter, 1985). In a social context, this can be equated with reputation. It is by utilizing the trust built up by the reputation of a close associate that the SME manager gains access to resources outside his own social domain. On a more general level, scholars have discussed reputational systems (Whitley, 1992). Reputational systems tend to be found in institutional contexts, since it is within these contexts that a reputation is built. One powerful vehicle for the configuration of a resource chain may thus be the profession of the entrepreneur. As such, the crystallization of economic activities may be seen as heavily embedded in social relations (Granovetter, 1985). As the above illustrates, the personal network of an SME manager plays a crucial role in his ability to find and get access to external resources. It has even been suggested that this is his most valuable asset (Johannisson & Peterson, 1984).

The commitment of resources presents an even larger problem in the configuration of resource chains. Commitment calls for responsibility of resources. Commitment to a resource chain leads to interdependence, relative to the size of the commitment. As such, the decision to commit the firm to a resource chain will depend on at least three factors, relating to both risk and opportunity: a) the size of the commitment; b) the knowledge gained either from the personal experience of the SME manager or through other sources; and c) the visions and ideas of the SME manager. The first two factors refer to the risk of participating in a resource chain, while the last factor clearly refers to opportunities and incentives in terms of financial surplus, market position, etc. An opportunity is an idea about a desirable future state. However, opportunities do not exist per se, but are created and/or constructed by the entrepreneur. As pointed out by Henders (1992), network positions are not empty holes waiting to be filled in. The actors themselves are responsible for their positions and assigned roles. This illustrates the importance of enactment in the configuration of the resource chain. Enactment is thus a prerequisite for realization.

The commitment of resources involves the formalization of relationships which were previously informal and even personal. Business exchange becomes a vital part of the relationship.

The "strength of weak ties" seems to play an even greater role in the configuration of international resource chains. Entrepreneurs, like everybody else, obtain information and make judgements based on interaction with others. The loose and changing network of contacts is used as a platform to create dynamic information through multi-linked interaction. Case studies show that firms which internationalize instantly often do so on the basis of "old" ties to buyers and intermediaries which an actor brings into a new venture (Mietela & Törnross, 1992). It is essential for resource-weak SMEs to be flexible in relation to changes in technology, market opportunities and changes in demand, without committing internal resources "blindly". Therefore, subjective judgements of external actors' intentions, reliability and commitment are potentially important qualities in constructing the resource chain.

The way the SME manager configures the resource chain depends on the activities of his surroundings. This implies that the configuration of the resource chain is not purely a product of design. On the other hand, it is not limited to readily available resources, either. Rather, it is constituted through a series of trial-and-error processes, in which the configuration is jointly shaped by the interplay between the entrepreneur and network resources. Configurations thus cannot be viewed as something developed solely from a plan or by design. Rather, realized opportunities are the outcome of the interaction between the SME manager and the resource controllers accessible through his personal network. Thus, configurations are the realized strategic possibilities of a frame of possible configurations, analogous to Mintzbergs´ (1987) notion of strategy as a frame. They are the result of mutual problem-solving, the solution of recurring task-partitioning problems and similar challenges in the configuration process. This process has elsewhere been described as a problemistic search (Cyert & March, 1963). This type of search gains importance in those cases where there is a major imbalance between the importance of strategic decision-making and available information and knowledge. Information levels tend to be high at times when the importance of decisions is low, not least in turbulent industries.

4.2.2 Organizing international resource chain activity

The organization of resource chains poses a challenge to conventional thinking, particularly from the point of view of management discipline, partly because incremental configuration is a key feature, partly because external incentive structures change traditional ones, and partly because the extraction of value from core skills is rooted in the management of supplied skills. Thus, the capability of the firm is critically dependent on its mode of interaction with other firms. In the resource chain, activity is based on collaboration with interdependent decision units, and the main role of the SME is that of a coordinator of complementary resource controllers in a dynamic division of labour rather than that of a centrally controlling hub firm, as in the organization of Japanese Keiretzus (Kristensen, 1994). In the international resource chain, the organizing context is fluent and transitory. Westley (1990) describes it as follows:

> "Series of interlocking routines, habituated action patterns that bring the same people together around the same activities in the same time and places." (Westley, 1990, p. 339)

As such, typical managerial activities, such as coordination and control, are not supported by the authority structure found in bureaucratic settings. Therefore, the function of the resource chain does not rest on legitimized power. In addition, the role of resource dependency as a vehicle for authority may be challenged. Although the positioning towards suppliers and buyers may be powerful in the short run, these positions seldomly mirror unique possession of resources. SMEs seeking to position themselves by blocking the access of buyers to suppliers may be bypassed by the actors and excluded from the resource chain. This mechanism has been described at length by Laage-Hellman (1992).

Scholars have previously characterized entrepreneurial management as charismatic (Smircich & Stubbart, 1985). Charisma has been defined as *"the ability to persuade*

114

others to enact realities that further the interests one wish to pursue" (Morgan, 1986, p. 176). In this sense, authority rests on the acceptance of the members of a group, e.g. a resource chain. Management is supported in the resource chain through the pursuit of activity. By providing knowledge and information about needs, the SME creates stable demand and supply conditions and reduces the impact of uncertainty and information for the other resource chain participants[12]. This is the central thrust of the SME. In return for access to externally-controlled resources, the SME offers demand stabilization, and thus reduces risk, as seen from the viewpoint of suppliers of skills and resources.

This process has a strong parallel to what Cyert & March (1963) describes as coalition management. From this perspective the managerial process is looked upon as one of providing inducements to those in possession of resources in favour of gaining access to these resources. Here, the managerial process is characterized by compromise decision processes and dialouge (Thompson 1967). The process of netting out the interests of each resource holder while maintaing streams of organized action will here be referred to as coalignment, analogeous to Thompson (1967).

The coalignment of resources to rationalize the efforts of the resource chain presupposes some degree of mutual adaptation. The pursuit of activity must change from being general to becoming more structuralized, in order to fit into the system of existing relationships between core and supplied skills within the resource chain. As actors gradually come to share a grammar for routinizing activity, relationships are formed and specialized to handle certain activities efficiently. Consequently, while resource chains will run easily in these routinized pathways, it becomes increasingly difficult to counter them (Håkansson, 1989).

The emergence of external resource controllers plays a central role in the development of the resource chain as whole, but also in the strength of the SME. By strengthening the capabilities of the external firm and/or increasing the amount and/or quality of resources available, the SME also ensures its own possibilities in

---

[12]   This has been referred to elsewhere as the raison d'etre of firms (Knight, 1921; Thompson, 1967).

the resource chain. It is therefore crucial for the SME to choose a role which will enable it to develop the resources attached to the resource chain while simultaneously legitimizing its position in relation to other firms. The function of this role is to maintain a position vis-à-vis other firms, which again makes it possible to maintain a system of role expectations from other firms (Andersen et al., 1994). The SME has a choice of several strategies for mobilizing the resources of external resource controllers, which rest on other foundations than those of the administrative hierarchy (Metcalfe, 1981; Lorenzoni & Ornati, 1988).

4.2.3 Development of the resource chain

The routinization of activity also helps the development of international activity, since routinized activity tends to develop its own interia. The inclusion of new actors, resources and activities is contingent on the existing setup of the resource chain. Thus, internationalization mirrors a process of path-dependency, in which initial decisions contain several consequences for the further development of international knowledge and the subscription of action. Both the organization task and the international expansion of the SME depends on its flexibility to meet the needs of suppliers, intermediaries and customers - in short, its ability to collaborate and combine complementary resources, actors and activities, and learn from these. It can be seen from this that there are two challenges to the international market expansion of SMEs: a) their dependence on the capabilities of supplied skills, and b) the scarcity of coordinating resources in the SME. These points will be addressed in turn below.

The above arguments concerning resource chains imply that international market expansion hinges on the ability of the SME to interpret resource utilization in various contexts and communicate this to other customers, thereby achieving a competitive advantage vis-à-vis competitors. In this sense, previous exchange relationships are used as stepping stones to subsequent exchange. The firm becomes an arena for the exchange of contextually bounded information. Its market rationale becomes the winning of resources in a world of imperfect knowledge.

From this perspective, the SME resource chain can be thought of as a configuration of internal and external relations, in which the ownership-controlled resources of the firm have contextual rather than absolute value. It is through this market-bound configuration of internal and external resources that the firm gains its ability to generate new activity. Consequently, the potential of new relations must be assessed in relation to their contribution to the generation of new activity, either by maintaining or expanding the degree of coherence in the firm's relationships. It is the constant renewal of knowledge of the utilization of resources which constitutes the basis on which the firm can conduct business. And it is through the capabilities of this base that increased international expansion is ensured. As such, the development of a resource chain is limited by the lack of capabilities of resource chain partners and the lack of development of these capabilities. This may present general problems of specialization and flexibility. Thus, the very ties which initially supported and made internationalization possible may also be those that hinder further expansion. Johanisson (1988) has called this the rubber-band effect. It therefore becomes increasingly necessary for the firm to establish relations with new resource controllers during international market expansion, and also to develop existing ones.

On the other hand, the international development of knowledge in the network also results in a process of heterogenizing. This is a regenerating process, where the actors try to utilize new dimensions of the resources involved, or utilize known resources in a new way in current activities, by adding new actors to the present setup, thereby altering the configuration as a whole (Håkansson, 1989).

Seen from this viewpoint, the crucial task of SME management in the internationalization process becomes one of balancing the diversity generated from existing exchange relationships, and utilizing the potential changes stemming from the introduction of new relationships. This indeed marks a balance between innovation and rationalization. Existing relations form the strategic frame from which new activities are generated. The more stability introduced into this frame through, for example, the interorganizational specialization of assets and other means of mutual adaptation, the more certainty can be introduced, which again allows for long-term planning and possible scale benefits from cost efficiency.

Specialization, on the other hand, necessitates the structuralization of activity, because resources are devoted to only a few potential exchange possibilities. This introduces rigidity in exchange, which is anathema to both flexible production patterns and innovation. This has clearly characterized business conditions over the past few decades, and, with increasing competition forcing firms to constantly improve existing procedures, it is important to avoid resource dependency. Moreover, specialization is the opposite of generalization. Too close an adaptation to the idiosyncrasies of one exchange relationship diminishes the contribution to other relationships.

As the number of activities in SMEs grows, and become increasingly diversified as a function of the participation in multiple business systems, so do the demands on the SME. Related to this problem is the scarcity of coordinating resources (Sørensen, op. cit.). The SME manager largely coordinates on the basis of the dialogue and personal relations to external resource holders. However, there is an upper limit to the relations which SME managers can maintain. Thus, the continuing international expansion of the SME depends on how the diverging demands of flexibility on collaboration throughout the resource chain are counterbalanced by the firm's ability to maintain and test the value of its own competence. The role of the SME in the development of the resource chain can therefore be described as that of a broker who attempts to satisfy the mutual interests of both parties while retaining a profit margin for himself.

5. Concluding remarks

In the above, several concepts have been developed to describe and assess the practices of international organization and development pursued by SMEs. It has been pointed out that any study of SMEs' organization and development of international activity must include their relations to external resource controllers, and that the organization of activities can be seen as the institutionalization of a shared grammar, which makes it possible to:

a)   routinize activity and b) develop shared skills which can be further used in developing new capabilities.

Thus, the organization and development of international activity takes place in resource chains, in which actors combine their skills by means of shared understandings and rationalized conduct. Moreover, it has been argued that the study of organizations among discrete economic decision-makers must take into consideration both the institutional context and the entrepreneurial logics of these decision-makers.

CHAPTER 4

NORDEX FOOD A/S

General profile

Nordex Food is a small firm situated in Dronninglund, in northern Jutland, Denmark. The firm produces and markets various types of cheese and other dairy products under the brand names "Dairyland" and "Arkadia". The firm's main product is feta cheese, a white cheese conserved in brine and produced from cow´s milk. The firm also produces butter, moulded cheese, and a number of special cheeses of Middle Eastern origin, such as Halloumi cheese and Balkan cheese. In 1993, the firm had a turnover of DKK 414 million.

Nordex Food has 101 employees, 75 in production and 26 in administration. The firm is formally divided into Nordex Food A/S and Nordex Holding A/S. The former is responsible for all trading activities, while the latter, a holding company, owns and operates three dairies.

Background, development and present status of Nordex Food A/S

The history of Nordex Food starts with Ørum dairy, which was owned by JBK. Following the success of the ultra filtration method, Ørum dairy expanded into controlling 9 dairies, which in 1983 had a turnover of DKK 800 million.

Meanwhile, as Ørum Gruppen was enjoying its success, the cooperatively owned dairies continued the process of rationalization which had begun in the 1950s. Up to the early 1990s, the cooperative part of the Danish dairy industry underwent massive rationalization, with the result that milk production is now concentrated in increasingly fewer hands: In 1992, more than 95 per cent of the milk produced in dairy farms was delivered to two cooperatively owned firms - Mejeriselskabet Danmark A.m.b.a. (now MD Foods) and Kløver Mælk A.m.b.a. Cooperative dairies are owned by the dairy farmers, whose basic interest is to obtain profitable milk prices. The management of the leading cooperative dairies convincingly argued that larger production units would create more rational production conditions, thus increase the prices paid to the dairy farmers.

The success of Ørum Gruppen in the late 1970s made it possible to offer higher milk prices to its associated dairy farmers. This led to painful questions being asked at the large cooperatively owned dairies. Dairy farmers connected to MD Foods demanded to know why the substantial and expensive rationalization and centralization process was necessary, when medium-sized producers such as Ørum Gruppen were able to earn higher profits and pay more to their dairy farmers? Eventually, in 1984, MD Foods acquired Ørum Gruppen from JBK. The dairies controlled by Ørum Gruppen were closed down, and the delivery contracts with the independent farmers were transferred to Akafa, a large feta cheese dairy controlled by MD Foods. As part of the deal, JBK also signed an agreement in which he commited himself not to start up feta production within the next 10 years.

The takeover came as a surprise to the management group at Ørum Gruppen, who had previously seen themselves as the flagship of the private dairy sector. Also, customers were afraid that the dominant position of MD Foods would favour their already active intermediaries, and that the takeover would lead to an industrial shake-out.

On the basis of the supportive environment at Ørum Gruppen, a group of four former employees, together with a Lebanese cheese importer, decided to start on their own, and in 1984 they formed Nordex Food.

One of the former managers of Ørum Gruppen, Keld Petersen (KP), became Managing Director of the new Nordex Food. The initial idea was to be an internationally-oriented trading company, selling a broad range of dairy and meat products in the Middle Eastern market through the contacts and relations built up by Ørum Gruppen.

The firm grew rapidly during the first years of its existence, thanks to the lucrative Middle East market, and began hiring back the former personnel of Ørum Gruppen. In addition, two dairy technicians were hired as quality and product development managers. Several skilled technicians and dairy engineers who had worked in other dairies that had been acquired and closed down were also hired.

In spite of the turbulence surrounding the firm, it has been able to grow substantially and consolidate, as shown in figure 4.3.

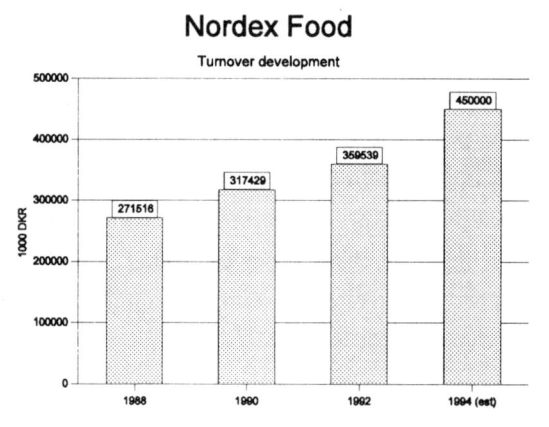

Figure 4.3: Nordex Food: Turnover 1988-1994

Turnover amounted to DKK 414 million in 1993 and is expected to exceed DKK 450 milion in 1994. Uf feta, with almost 50 per cent of total sales, accounts for most of this. Halloumi, traditional feta, blue cheese and a number of other minor productions account for a further 15 per cent, while the rest is accounted for by the firm's trading activities.

Production is based on short-term sales forecasts, and is contingent on a continuous inflow of milk and outflow of dairy products. The effectiveness of the information flow between the sales and production functions plays a vital role in this. The coordination activities between these functions are therefore frequent and based on mutual adjustment, furthering the demand for a flexible and adjustable organization,

122

capable of coordinating activity between production, marketing and the market intermediaries.

The sales function is divided into three sales areas:

Export A	*Covers sales to the Middle East and a few other countries. It is responsible for the product range at Nørager Dairy and Østerbølle Dairy.*
Export B	*Covers sales to Europe north of the Alps, Africa and North America. This sales area is responsible for the product range at Katrineholm Dairy.*
Export C	*Covers England and Europe south of the Alps and a few other countries. The export division exports cheese from all dairies. In addition, this sales division is responsible for marketing activities.*

Besides these functions, Nordex Food established a sales subsiduary in the UK in 1993, manned by the personnel of a former wholesaler. Also, the firm has established a new sales function aimed at the retail chain.

Products and Markets

Today, Nordex Food produces and markets a range of cheese types and other dairy products. Feta cheese is the most important product, accounting for more than 50 per cent of turnover. All in all, the firm produces and trades 22,000 tonnes of dairy products a year, of which around 50 per cent is produced by Nordex Food. The remaining 50 per cent is supplied by producers with whom Nordex Food collaborates. These include Mejerigaarden, MD Foods, Randers-Viborg Dairy, a German dairy, and producers of ethnic food products. Together with these producers, Nordex Food has developed a range of products which are marketed under its own brand name. These products include butter, canned cream, margarine and sausages. Collaboration also extends to other areas. For example, the firm has signed an agreement with Randers-Viborg dairy to market their products through Nordex Food UK.

Nordex Food markets its products in Denmark, but most of its turnover is generated through its international operations. However, Nordex Food started out as an internationally-oriented trading company, so the export ratio has always dominated total turnover. In 1985, approximately 99 per cent of the turnover was derived from international activity. In 1993 this figure amounted to 97 per cent.

The firm mainly exports through foreign intermediaries. Since 1985, Nordex Food has establised relations with more than 200 intermediaries in 50 countries. Approximately 75 are situated in Europe alone. Exports can be divided into three geographical areas: Europe, The Middle East, and Overseas, which includes the USA and Latin America. These areas differ widely as regards purchasing behaviour. In the Middle East, importers are normally very large trading houses, which operate through competitive bidding and purchase in large quantities. Moreover, imports of feta cheese are often determined by legislation in these countries, and since European feta is competitively priced compared with local producers, it is relatively easy for the trading houses to resell. Consequently, intermediaries are neither interested in nor willing to develop specific agreements with feta producers. There is a strict division of labour between producers and the Middle Eastern trading houses: The trading houses buy the cheese and handle all resale activity. There are constant negotiations over price and delivery quality with these trading houses, as well as with the local authorities. This is therefore an important element in doing business with Middle Eastern trading houses. One of the owners of Nordex Food, marketing manager Jørgen Ugilt (JU), compares selling to the Middle East with the situation at a horse fair:

> *"It is like horse-dealing: You negotiate prices over the phone, and you have to keep the dialouge going and barter with the customer about the price each time, until you are able to finish the deal."*

[Jørgen Ugilt]

EEC/EU export restitutions distort normal conditions in the Middle East, and make it difficult for exporters to establish a more permanent position in this market. Since demand depends on continuous EEC/EU subventioning, long-term planning is a risky operation. Moreover, as a result of the GATT trade negotiations in 1994, it was decided to reduce restitutions to feta cheese substantially over the coming years. This will lower the profitability of feta exports from the EEC/EU, as well as make it possible for cheese producers outside the EEC/EU to enter the Middle Eastern market (applies mainly to producers from New Zeeland and Australia). At the moment, the Middle East accounts for approximately two thirds of turnover. The European share of total turnover has grown substantially over the past three years, however, along with the general growth in turnover. This has reduced the firm's dependency on the Middle East. This development is shown in figure 4.4 below.

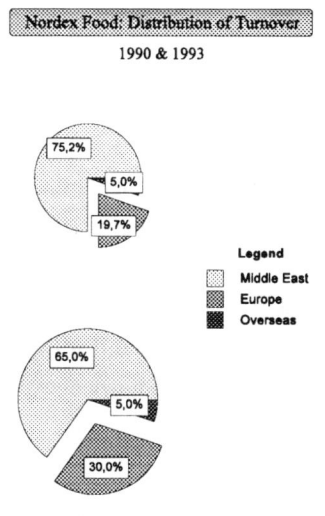

Figure 4.4: Nordex Food: Turnover development
Note: The size of the sectors is proportional to turnover

The figure shows that the relative share of turnover derived from the European market has increased by 10 per cent, with that of the Middle East declining by a similar amount. Measured in absolute figures, however, Nordex Food has managed to double its income from the European markets between 1990 and 1993.

The Nordex management sees the European markets as the basis for ensuring long-term growth, and the firm aims for 50 per cent of total turnover to come from European sales. The target groups for feta cheese in Europe are ethnic immigrants of Middle Eastern origin. However, a growing number of "native" Northern and Central Europeans have also begun to buy feta regularly, which suggests a strong growth potential in the European market.

Nordex Food has based its expansion in the European market mainly on the strenghtening of existing relations to independent foreign intermediaries and retail chains. On the basis of these efforts, Nordex Food has managed to establish a strong market position in Europe. A substantial part of feta imports to The Netherlands and Germany comes from Nordex Food, and the firm has a strong position in both the UK and Scandinavian markets.

Organization of exports - development and organization of relations to European intermediaries

In 1985, Nordex Food began to look for additional business opportunities in Europe. During this period, JU and the sales and marketing managers travelled around Europe, making contact with potential ethnic wholesalers. The firm had no prior experience of this customer group, since Ørum Gruppen mainly did business with Middle Eastern trading houses, and knew very little of the activities taking place in the domestic marketing channels. Thus, their knowledge of these customers and how to serve them was at a minimum.

> *"When we started out, we were very open-minded, as we knew absolutely nothing about the segment. I had never before visited an ethnic wholesaler, nor did I know where to find one. If you are about to develop an international network of Turkish wholesalers, there is no marketing textbook, any telephone list or any thing else to help you."*
>
> [Jørgen Ugilt]

There are between two and three million Turks in Germany, one million of which live in the Ruhr District alone. More than 2 per cent of the Dutch population, or 350,000 persons, are of Turkish origin. Although Turks form the largest single ethnic group of emigrants, the total number of immigrants of Middle Eastern origin in Europe is much higher.

Feta is an important ingredient in the Middle Eastern kitchen. Both Turks and Greeks eat feta cheese at least twice a day. Feta is used in various forms: fresh, in salads, or in pastry. A number of specialty or "ethnic" stores have thus appeared in the wake of the immigrants. These stores have an assortment of groceries, mainly imported from Turkey and Greece, including wine, spices, etc. They are mostly found in large industrial towns, where the concentration of Middle Eastern immigrants is highest. Normally, these stores are run by families, who later help other members of the family, or sons of relatives, to do the same. Ethnic shops are thus interconnected in a net of family and kinship ties stretching across regional as well as national borders. These retailers create their own business community, where competition and collaboration go hand in hand. Many wholesalers both import and retail products. Imported products are distributed to other wholesalers, who collaborate in purchasing and transportation arrangements. For example, some German ethnic wholesalers have established their own trade and transportation organization, which supplies a large number of Turkish and Moroccan wholesalers with wine, spices, marinated olives and other specialities. Basic provisions such as beans, rice and cheese are purchased from local producers, however. This is because the exportation of these products is forbidden in a number of Middle Eastern countries, because local producers cannot satisfy domestic demand.

At the local level, such as in large cities, trade is organized through large fairs (in German: Grossmärkte), where Turkish and other ethnic retailers and wholesalers meet weekly to socialize, exchange information and do business.

In 1986, Nordex Food exhibited an assortment of feta cheese at the Anuga food fair in Köln. There, they were contacted by a Turkish wholesaler who was interested in their product, but who also told them that their cheese products would not suit the taste of his Turkish customers. He offered to advise them regarding Turkish tastes and to help them in developing cheeses tailored to the Turkish ethnic market. JU accepted gratefully, and the following months saw a hectic round of phone-and-telex-based communication between the Turkish wholesaler, the product development manager, and JU on various aspects of the marketing of feta cheese, including slicing, packaging, tastes, consistency, etc. Nordex Food sent samples of the cheese for further comment by the Turkish wholesaler. During this period of product development, JU also learnt more about Turkish business customs and the buying behaviour of the market in which they were about to establish themselves. After about 6 months, Nordex Food was finally able to export a feta cheese which suited the taste of the wholesaler's customers.

In the following period, the firm established relations to wholesalers in Germany, The Netherlands, the Scandinavian countries, France, Spain, Italy and the UK, helped by the initial contact to the Turkish wholesaler. JU, and Nordex Food in general, gradually became convinced that they had a product which could meet the needs of Turkish wholesalers better than that of their competitors. It was therefore decided to develop a more systematic distribution network of wholesalers to cover countries with a heavy population of Middle Eastern immigrants. Consequently, JU began to travel around Europe to locate and evaluate potential wholesalers, eventually establishing more than 75 business relations. Through these initial dealings, JU learnt that business in the Turkish tradition is largely conducted in a social context, with specific rules of etiquette. Business deals are concluded together at social occasions, e.g. coffee drinking, family visits, and business chatting.

> *"This is how business is conducted in the Middle East. They like to talk and visit customers and drink coffee. Our business conversations involve a number of social affairs too... Business affairs are not tightly scheduled as we are used to. I never know what will happen (when I visit) a customer, and when I can proceed to the next customer. I therefore also always plan everything a little loosely during business visits."*
>
> [Jørgen Ugilt]

Contracts are not customary with ethnic wholesalers. However, this doesn't mean that it is easy to enter or leave a business relation once it has been established - in these contexts, reputation plays a major role. News travels fast in this highly interconnected network of wholesalers, and opportunistic behaviour becomes known almost instantaneously. The conventions and social structure of the ethnic groups form an entry barrier which is hard to penetrate. The information network, family and kinship ties, and the business traditions and methods of ethnic dealers make it difficult for an outsider to achieve acceptance and become a trusted business partner. For insiders, however, the Turkish society of wholesalers supports and provides members with valuable information, as well as a medium for marketing communication. JU discovered this when Turkish wholesalers began contacting him after his first sales to the wholesaler he met at the Anuga fair.

> *"The wholesalers came shortly after the beginning [of this initial sale] and there, the transient nature of the segment is obvious. Other Turkish wholesalers from different parts of Germany, and even from Austria and the Netherlands, phoned to know whether they could have a sample of the product, and perhaps market the product as well."*
>
> [Jørgen Ugilt]

In addition to the general exchange of information, a number of issues are discussed during business visits. In general, wholesalers have confidence in JU and treat him as a member of the community, which means that he is expected to listen as well as provide information and participate in social activities. Wholesalers are especially eager to know how much other wholesalers sell, and whether they sell as much as their colleagues. JU also gets told immediately if there are problems, or if they are dissatisfied with something. Other things which will affect business, such as a generational change or a wholesaler who is about to close down or hand over his business to somebody new, are also discussed during JU's business visits. This information keeps him up to date with the distributors, and he will often be able to take care of problems or exploit opportunities immediately. Furthermore, by acting on this information, JU earns the reputation of being a reliable business partner who respects traditions and is genuinely interested in their affair. Thus, frequent contact with the ethnic wholesaler community helps JU maintain a reputation as a respectable and reliable business partner, and thus furthers the commitment of the wholesalers to the Nordex Food products.

The information and personal contacts are also used for other purposes. JU uses his relations to wholesalers in tracking down and evaluating potential new wholesalers in other parts of Europe, in addition to bank information (in order to qualify for insurance by the EKR[13]) and his personal impression from visiting their businesses. Wholesalers must have storage facilities suitable for storing cheese in order to be accepted as partners. The relationships are always developed gradually. Normally, they start with the shipment of a single pallet of cheese and are taken from there. The largest wholesalers buy truckloads on a weekly basis. Shipments are organized on a weekly delivery basis, so wholesalers are strongly urged to adopt fairly stable ordering patterns. Otherwise, production planning becomes difficult.

The information JU obtains helps him keep track of competitors' moves. On the other hand, it is very difficult for Nordex Food to develop any special arrangement with importers and wholesalers. Any hint of exclusive agreements travels fast within the wholesaler community. Thus, the success of Nordex Food in this market also depends on its reputation among Turkish wholesalers.

Besides the Turkish community, the firm also serves two other customer groups: Greek wholesalers, whose main customers are Greek restaurants and retailers, including supermarkets, speciality stores and retail chains, and "native" central and northern Europeans. In addition to the Turkish product line, JU has also developed a brand of Uf feta called "Arkadia", which is mainly aimed at Greek restaurants in Europe. Greek restaurants are normally owned by Greek immigrants. Although business methods and principles are very similar to those of the Turkish wholesalers, it is a completely separate market. Greeks and Turks have a long history of conflict, which, in 1974, culminated in the division of Cyprus into a Greek and a Turkish sector. The disputes between these two countries are also reflected in relations between Turkish and Greek immigrants in foreign countries. Thus Turks and Greeks do not shop in each others' shops nor eat in each others' restaurants.

This dispute has led Nordex Food to develop two different brands of feta - one for the Turkish community under the brand name Dairyland, and produced by a dairy of the same name, and another for the Greek community (and European Supermarkets) under the name Arkadia, with Nordex Food named as producer.

---

13   Eksportkreditrådet (The export credit council)

The Greek segment is dominated by fewer, but larger wholesalers, who supply Greek restaurants mainly with wine, spices, olives and cheese. The feta cheese bought by Greek restaurants differs from that of Turkish wholesalers and restaurants. Greek restaurants normally use the less expensive Uf feta in restaurants in Europe and in tourist restaurants in Greece. These are mainly frequented by North and Central Europeans, who generally can't tell the difference.

Nordex Food has also developed export relationships with Greek wholesalers in a number of European countries. Like their Turkish counterparts, Greek wholesalers form a "closed" segment of interrelated businesses, knitted together by family and kinship ties. JU located the Greek wholesalers through Greek restaurants, and has gradually been able to establish a foothold in this enclave similar to that in the Turkish community. Their business traditions are also very much similar to those of the Turkish wholesalers.

These wholesaler relationships are a valuable asset for Nordex Food, as they give access to a wide range of ethnic stores, which cannot be reached otherwise. It takes a lot of resources to develop these relationships, but once established, they are usually very durable. As such, therefore, they should be regarded as market investments. Nordex Food thus takes particular care to support wholesalers and keep them satisfied, adjusting to their business norms through effective deliveries and quickly responding to problems and requests. This has had mutual benefits: A number of the wholesalers started out at the same time as Nordex Food, and their businesses have thrived as their relationship with Nordex Food has developed. JU explains:

> *"We have had our customers for a number of years. I am always afraid to establish a new relationship to a wholesaler and I therefore try hard to maintain already established relations. We know these customers, how they order and how they pay."*

[Jørgen Ugilt]

Turkish households are usually very large, often with 10 persons or more, but most shopping decisions are made by one person. Thus, for the Turkish wholesaler, one customer represents a relatively large amount of purchasing power. The wholesalers' relations to customers are often based on family and kinship ties, involving shared experience and knowledge of personal affairs. Nordex Food does little to control the market efforts of the wholesalers, since it lacks sufficient knowledge and anyway has no possibility of interfering in these business activities. They therefore acknowledge that they must trust the abilities of their intermediaries, and that their only influence on the business relationship is through the careful selection of wholesalers and support of their efforts.

However, through a restrictive policy of payment on delivery, Nordex Food does attempt to protect its interests. Experience with non-payment and sudden business closures has taught Nordex Food to deliver goods only after having received payment for previous deliveries. Thus, wholesalers are evaluated via an internal credit assessment, based on general impressions of solidity and recent ordering behaviour.

Trust between the partners occurs gradually - relations to wholesalers tend to develop in a specific pattern. The initial phase is characterized by a number of meetings within a short span of time. This is to make the wholesaler really feel that Nordex is backing him up. In the next phase the relationship stabilizes; ordering procedures become internalized and purchasing starts to follow a regular pattern. In this phase, the personal interface between JU and the wholesaler decreases, as the weekly orders, etc., are handled via standard procedures.

The third customer group consists of "native" central and north Europeans. These customers acquired a taste for feta cheese from holidays in Turkey and Greece, and on their return have added it to their standard stock of groceries. Both in Germany, the UK and Scandinavia, feta cheese is fast becoming a standard food item in the homes of the younger generation. Nordex Food markets a special range of feta products under the brand name "Arkadia" aimed at this customer group.

Europeans mainly buy their groceries in supermarkets, which are increasingly owned by large retail chains. The purchasing behaviour of retail chains is fundamentally different from Nordex's other customer groups, and requires a different sales approach. Retail chains have undergone massive reorganization over the past decades, and many have become strongly internationalized, e.g. Aldi Tengelmann (Germany), Carrefour (France), Dansk Supermarked (Denmark), and Sainsbury (England). These chains dominate the retail business in most Northern and Central European countries, and they have introduced several rationalizing practices which have affected business conditions for producers by eschewing dependency in favour of retail chains. They typically have a centralized purchasing policy in order to benefit from scale advantages. Often, retail chains promote own-brand products in order to strengthen their market image, and to increase their bargaining power over suppliers, who are thus unable to develop an independent image towards end users. Their interests are reflected in their purchasing behaviour, which differs radically from that of the Greek and Turkish wholesalers.

In line with the growth of Nordex's international commitment, a number of practices have been developed to routinize its activities. The purchasing habits of wholesalers and retailers follow quite distinct logics, however, and Nordex Food has therefore had to adopt different procedures for handling these two categories of customers. JU explains this difference in the following way:

> *"With the Turkish and Greek wholesalers, it is important to take time for the social aspects of business. Time is only of small importance, and the customer expects me to stay all day when visiting him. When making appointments with the purchasing manager of ALDI, on the other hand, you are told by his secretary that he has time to see you between 10.00 to 10.15 p.m. Eight minutes past ten, he begins to look at his watch, because he has an appointment with another sales representative waiting outside."*
>
> [Jørgen Ugilt]

Nordex Food has attempted to serve this segment through the existing sales organization; this has only had limited success, however, because marketing strategies for ethnic wholesalers and large retail chains are incompatible. The firm has therefore recently decided to establish a sales function with sole responsibility for retail chains.

Strategies for reducing the complexity of international activities

The growth of Nordex Food's engagement in European markets has led to a complex sales situation with multiple business practices and relations, which makes heavy demands on the time and efforts of the sales department. Because of his close personal interface with wholesalers, JU travels at least 80 days a year, and the wholesalers are also invited to Nordex Food in Dronninglund. In general, this time-consuming way of doing business is a growing problem in Nordex Food, and has forced the firm to begin to think of alternative organizational set-ups, e.g. delegating more responsibility and simplifying the coordination and conclusion of activities. At the same time, however, Nordex Food wants to maintain the flexibility which personal contact makes possible. This has led to conflicting demands on the organization of international activities.

One solution has been to find local collaboration partners with complementary skills and let them take over some of the obligations of Nordex Food. This has been done with some success in The Netherlands, where a trading agency has taken over a number of the activities normally undertaken by the firm itself. Another solution is to establish joint ventures with wholesalers, or establish subsidiaries under the management of former wholesalers. This has been done in the UK, where the firm established a sales subsidiary in 1993 based on a relation to a retired wholesaler. Today, two former managers of the wholesaler are employed in Nordex Food UK. Nordex Food also considers the possibility of extending relations to selected intermediaries in joint venture partnerships.

It has also been necessary to use trading agencies in markets where cheese imports are restricted by legislation. The following describes the development and organization of business relations to intermediaries in Finland and The Netherlands.

Collaboration with Hoers Agenturen

Hoers Agenturen is a Dutch trading company, dealing with basic provisions such as cheese, rice and beans. It mainly sells to ethnic wholesalers in the Netherlands, who resell to a large group of immigrants of Oriental and Middle Eastearn origin.

Mr. T. Hoers (TH) started Hoers Agenturen with his wife in December 1989, soon after his former employer went bankrupt. Their daughter has also recently become an employee in the firm. Hoers Agenturen is situated near Breda, at the private address of the Hoers family.

Hoers Agenturen represents two firms: Nordex Food and Borlim, a Belgian producer of rice and beans. The product range includes various types of rice and beans, feta cheese and biological (moulded) cheese. The agency sells mainly to wholesalers, and does business regularly with around 35 Turkish, Chinese, Indonesian, Moroccan, Syrian and Dutch wholesalers.

TH's previous job was as sales manager in a similar line of business, and he started Hoers Agenturen on the basis of his former business relations from this firm. But while his former employer did business with both wholesalers and retailers, TH decided to deal only with wholesalers, and is still doing so four years later. Hoers Agenturen has been growing steadily since its establishment. The firm had a turnover of NLG 17 million in 1993, two thirds of which came from rice and beans.

In 1989, TH was asked by one of his Turkish wholesalers whether he had any contacts or knew anything about a brand of feta cheese called "Dairyland". TH could vaguely remember the name from his earlier visits to Turkish retailers, but had never had any direct contact with Nordex Food. He was, however, eager to find new areas of business, and he saw possibilities in feta cheese, since he was already serving a relevant clientele of wholesalers with his present product line. Also, TH saw possibilities for both Nordex Food and Hoers Agenturen in strengthening their position vis-à-vis wholesalers as regards payment problems. Consequently, in 1989, he contacted JU, and suggested that he took over the representation of Nordex Food in The Netherlands. At that time Nordex Food had only a few customers in Holland. Several of their customers had closed, and the firm was left with a number of outstanding payments. On the other hand, Nordex Food did not normally work with trading agencies. Despite this, TH was able to convince JU that a reasonable business arrangement could be made, and they made an appointment to meet each other in The Netherlands.

Thus, the relationship got off to an excellent start. TH also told JU that he had no experience regarding cheese, but that he had experience of working with ethnic wholesalers and access to a number of customers who would probably be interested in the Dairyland feta. Nordex Food were not unduly worried about the lack of experience, however - the collection of outstanding payments had more than convinced them about the qualities of Hoers Agenturen. JU backed up TH from the start by paying a number of visits to him and his customers, and by providing him with technical assistance where necessary. JU also invited TH to participate in their stand at the Anuga food fair in Köln, where a number of Hoers' potential customers would also be participating, and invited TH to Dronninglund in 1990, where he received some basic training in cheese production, qualities and types. TH has since visited Nordex Food a number of times, both alone and together with customers, and through these visits has increased his knowledge base.

After Hoers Agenturen took over in The Netherlands, feta sales increased substantially, and Dairyland has become established as the leading feta brand in The Netherlands. Hoers Agenturen and Nordex Food have widened their collaborative efforts to include making joint marketing decisions, such as product range, customer target groups, etc.

As a result of their combined efforts, they have been able to outperform a number of other producers from Germany, Belgium and Denmark, including MD Foods. TH believes that the reason for the success of Nordex Food stems mainly from their product quality and their ability to cooperate with everybody, including Hoers Agenturen and (in relation to feta cheese, mainly Turkish) wholesalers. The Turks in particular see quality as a major issue, differing in this respect from Dutch customers. As regards product quality, Nordex Food clearly have a market differential, which is well known in the Turkish community:

> *"Believe me, Turks have tried numerous other types of feta cheese. A couple of years ago, there were four Turkish agro-engineers, who tried to start a production of feta in Holland, subsidized by the Dutch government. Today they have closed down the factory again."*
>
> [Theodor Hoers]

This is very different from MD Foods' approach, who try to sell their products by lowering prices. MD Foods often "dump" excess production which they have been unable to sell in the Middle East on the European market. Product quality often fluctuates, which damages the reputation of their products in the Dutch market. Nordex Food, on the other hand, adapt to the business practices of ethnic wholesalers, and react swiftly to complaints about product quality, which has strengthened their reputation among wholesalers. This is illustrated by the marketing of a German make of Mozzarella cheese in the Dutch market, which Nordex Food had produced under its own name. The cheese did not live up to expectations, and both Hoers and Nordex Food received several complaints about the quality of the product. According to TH:

> *"After some months we found that the quality had dropped. The cheese had too much mould in it, and the colour was not right. Nordex Food decided then to start its own production of pure Nordex products, as they were afraid that the reputation of their trade mark would be affected by the inferior quality of the German Mozzarella."*
>
> [Theodor Hoers]

Today, daily communication between Nordex Food and Hoers Agenturen consists is handled mainly by telefax. Routines have been developed, and the trade process is thoroughly organized, including payments and delivery. TH still meets JU at least four or five times a year, however, and together they visit the wholesalers in order to show their interest, socialize, and receive general information about the market situation. TH and JU put a lot of time and effort into these meetings, which normally involve a complete day of socializing, and eating huge meals!

> *"This is extremely important for the Turks. If we refuse a dinner invitation it could mean an immense degree of trouble, as this again could be interpreted as a dislike toward the person, caused by the colour of his skin. We always hope they forget to invite us to dinner, but they never do."*
>
> [Theodor Hoers]

JU and TH have similar ideas about how the ethnic segment should be served, and share their knowledge in this field. Knowledge about particular customs and details is especially important in relation to religious events, such as Ramadan[14], and rules of courtesy when doing business. It is also important to prepare visits and give advance warning to customers, rather than just "dropping by", which relates to the general "underdog" situation of foreigners in Holland: Dropping by could be seen as though JU and TH were only prepared to use spare time rather than "prime time" on Turkish dealers.

The business relationship between Nordex Food and Hoers Agenturen has gradually changed character over the years. From just taking care of payment problems, TH has gradually widened his responsibilities to other areas. Today, TH see the relationship with Nordex Food as the one with the greatest growth potential. TH thinks that, within a couple of years, this collaboration could lead to the establishment of a sales agency with joint ownership.

Collaboration with Gula Huset Ab

Gula Huset is a manufacturer of cosmetics and products for personal care, as well as an import agency for cosmetics, personal care products and fancy foods. The firm, which is situated on the outskirts of Helsinki, Finland, was established in 1925 as a producer of shampoo powder, and has gradually moved into other areas, such as cosmetics, fancy foods, liquor, etc. Only a small production of skin cream remains, however, and today, Gula Huset is mainly a trading firm. The turnover in 1993 amounted to FIM 70 million, about 25 per cent of which came from the sale of cheese. The firm employs 40 people, and is divided into three business areas: food products, grocery products, and duty-free products. Products are forwarded to a number of retailers, including retail chains, restaurants, hotels, perfumeries, tax-free shops at ferries and airports, etc.

---

[14] The 9th. month of the Muslim year, during which no food or drink must be taken between sunrise and sunset. The Muslim year is based on the movements of the moon, and Ramadan takes place at different times each year.

The Finnish market for imported cheese is highly restricted. Cheese imports are regulated through bilateral trade agreements between Finland and a number of cheese exporting countries, and is administered by the Finnish Ministry of Trade and Industry. Around 80 per cent of total cheese imports come from EU countries, while the remaining 20 per cent comes from countries outside the EU.

The Ministry of Trade and Industry decides which retailers can import cheese and how much they can import. At the retail level, four large buyers have approximately 95 per cent of the total cheese market. These are Kesko, a large retail chain, SOK and EKA, both cooperative organizations, and T-Group and Stockman, which controls a number of large supermarkets (megastores).

In addition, Valio, Finland's largest producer of dairy products, produces an assortment of foreign cheese types, including feta. These are not considered as imported cheese, however, and add to the competitive situation of the market for imported cheese; this is growing, and today accounts for approximately five per cent of the total market for cheese in Finland (excluding cheese from Valio).

Feta imports are the fourth largest in Finland. End users are mainly Finns, there being only a very small number of immigrants from the Middle East in Finland. The strong preference for feta cheese is mainly explained by the large number of Finnish tourists to Greece and Turkey. Feta cheese is mainly sold in supermarkets and speciality stores, who market the cheese as a fancy food.

The Finnish trade in imported cheese is organized in the following way: Retailers with import licences order through foreign cheese agencies, who normally have concessions for a number of cheese products. Thus exchange takes place in long-term relationships between relatively few actors.

In 1985, Gula Huset Ab decided to expand to fancy foods. The firm had some prior experience in importing fine foods, and saw this as a major area of growth, which supplemented the existing business well. The firm acquired the Oy Innzano agency in 1985, and established a fancy food division, which was led by Hans Petterson

(HP), one of Oy Innzano's former owners, who is also responsible for this division today.

Through this, and a number of subsequent acquisitions in the following years, Gula Huset both gained control over a number of agencies and acquired import licences. Besides strengthening its market position by taking over the agencies, Gula Huset introduced business methods used in the marketing of personal care products, which were new in relation to cheese marketing. These included a field staff of sales consultants and a programme for helping retailers present the cheese to consumers. The sales consultants partcipated in fairs and set up demonstration stands in supermarkets.

The efforts paid off. In 1990, Gula Huset became the second largest cheese import agency in Finland, and the cheese trade had grown into an important business area for the firm. Around this time, the largest import agency, E. Teppo Oy, contacted Gula Huset and offered them their business. Gula Huset accepted, becoming at one stroke the largest Finnish cheese import agency, with control over relations to foreign cheese producers, amounting to 70 per cent of imported cheese.

The strong position of the firm was considered a threat by several of cheese producers, who regarded the concentration of agencies as eroding their possibilities for influencing sales. In 1990, these considerations led a number of Danish, German, Dutch and French producers to establish their own sales agencies in Finland. As a result, Gula Huset's market share fell to 50 per cent of the Finnish market, a market share which the company holds today.

> *"Following our increasing size, a number of our suppliers, among them Tholstrup Cheese, disappeared. It all started with Tholstrup Cheese. They belonged to Einar Teppo, the same import agency that represented Nordex Food. It was firms like Tholstrup which established their own sales office in Finland. Subsequently, a number of producers followed, who imitated Tholstrup. In this way, our market share diminished to 50 per cent. We have been able to consolidate this position for some time now."*
>
> [Hans Petterson]

In 1987, Gula Huset acquired the Nordex Food agency, along with a number of other agencies. Arkadia, the brand sold in Finland, was already established in the Finnish market when Gula Huset acquired the import agency. In 1989, HP met JU for the first time at the Köln food fair, and explained the takeover and the intentions of Gula Huset. They later met in Finland, which proved to be a positive meeting for both parties. Nordex Food, who liked the aggressive style of Gula Huset, was willing to collaborate with them, and shortly afterwards, the Finnish firm decided to make Arkadia feta their leading brand in this cheese type. Sales of Arkadia grew, and the two firms eventually established a relationship which has become important for both of them.

The content of the relationship gradually developed. Nordex Food supported Gula Huset in their marketing efforts in Finland, and a number of experiments were made with the brand name, though with limited success. HP has also started to use Nordex Food as a showroom when introducing new customers or introducing new products to existing customers. These meetings are carefully orchestrated with Nordex Food, and normally include staying at Dronninglund Castle, visits to dairies, and social activities. HP is in Denmark about ten times a year, where he visits Nordex Food and a number of other suppliers in different product areas, such as jam and fish. Today, more than 95 per cent of the feta cheese sold by Gula Huset comes from Nordex Food.

> "In principle we represent other feta cheese types, but we do not do anything to represent these types. It is obvious, if anyone should ask for another brand, a German feta cheese for example, then we can make delivery....There are customers who want a specific brand and nothing else, and that is exactly the strength of a broad assortment. At the same time however, one has to concentrate on a number of core products, and do less for the marginal products."

[Hans Petterson]

The development of the Gula Huset-Nordex Food relationship coincided with the concentration of the Finnish retail structure in fewer hands - larger purchasing units were formed in order to strengthen their bargaining power with suppliers. The large purchasing centres demand discounts on established brands from the import agencies, and are increasingly using own brands as a way of increasing their control over their market image. The more retail chains slim down and specialize in core business areas, the more activities are carried out together with other firms, such as import agencies. This means that more responsibility is delegated to suppliers, which in turn requires an increasing degree of coordination between retail chains and their immediate suppliers. This development especially favours large agencies, such as Gula Huset, which gain in importance as a result of their broad product range, volume, and number of contacts. Another aspect of this development is that it has transformed Gula Huset from the more passive role of a traditional intermediary into participating in activities directly related to production. This has also affected its role towards suppliers.

As a result of these changes, Gula Huset has expanded its activities, from marketing other firms' cheese products to acting as a consultant to the large purchasing centres in the development and production of own-brand cheese products. Thus, the supplier-intermediary relationship is changing - as Gula Huset begins to use cheese producers as sub-suppliers in relation to specific activities, the production and distribution roles of the firm are gradually merging. The following example illustrates this changing pattern of roles: Kesko contacted Gula Huset in search of a supplier of "Nya Skärgård", a Port Salut cheese, to be marketed under its own trademark. The cheese was earlier produced by a dairy owned by Kesko, but it was considered peripheral to Kesko's main business activity and shut down. After trying a number of other dairies, Gula Huset and Kesko finally decided on Nordex Food, since their cheese came the closest to the original Port Salut produced by the retail chain´s own dairy. Today, Nordex Food makes the cheese for Gula Huset, who resells it to Kesko. The likelihood of EU membership in the near future probably spells the end of import restrictions on foreign cheese, and cheese imports are expected to increase markedly (MTTL 1993). The future prospects for Gula Huset vis-à-vis its suppliers will be heavily influenced by the expected changes in business conditions brought about by EU membership. The role of the firm will probably change in the direction of taking on more service activities in relation to both suppliers and customers. This could also lead to a closer relationship between Gula Huset and Nordex Food. One possible development is that, with quick delivery increasing in importance as a sales parameter, Gula Huset could become a wholesaler with storage facilities. These facilities could eventually be developed together with Nordex Food and a few other of Gula Huset's core suppliers in the area of fancy food.

ANALYSIS OF THE NORDEX FOOD CASE

This case indicates that, in general, cheese production is a cross-border activity in which no clear international division of labour is possible. Although cheeses are normally local in origin and consumption is based on food traditions related to specific cultures, producers are interconnected through complex international networks of producers, intermediaries, and users. In addition, the network displays a pattern of dynamic specialization, with a large degree of indeterminedness concerning the distribution of production tasks. Various activities are concluded and coordinated with actors in other countries, and actors often take on various roles in different activities. This pattern is also evident in the internationalization of Nordex Food, which cannot be seen independently of the existing competences and interests developed in Ørum Gruppen, and earlier in the dairies in the local areas. Both the local area and the actors connected to the worldwide production and distribution of feta cheese, contain a number of competences which Nordex Food has been able to draw on and configure into concerted activity.

Thus, the competences and skills of Ørum Gruppen did not disappear when this firm was taken over by MD Foods, but could relatively easily be re-established by another firm. Rather than seeing them as bound to the core of the firm, therefore, they should be seen as vested in the relations developed to other actors. This example shows that relations endure beyond exchange transactions, and are thus not merely the outcome of them. Rather, they both reflect and drive transactions. Relations to actors are joint investments in market assets which the exchange party has an interest in preserving, since they represent established routines and bonds of trust. Thus market assets can be re-established and used in new activities. Through the personal relations of former Ørum Gruppen employees, Nordex Food was therefore able to recreate some customer relations relatively quickly, and thus re-establish the resource chain, enabling the specialized core and supplied skills to again participate in value-adding activity.

An interesting point in the configuration of the resource chain is that it was not re-established for the purpose of exporting feta cheese. Rather, it was capitalizing on the established routinizations for carrying out activities in a broad range of foods, e.g. chickens, canned cream and other products. It was not until later that feta cheese came to dominate the exchange activities again.

Turning to the organization and management of international activities at Nordex Food, the business practices of the European network of cheese producers correspond to the development and organization of business activities explained above. Nordex Food operates on the conditions of the network, establishing and constantly reconfiguring a loosely coupled activity frame within which, given the limitations of production capacity and the relational access to and availability of external competencies and resources, activities can be carried out within a short period of time. The firm's strong market position, especially in the European markets, depends on its ability to interpret and organize activities in accordance with the market logic of the ethnic wholesalers. Through a number of trial-and-error activities, the firm has gradually developed a relational position and sufficient market knowledge to build up a resource chain in which the competencies of the ethnic wholesalers are matched by the internal skills of Nordex Food. New activities are often the product of collaborative ventures between Nordex Food and a market intermediary, such as Hoers Agenturen or Gula Huset. In this sense, the firm draws on external competencies, and uses these to develop new projects, which are eventually formed into product lines. The international development of Nordex Food also illustrates the development of network competences. The internationalization of Nordex Food has enabled the firm to acquire knowledge of the business practices of the ethnic community in Europe, and to use this knowledge in improving their competencies in product development. Thus, from being a trading company based on contacts to the Middle East, interaction with the ethnic community in Europe has led to the development of competences in production and product development. Today, the skills of the firm are intimately linked to the routines developed in relation to this market segment. Thus, the trial-and-error processes in network interaction have resulted in a new relationship profile, which clearly distinguishes the firm from its most important competitor: MD Foods. Whereas the European marketing strategy of MD Foods is to sell feta cheese on a bulk basis through competitive pricing, Nordex Food´s strategy is to treat feta as a brand and sell it through the ethnic wholesalers, using their resources.

These activities are often initiated as a result of the relationship dialogue, rather than being the product of decisions made by a single actor. Personal, direct interface therefore plays an important role in the development and organizational set-up of Nordex Food. This is evident not only in relation to the development of new products or product lines, but also in the development of administrative routines for handling daily operations between the firms. Through frequent personal contacts, the infrastructure is developed for the telegraphic style of interaction which characterizes daily operations, where the firm is swift to react to any disturbances to the established order, thereby assuring customers and intermediaries that their expectations will be met. In addition to the development of Nordex Food's international engagement, JU has gradually built up a shared knowledge base together with intermediaries. The strength of this arrangement has been an "intensive" dialogue between Nordex Food and its market representatives, which has enabled Nordex Food to meet their (often diverse) demands. Consequently, Nordex Food's international engagement in Europe has gradually developed into a complex structure, which is roughly outlined in figure 4.6 below.

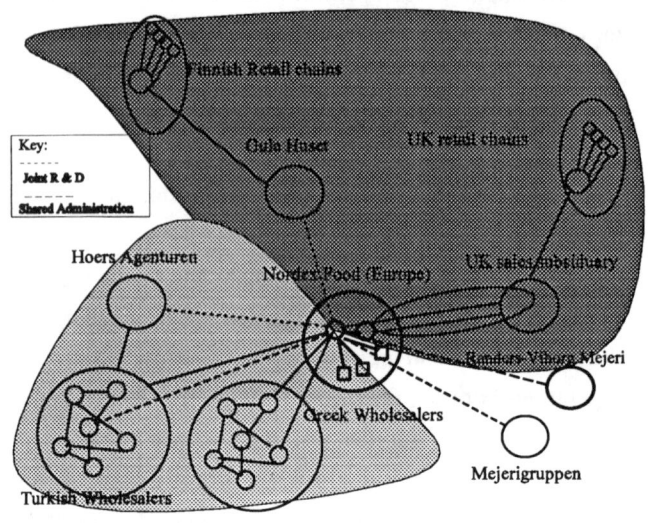

Key:
Joint R & D
Shared Administration

Finnish Retail chains
Gula Huset
UK retail chains
Hoers Agenturen
Nordex Food (Europe)
UK sales subsidiary
Randers-Vibarg Mejeri
Greek Wholesalers
Mejerigruppen
Turkish Wholesalers

Figure 4.6: The Focal network of Nordex Food

Nordex Food operates in two distinct business areas, characterized by different buying practices and thus also by different demands on suppliers. This is illustrated in figure 4.6 by means of the two shaded areas. As can be seen from Nordex's focal network in figure 4.6, the firm draws on a number of different relationships, all of which emanate from the department headed by JU. The complexity of the Nordex Food distribution network has underlined the need for administrative routines to reduce this complexity and rationalize business practices. These have generally been established on a personal level between JU and the wholesalers, backed up by an administrative body of assistants who take care of routine ordering, shipment and production planning together with the dairies. These routines have increased in value with the growth in the number of established relationships, and form the basis for rationalizing business conduct. At the same time, these efforts have furthered the structuralization and specialization of activities. The development of new relationships is becoming increasingly dependent on previously established routines. In an attempt to maintain close and frequent interaction with the Turkish wholesalers, some of the procedures for concluding activity gradually increase in importance at the expense of others, leading the firm to establish additional arrangements in

146

order to maintain the dialogue. These include a division responsible for dealing with the retail chains, a sales subsidiary in the UK, and a market intermediary in the Netherlands, which may in the long run also become a joint-venture sales subsidiary. However, these investments are gradually changing the organization of activity into a specialized and more functional, but less flexible form. This can lead to problems in the future, because, at the moment, contacts to wholesalers are strongly based on personal contacts and the experience of JU, and flexibility, in terms of adapting to the personal and varying needs of business partners, is an issue of major importance.

Another task facing the firm is to develop competences in dealing with retail chains. So far, the firm has been fairly successful with the ethnic segment, but the routines and competences developed here are less useful in relation to the retail chain segment, which is only organized to deal with suppliers who can either a) offer brand names, supported by substantial promotion budgets, or b) offer products produced under private labels. So far, Nordex Food has little experience in this form of international activity, and their present marketing competence seems inadequate in this context. A major challenge for Nordex Food is thus to develop skills and draw on complementary skills in this area, while maintaining their present activity level in the Middle East and the ethnic segment.

CHAPTER 5

HWH Production A/S

General profile of HWH Production A/S

HWH Production A/S is a small firm situated in Hadsund, in northern Jutland. The firm produces a front-lifter system for tractors, including a control console and a number of appliances for the maintenance of outdoor areas. Its customers are mainly firms and public organizations which are responsible for the maintenance of outdoor areas used by municipalities, farmers, building constructors, housing associations, producers with geographically extensive production facilities, etc.

The firm currently employs approximately 25 persons, including an administrative staff of two, 3 draughtsmen, and approximately 20 workers in the assembly, maintenance, purchasing and storage departments. The firm is owned by Henning Westergaard (HW) and Hans Jacobsen (HJ). Turnover is approximately DKK 15 million.

Background, development, and present status

The firm was established in 1977 by HW. Prior to the establishment of HWH Production, HW had worked in his father's firm, Hadsund Traktorlager (est. 1959), repairing and trading agricultural machines, such as tractors, harvesters, etc.

In 1964, Hadsund Traktorlager started a production of high-pressure cleaners for agricultural and industrial use. This production was initiated by HW's younger brother, Knud-Erik Westergaard (KW), and became so successful that KW decided to start his own firm, KEW, which is today a medium-sized firm producing and selling high-pressure equipment worldwide, both for industrial and private use. In

1988, KW was forced to sell his shares in KEW, and is today involved in the production of battery-driven cars, marketed as KEWets.

HW continued the family business together with his father, but in 1977 decided to start his own firm as well, HWH Production A/S, in the same line of business. In 1977, the firm won an order from Mariager town council to deliver a number of tractors fitted with a revolving brush and a control aggregate for sweeping cobblestones, since the streets in the historical part of Mariager are paved with this material. However, HW found that there was no suitable product on the market which was able to sweep cobblestones effectively. Consequently, he decided to develop a system himself, and succeeded in constructing a hydraulic front-lifter system with adjustable pressure, which could be adjusted from inside the cabin of the tractor, and which was able to sweep both streets paved with cobblestones and a number of other surfaces.

The product concept turned out to be a success, and HWH was able to deliver a similar system to a number of Danish municipalities. The firm continued to develop the product, and expanded the number of appliances which could be controlled by the system. The present range includes both snow-sweepers and lawnmowers. Based on the initial success, HW decided to specialize in this line of business. At that time, the firm had 5 employees and a turnover of under DKK 1 million.

The development of the HWH concept
The experiences accumulated from solving the problems of different municipalities furthered the development of the front-lifter principle, and gradually formed the core concept of the product. HW's idea was to fit a control console to which various appliances could be attached. In this way, customers would be able to reduce their investments in specialized equipment and change appliances relatively fast and easy. Together, the control console and one appliance would be more expensive to buy than a specialized machine, but the more appliances the customer bought, the relatively cheaper it would be. Moreover, it would be relatively easy to upgrade to new or improved appliances, and not as costly as fitting a completely new appliance on a tractor. Compared with the product range of competitors, this was a novel idea.

HW hoped that this ability of the HWH product line would especially interest smaller municipalities with tight budgets, or customers who for other reasons wanted to avoid too-specialized equipment.

Thus, HW hoped to establish switching costs, and hereby build up a core of regular customers, who would come to the firm with specific maintenance problems and have HWH Production develop a product tailored to meet their specific needs.

> *"You could say that, in principle, we sell an idea, rather than a physical product. When customers have bought our console once, they can always find appliances which can be tailored to meet their specific needs."*
>
> [Henning Westergaard]

Customer-driven product development

Product development at the firm is based on customers' requests for appliances to solve specific problems. The idea was to meet specific customer needs together with experts from the area in question, and later to adapt the product or technical solution to other areas. In this way, the firm would gradually build up its competencies and potential product programme.

The firm has developed a number of customized products whose technical solutions were later used in connection with other customers. One such example is Aalborg Airport. This is a relatively large airport, with both civilian and military functions, and which has NATO status. The airport is situated near Limfjorden, 10 kilometres from Aalborg. Fjords and other types of coastal areas are often heavily infested with birds, who are attracted by the abundance of fish in the area. However, massive flocks of birds are a problem for jet aircraft, as birds can get sucked into the engines and cause damage during landing and take-off. This can result in serious accidents. Aalborg Airport thus needs an effective means of keeping birds away from the airport runways. Research in the area led to the conclusion that runway areas could be made uninteresting for birds if the grass was cut to a certain height. The Airport management contacted HWH and discussed the problem with them. After some initial investigation, HW found that ornithologists at the Kalø bird research centre and the European birdstrike commission had a substantial knowledge of bird behaviour. With their advice, and through experiments conducted together with ornithologists from the Kalø bird research centre, HWH Production developed a grass mower which cut the grass to the specified height, and which, in addition, deposited the straws so that they formed a pattern on the ground which birds found unappealing to land on. Through this order, HWH also became automatically registered as a NATO supplier, with permission to supply other Nato airports. The lawn mower appliance has later been sold to a number of other Scandinavian military airports with similar problems, e.g. Bodø NATO airport in Norway. The reason for the specific Scandinavian interest is that Swedish and Norwegian airports are often situated near the coast, due to the mountainous nature of the two countries.

A number of other technical solutions include: snowploughs designed for specific purposes, weed removers, and rotating sweepers, which can sweep pavements while being operated from a tractor driving in the street. Today, the product range includes appliances for all-season outdoor maintenance. This also means that the composition of demand is contingent on variations in the seasons:

> "We have a product programme which resembles the four seasons by Vivaldi. The less snow received, the longer the grass. The latest years, our lawn mower product line has dominated over the winter appliances. This however changes over time."

> [Hans Jacobsen]

The internationalization of business activities
In 1979, the firm exhibited the front-lifter system at the international industrial fair in Herning, where they were contacted by Broddway, a large Swedish firm. The representatives of this firm were especially interested in a lawn mower which could be mounted on a specialized vehicle for use in motorway maintenance, and the HWH product met this need perfectly.

Before it would accept HWH as a supplier, however, Broddway demanded extensive product documentation, including blueprints, manuals, etc. This is standard procedure in the public sector, because customers want to ensure that spare parts can be produced by other suppliers should the original supplier close down. HWH had to employ a draughtsman to meet the firm's demand. This investment marked a watershed in the HWH's business practices. With the help of its new employee, the firm gradually began to build up a library of designs, which made it easier for the firm to approach larger customers and to operate on an international basis.

> *"The Swedish order was the first one. Now we are met by a claim for documentation each time we approach a larger customer. Our documentation has to be O.K. Larger customers ensure that this is the case before they even enter into a relationship with a supplier."*

[Hans Jacobsen]

Side by side with the customized machinery, the firm also started a product line of standardized appliances. Here, HWH functions as a subsupplier of specialized machinery to large German suppliers of outdoor machinery. This has grown into two complementary, and sometimes competing, lines of business, which make both complementary and competing demands on the HWH production function. It also divides the firm's management into two interest groups: HW, who is interested in the product development activities, and Hans Jacobsen (HJ) who believes the long-term interest of the firm lies in maintaining stable relationships with large customers.

The sucessful export to Sweden made HW realize that the product had an international market potential. He therefore decided to look for intermediaries in other countries who could represent the HWH product concept.

The role of trade fairs in developing an international engagement
During the 1980s early 1990s, HW visited a number of fairs on the lookout for potential intermediaries. International trade fairs play a central role in this line of business for a number of reasons. They give firms the opportunity to demonstrate new products to potential customers and keep existing customers updated on new developments. Moreover, they play a central role in the organization of business activities. A number of intermediaries meet with their suppliers at these fairs and use

the opportunity to exchange information and discuss business matters. Moreover, trade fairs function as markets for dealer contracts. A number of intermediaries and producers visit fairs mainly to establish new contacts to dealers and suppliers.

HW made a number of contacts to potential intermediaries during these visits. These were later sorted, based on HW's experience from his father's firm. HW found it relatively straightforward to evaluate potential intermediaries of this type. The firm's international engagement thus gradually emerged from the relations established by HW at international trade fairs. The business prospered during this period. Exports became a substantial part of turnover and the main contributor to turnover development. In 1988, exports amounted to more than 40 per cent of total turnover, or DKK 6 million. In 1992, two thirds of turnover was generated through export sales, amounting to DKK 10 million. At the same time, Danish municipalities experienced budgetary cutbacks. Due to a number of mild winters, this became one of the areas in which councils could make budgetary savings without incurring the wrath of public opinion. This led councils to cut their expenditures on outdoor maintenance, which substantially depressed the market for this type of product.

In 1993, foreign sales dropped sharply, as the devaluation of the Finnish Mark, the Swedish and Norwegian Crowns, and the English Pound began to affect market prices in these countries. This meant price increases of up to 30 per cent to the end user. However, the firm still managed a turnover of DKK 15 million in 1993, and an export ratio of approximately 30 per cent.

Products & customers
HWH Production's product range consists of the front-lift system and a number of specific appliances. At present, the firm makes four main groups of appliances: Snowploughs, lawn mowers, weed rippers, and sweepers. Prices range from DKK 7,000 - 72,000 per appliance, excluding the hydraulic front-lift system, which comes in five different versions: a universal system for tractors under 35 h.p., two specialized models for sweeping and weed-ripping, and two universal models. Prices for front-lifter systems range from DKK 14,000 - 37,000. Although appliances are

standardized to some extent, they are normally produced in very small batches, which are customized to the specific needs of the customer in question.

The firm aims at a wide range of customers, including municipalities, farmers, airports, building contractors, etc. Especially appliances used for sweeping, lawn mowing and snow clearing have been exported, while the more specialized appliances have only been sold in a limited number.

EXTERNAL RELATIONS

Organization of Production: Relations to suppliers

The components used for the system are largely produced by local subcontractors, while HWH Production is responsible for specifying the components and designing and assembling the products. HWH bases the major part of production on suppliers who produce to its specifications. Approximately 90 per cent of the components are made by suppliers, while HWH concentrates on assembly and the production of specialized parts in very small batches. This way of producing is traditional among Danish manufacturers of tractor appliances. Firms are generally small, seldom having more than 50 employees, and are characterized by a substantial proportion of skilled workers and a large degree of customization. Product components are mostly standardized, and a number of producers use a standard assortment of components in assembly. Often, large parts of production are carried out by a network of small firms which are used on an ad hoc basis. These are often blacksmiths specializing in specific forms of production, and with a specific profile in machinery and know-how.

HWH mainly uses local suppliers, selected on the basis of personal knowledge and experience. Coordination with these suppliers is flexible and ad hoc. HWH tries to keep the number of components small, and uses standard components as much as possible. This keeps storage costs low and production planning less complex. The local suppliers form a flexible, low-cost production system for the firm, which makes this delivery policy possible. On the other hand, the firm can easily supplement suppliers with its own production if necessary.

HWH uses three local suppliers for most of its components: JKF, Sand Production, and Borup Andersen, all of which are subsuppliers as well as "core firms" in numerous other relationships. These suppliers are used regularly, and together they form a stable production base for the firm:

> *"The components manufactured by subsuppliers will always be produced outside HWH. We are not interested in these lines of work, as they involve specialized machinery which we are not prepared for nor can afford to buy. Consequently, these tasks would have had to be done manually by us, which would increase the production costs substantially. We always use the same suppliers, as they know our quality standards and the dimensions in which we normally order components. As such, the components are ready to be mounted when they arrive, and we do not have the kind of calibration problems one always has with new suppliers who have to be taught the tolerances each time..."*

[Hans Jacobsen]

HWH purchases approximately DKK 1.5 million worth of components a year from these suppliers.

Organization of exports: Development and organization of relations to foreign intermediaries

In Denmark, customers are served directly by HWH, while foreign customers are served through a net of independent distributors. The intermediaries used by HWH fall into two categories: large industrial customers, for whom HWH functions as a subsupplier, and independent intermediaries, who are often tractor dealers.

This division of intermediaries is also reflected in the internal divison of export activities in the firm. Whereas HJ mainly serves the large industrial customers, HW is more interested in serving the specific needs of the latter group, and thus in the development of new products. In the following, we will focus on the relations of HWH Productions to this latter group of intermediaries.

HWH Production uses tractor dealers and dealers of agricultural machinery to promote their products. Tractor dealers serve a central function in the local areas. The harvest season is short and intense in Scandinavia and Northern Europe, due to the climatic conditions in this part of the world. This leads to an intensive use of machinery, which in turn calls for an effective service back-up. This makes for close relations between tractor dealers and their customers, and dealers often have a professional background as farmers.

From his experience at Hadsund Traktorlager, HW knew that this type of dealer is often consulted by purchasers, farmers and other customers. The industry is characterized by a small distance between wholesalers and manufacturers, and a tradition for tailoring appliances to the specific needs of customers (Jensen & Thomassen, 1988). Dealers and customers often have a long-standing relationship, involving service contracts, regularly purchases, etc. Dealers are therefore eager to adapt to their customers´ specific needs, and supply high quality goods and services, etc. Apart from the technical side of the products, therefore, dealers are also interested in providing an appropriate service, relating to product capabilities, repairs, etc. From his knowledge of the business conditions of tractor dealers, HW realized that a simple, modular design for the front-lifter system would be an important asset, enabling local dealers to carry out repairs relatively quickly. Thus, the system was constructed from standard components already on the market, and assembled with nuts and bolts rather than rivets and weldings. Furthermore, the use of electronic components was avoided, since this was outside the technical capability of the local dealers.

In the 1980s and early 1990s, HWH established contact with dealers in 12 countries, including all the Scandinavian countries, Germany, The Netherlands, France, Switzerland, Spain, Italy and Belgium. A number of relations established early on in the internationalization process have either been terminated or replaced, mainly due to a lack of interest and/or sales effort on the part of the intermediary.

The changing role of intermediaries in the buying process

The agricultural machinery industry has undergone several changes in recent changes. From being mass produced, agricultural machinery is now increasingly customized. Various types of equipment are produced in small batches, sometimes even tailored to the needs of a single customer. This has given the intermediary a more interactive role, helping the customer with the specification of his needs and overtaking the dialogue with the producer. Producers and intermediaries are therefore developing a broader relationship, and the position of the intermediary has gained in both importance and power. This has led to increasing coordination between HWH Production and dealers, since the product is normally produced to order, and tailored to meet the specific needs of the individual customer. For intermediaries to be able to translate customer needs into product capabilities, therefore, it is important that they have a substantial knowledge of both the product concept and the firm's product range. As part of establishing a new dealer relationship, therefore, the firm always invites some of the employees responsible for maintenance (normally also including the firm's owner) to visit HWH Production for training in the product. The training programme usually lasts one week, during which the dealer's employees receive basic training in the front-lifter system and the firm's other products, and help out in assembling new machines. During the training programme, intermediaries come to meet the production staff at HWH Production and get to know who has specific know-how of what product. Intermediaries later utilize these relations when contacting HWH about specific issues. In this sense, HWH Production is comparable to a workshop, where appliances are assembled by production teams in cooperation with the intermediaries.

The following examines the firm's relations with two intermediaries, both of which are independent tractor dealers. These are: Eik & Hausken in Norway, and Homburg Machinehandel in The Netherlands.

Eik & Hausken A/S

Eik & Hausken A/S is a Norwegian firm situated on the outskirts of Oslo, dealing in tractor sales and maintenance. The firm is an import trading agent for Fiat and Ford tractors, which account for more than 60 per cent of its business, and a number of appliances - including those of HWH Production - and spare parts, which account for the remaining 40 per cent. Turnover in 1993 amounted to NOK 17 million, which was an increase of more than 40 per cent over the 1992 figure. The main reason for this increase is that the firm took over the agency of another importer on January 1st., 1993.

The firm is owned by Tore Jacobsen (TJ), who took over the firm from its former owners in 1991. TJ has been employed in the firm since 1984, and in 1988 became manager. The firm has 9 employees, mainly involved in sales and maintenance.

Most of Eik & Hausken's customers are farmers, who contribute approximately 50 per cent of turnover, and housing associations, golf clubs, municipalities and institutions, who together account for the remaining 50 per cent. Both agricultural and public sector spending has been declining for some time. This decline in the firm's business area is reflected in Norway's import of tractors, which has decreased from 9,000 tractors a year in 1987 to only 2,200 in 1992. Eik & Hausken has therefore begun to look for other business areas, and now specializes in golf equipment, which is a growth area in Norway. Norway currently has 25 golf courses, with 25 more under construction, 5 or 6 of which are expected to be finished during 1993. Golf courses typically invest NOK 4-5 million in specialized equipment for area maintenance. Consequently, TJ is currently establishing relationships with a number of English producers of specialized equipment for golf course maintenance, including special lawn mowers, etc.

Customer relationships are normally of a long-standing nature. Customers usually buy technical solutions rather than tractors, and use Eik and Hausken as advisors. A product which fits the customer's needs is therefore more important than a specific brand of tractor and appliance.

Eik & Hausken only keep a small stock of spare parts and demonstration models. Due to increasing customerization, it is not usual to have tractors in stock.

> *"We have a fairly intensive dialogue with suppliers when a customer orders a product. This is in fact initiated from the ordering of the tractor, which is*

*also to an increasing extent fitted to the individual wants of the customer.
Today, tractors and appliances are ordered simultaneously."*

[Tore Jakobsen]

Eik & Hausken A/S: Collaboration with HWH

The relationship to HWH Production was more or less established by chance. HWH originally had another main importer in Norway, who asked Eik & Hausken to rebuild a tractor model. Eik & Hausken were interested in the product as a supplement to their existing product range, and began to purchase snowploughs and sweepers through the importer. As sales of the HWH appliances climbed, Eik & Hausken came to sell all the appliances purchased through the importer. When TJ discovered this, he contacted HWH Production directly, and they agreed that Eik & Hausken could take over the importation. Between 1985 and 1988, Eik & Hausken sold a large number of smaller tractors (30-40 h.p.), mounted with HWH's front-lift system, to Norwegian housing associations and municipalities. In 1989, the market for tractors began to decline, and sales of front-lifter systems dropped. During the past three years, only a few tractors with front-lifter systems have been sold.

The main customers for the front-lifter system are housing associations, small municipalities, nurseries, and, to a smaller extent, golf courses. However, HWH's product is faced with competition both from specialized machines and other front-lifter systems. Municipalities prefer specialized machinery, which suits the hilly terrain of Norway best. Also, Norwegian municipalities often have fairly large budgets, and thus don't need to worry about the economic benefit of having tractors fitted for a multitude of purposes. In Norway, the front-lifter system is thus seen as just another specialized piece of equipment, suitable for specific sweeping and snow-clearing tasks.

A number of Swedish and Italian suppliers have a front-lifter system which could meet the needs of this customer group just as well. The Swedish producer in particular is more competitive than HWH Production, owing to the devaluation of the Swedish Crown, and offers the same quality. Eik & Hausken sells the HWH product to housing associations and nurseries, where it is considered to be the most suitable product. TJ prefers HWH products for this customer group because of the stable relationship to HWH Production and the know-how already acquired about their products.

> *"The primary reason why we sell the products of HWH is that we have stable relationship to the firm, and that we know the technical [ability] of its products. For the customer, the product is not that important. In 90 per cent of the cases, I would probably be able to sell something else."*
>
> [Tore jakobsen]

TJ and several others from Eik & Hausken have visited HWH Production over the years, and have been visited by them in Oslo. Eik & Hausken personnel therefore know who to contact at HWH with regard to specific activities, and make use of this knowledge in relation to sales. In addition, TJ has taken customers to visit HWH Production in order to have a specific product demonstrated. Apart from this, however, contact is not very intensive. Collaboration with HWH Production is initiated by customer contacts. Since it is based on current levels of demand, it is intensive in periods of rapid sales, but is now at a low level.

Eik & Hausken have attempted to develop joint market opportunities with HWH, but these activities have not been very successful. Eik & Hausken often get requests for a sweeper at the back of the tractor, instead of at the front. Having first tried other suppliers for this product, they decided to turn to HWH Production, who, however, did not have this product in their product catalogue. HWH had little faith in Eik & Hausken's sales figures, and were only interested if their expenses were covered. Moreover, they found the product idea technically problematic. Consequently, Eik & Hausken decided to develop the sweeper themselves, and have it produced by a local workshop.

Homburg Machinehandel B.V.
Homburg Machinehandel B.V. is a Dutch company situated in the industrial area of Stiens, a small town in the northern part of The Netherlands. Homburg Machinehandel is both a producer and wholesaler: In addition to its own production of drain cleaners, it is also the general agent for several international producers of agricul-

tural machinery, on similar terms as Eik & Hausken. The firm has 15 employees and in 1993 had a turnover of NLG 7 million. The firm was established in 1958, and is now managed by Mr. J. de Boer (JB), its owner since 1987. In 1990, the market for agricultural machinery stagnated, and the past few years have been characterized by recession, which has affected the activity level substantially. This forced Homburg Machinehandel to reduce the number of employees from 25 to the present number.

Homburg Machinehandel has in-depth knowledge of a relatively small number of suppliers. The firm specializes in crop protection and open area maintenance, and its customers are mainly farmers, contractors responsible for street maintenance (contracted by Dutch municipalities), municipalities, and sports clubs with outdoor facilities, such as soccer clubs, golf clubs, etc.

The major part of the firm's business activities is organized through 80-90 smaller tractor dealers scattered throughout Holland. Normally, these local dealers are specialized in tractors and tractor maintenance, and have only limited knowledge of specialized equipment for crop protection, etc. Homburg Machinehandel thus employs two salesmen, who act as consultants and visit customers together with a local dealer. In addition, the firm has a number of service contracts, and carries a stock of spare parts. Apart from its core customers, Homburg Machinehandel also sells directly to contractors and attempts to establish sales to municipalities. In addition, the firm has a small export of drain cleaners to Denmark. The Danish importer is HWH Production.

The product profile of the firm consists of its own product line and the complete product range of four international producers (two Danish, one French and one Italian) of agricultural machinery.

Hardi International is Homburg Machinehandel's biggest supplier, and HWH Production its smallest. The firm's main area of business is crop protection. The firm carries out a number of activities together with Hardi International, including joint promotion activities, where Homburg escorts customers to a hotel and conference centre managed by Hardi International. Homburg has also developed training facilities for sales personnel at the machinery stations. At the moment, the firm is trying to enter the market for sprayer systems to golf courses, which is a growing business area in Holland. These efforts are supported by Hardi UK, the English subsidiary of Hardi International, which is an important supplier of this type of equipment to the more than 2,500 courses in the UK. At the moment, there are only about 125 golf courses in The Netherlands, but additional courses are planned. Hardi have provided Homburg Machinehandel with prospect material as well as technical assistance in relation to these activities.

> *"We have a special arrangement with Hardi UK. They have a special prospect made especially for the sprayers, which we also use here. Besides that, they also provide us with technical assistance."*

[J. de Boer]

Homburg Machinehandel: Collaboration with HWH

The relationship between HWH Production and Homburg Machinehandel was initiated by HW, who met JB at an agricultural fair in Utrecht (Holland). HW was interested in importing the firm's drain cleaners. At the beginning of the 1990s, the Dutch government decided to forbid chemical spraying for weed prevention. This led Homburg Machinehandel to search for other methods of weed control. Through its business relations with HWH Production, Homburg Machinehandel already had a rudimentary knowledge of their product line, and knew that HWH had a product for the mechanical removal of weeds, so they contacted the company in Denmark. At that time, HWH had an intermediary in Holland which specialized in selling sweepers and snow-clearing equipment. HWH was not satisfied with this relationship and was eager to start up with Homburg Machinehandel. Homburg Machinehandel, on the other hand, were primarily interested in the weed ripper, as other HWH products were only marginally similar to Homburg's product range. HW was very interested in changing dealers, however, and Homburg Machinehandel eventually agreed to take over the agency from the other intermediary. The original idea was to start with the weed brush and then expand the marketing efforts to the other products.

HW subsequently invited the production staff to Denmark, where they received training in the company's product lines. Most of Homburg's employees have visited HWH Production in groups of three or four. HW has also visited Holland in order to introduce the product line to the salesmen there. Normally, contacts are initiated by Homburg Machinehandel, and only in relation to visits and to specific requests concerning the HWH product line. Pete Sitsemar (PS), who is responsible for supplier contacts, finds HWH extremely informative, and general characterizes the business atmosphere as friendly. Contacts are normally made through HW or HJ.

Up to now, sales of the HWH product line have not shown a profit. Sales-related expenditures and the income from the modest sales are more or less in balance. HWH Production has made various efforts to increase sales, but one problem is that tractors in Holland are often already equipped with a front-lifter system. The main problem, however, is that customer groups with the biggest potential as regards HWH products are marginal customers for Homburg Machinehandel. Although the firm has some experience in dealing with municipalities as regards sprayers, the sales task connected with the HWH front-lifter system is radically different. Normally, the sprayers and other products which municipalities buy are treated as annual expenses, and are the responsibility of the municipalities themselves. However, the HWH front-lifter system and associated appliances are seen more as investments and as such come under the jurisdiction of the central authorities. This means different buying routines, including a protracted and complex procurement process, involving different departments and a lot of administrative work. Homburg Machinehandel is not equipped for this type of business activity, and find it burdensome:

> *"We are not used to dealing with municipalities, so it is a handicap for us. Normally, when dealing with municipalities, you have to keep to the budget, and then you have to demonstrate again and again. That takes another year and then.... Normally we make an offer, and then within one or two weeks we know if he is interested or not. We are not used to waiting one or two years. That is the difficulty in selling this equipment here in Holland. Not for the product but for us. It is a quite different system of selling."*
>
> [Piet Sitsema]

Homburg Machinehandel have tried to overcome the difficulties of selling these products to municipalities, however. During 1994, the firm has planned a number of activities especially directed towards this group of customers.

In general, however, Homburg Machinehandel is not satisfied with the present situation, and if it proves impossible to sell the product line to municipalities, or to increase sales to some of the other customer groups, they will consider cancelling the arrangement with HWH Production. There is no written contract between the firms, as this is not customary in this line of business.

ANALYSIS OF THE CASE
The process of "learning by doing" plays a central role in the international development of HWH. The experiences gained in one relationship have subsequently been used in other relations. These experiences have gradually become routinized knowledge, which shapes the way in which HWH enact their international competencies. The initial order was largely the result of the business practices mastered by the firm. It was a project-based order, which relied on the skills and inventiveness of HW, and where the standard production tasks could be carried out within the existing production system. This initial experience has influenced the way in which HWH approaches international markets. This is evident in the extensive use of fairs as entries to new markets, but also in the lack of continuity in maintaining and developing contacts to intermediaries.

Judged on the basis of the above relationships, the present organization and management of the firm's international activities is characterized by instability and a small degree of complementarity and shared interests with market intermediaries. During the 1980s the business prospered, and HWH was able to start projects with intermediaries in a number of countries. Initially, this was easy. HW designed the product in such a way that intermediaries were mostly able to repair and modify products themselves, which reduced the interrelation necessary to a minimum, and avoided organizational overload. However, this also meant that relations developed on an arm's length basis, with little contact or joint problem-solving. HWH was therefore not able to develop joint product or market projects together with their intermediaries to the same extent as other suppliers. This is especially marked in the contrast between the modus operandi of Hardi International and HWH Production in the Homburg Machinehandel relation.

At first glance, the loss of interest seems to be caused by a generally mature and depressed market and the general economic depression in the countries where HWH Production operates. A closer look reveals that other suppliers are able to continue and develop their business with intermediaries, however. The reason for the difference is that the intermediaries studied here are not passive bystanders, waiting for the market to grow so that they can sell HWH products again, but are actively looking for new business areas, which may or may not include the HWH product line. This loss of interest has various causes. One reason is the mismatch between the intentions of the HWH product idea and the business profiles of the market intermediaries. Rather than adopting the HWH idea of a front-lift system in toto, intermediaries have selected specific parts of the product line which fit into their product programme. Their main customers are only marginally interested in HWH's product line, since they are not searching for multi-purpose products. Both customers and intermediaries prefer a trade-off relationship between the performance of a specialized appliance and the flexibility of a module-based front-lift system. Consequently, when they can afford it, they prefer specialized equipment for specialized purposes.

A related reason for the loss of interest in the studied relationships is that, as a result of market depression, intermediaries are gradually changing their business areas in order to exploit new opportunities. In the process, they also involve suppliers as consultants and joint-venture partners in specific projects. This was the case both at Eik & Hausken, who have approached British producers of golf course equipment, and Homburg Machinehandel, who are using the specialized knowledge and promotion material of Hardi International to gain access to a similar market as that of Eik & Hausken's in Norway. This is illustrated below in figure 5.1.

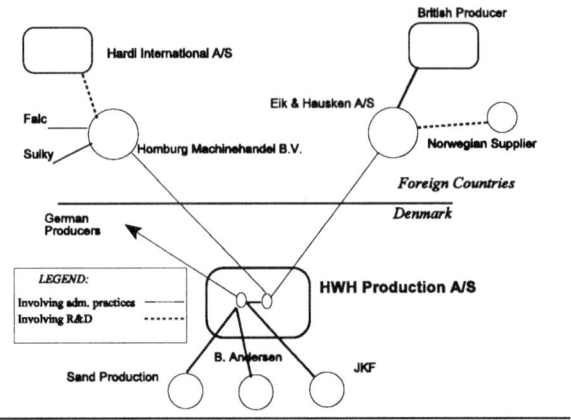

5.1: The focal network of HWH Production A/S

None of the studied intermediaries have involved HWH Production in their attempt to develop new business areas. HWH is mainly seen as a subsupplier in relation to unexpected upturns in demand or other such situations. In general, the dialogue between HWH Production and its market intermediaries only concerns problems and questions connected to actual exchange transactions, and this dialogue is normally initiated by the intermediary. Some attempts have been made by Eik & Hausken to persuade HWH to adapt an appliance to the Norwegian market, but the company was not interested, and Eik & Hausken are having the product made by a local supplier instead.

The experiences of the intermediaries and the general impression of the relationships at HWH Production clearly reveals a gap between interpretations of the relationships. While HW sees intermediaries as partners in marketing their front-lifter system and with whom HWH has an intimate and innovative relationship, intermediaries regard HWH Production as an occasional supplier of specialized equipment, which matches the special needs of a specific customer group, and which complements rather than completes their own product ranges.

In this sense, there is a strict line between the business area of HWH and that of its intermediaries in terms of a clear division of labour and a standardized exchange

166

routine. This business practice clearly differs from that of HWH Production at the beginning of its internationalization process. Here, the market differential of the firm was constituted by its ability to engage in a dialogue, and together with customers develop competitive products. However, while intermediaries still recognize the products as being competitive and of outstanding quality, their market differential, in terms of meeting the specific needs of customers, is vanishing. The dialogue between HWH Production and its intermediaries is one of few words, and no innovative activity is taking place in the relationships, at least not in the ones studied. There is little or no contact between HWH Production and the needs of end users, and there seems to be no dialogue between HWH Production and its intermediaries on this.

The difference between these practices makes alternative and increasingly incompatible demands on HWH. Whereas the tractor dealers want flexibility and ad hoc adjustments and the ability to meet their needs for collaborative activities on an ongoing basis, the larger producers are interested in standardized products, documentation and quality control. The firm is thus at a cross-roads, where it must make strategic decisions concerning the future direction of development.

The present situation is probably the result of a number of interrelated causes, which it would be difficult to identify in practice. One cause, however, may be the firm's rapid internationalization, which led to the hasty development and subsequent termination of a number of relations to foreign intermediaries. In the present situation, however, it is difficult to establish any form of relationship, as this would make an impossible claim on the resources of the company.

CHAPTER 6
Lux Perpetua A/S[15]

Lux Perpetua develops and sells lamps, mainly through retail outlets, such as hypermarkets and DIY stores. The firm has 11 employees and an annual turnover of between DKK 40-50 million. The firm's activities include design, marketing, administration and production planning. For other activities, Lux Perpetua relies heavily on collaboration with external sources. Production, including storage and packaging, is carried out via relations with vendors and producers. The product line consists primarily of low-priced lamps for the consumer market, of which the firm has more than 150 models. The firm exports mainly to Scandinavia, via independent intermediaries. At one time, thirty per cent of production was exported. In 1992, international turnover amounted to fifteen per cent of total turnover.

Background
Lux Perpetua was established by Svend Erik Poulsen (SEP). His professional background includes an apprenticeship as an electrician, and experience as a clerk, purchaser, and export agent in Denmark for a Swedish lamp producer.

In 1977, this firm went bankrupt, leaving SEP without a job. This was the primary incentive for starting Lux Perpetua. During a rainy holiday, SEP became interested in one of the lamps at the hotel where he was staying. He was convinced that it could be produced and sold in Denmark, and on his return he contacted Dansk Supermarked (DS), a large Danish retail chain, and offered them an option for

[15] Cover name

purchasing 5,000 lamps, for delivery four months later. This agreement marked the beginning of Lux Perpetua.

Organization of production and exports
The order presented SEP with an opportunity, but also with a problem. He lacked production experience, and had no interst in investing in production facilities, partly because of his former employers' experiences. The bankruptcy of this firm was partly due to the large specialized investments demanded by their main customer, IKEA, as the price for becoming their supplier. Because of the subsequent dependence of the firm on this one customer, IKEA had been able to depress prices to a level which eventually become unacceptable. Learning from this, SEP realized that investments should be minimized in order to stay flexible and avoid dependency on banks. SEP therefore looked for external suppliers. His basic idea was to subcontract all production activities and as much of the administration as possible, and to concentrate on lamp development and marketing.

Experiences and relations from previous jobs came in handy in solving this problem. SEP had relations to a number of therapy workshops for the physically and mentally handicapped in North Jutland County. These workshops were set up to activate handicapped people by giving them the opportunity to carry out simple production tasks at low wages. The workshop managment was presented with SEP's ideas for lamp assembly and found the task within their reach. This led to an agreement being made between SEP and North Jutland County. Next, SEP searched through his personal network for suppliers of materials. He was able to draw on several contacts from the time he made the rounds of international lighting fairs for his former employer. Relatively quickly, he found two German suppliers of components.

To make certain he could meet the obligations made to DS, SEP started coaching the mentally retarded on the shop floor, and personally coordinated activities in the therapy workshops. In this way, he became acquainted with both clients and administrators. He made it a daily routine to pay visits to the workshops, and also visited suppliers and customers on a regular basis, in order to monitor activities and adapt accordingly.

SEP succeeded in delivering the order to DS, and won a new order from the firm. Meanwhile, former customers of his previous employer interested in purchasing the lamp began to contact SEP, and in this way he gradually built up a customer base. His previous job experiences enabled him to communicate with these actors and understand their problems and needs. Through frequent contact, and by adapting and combining the interests of various actors, SEP thus managed to maintain a stable production pattern. All interests were met, and the actors gradually included the lamp assembly activites in their planning. SEPs basic idea was still to stick to his personal capabilities and leave production to suppliers and customers. Additional tasks were therefore delegated: storage facilities were rented, and a forwarding agent was brought in to handle freight documentation and daily order handling. In this way, SEP managed to concentrate his efforts on product development and marketing activities.

Formalization of Lux Perpetua: The birth of an organizational structure
Although SEP continued to delegate as much as possible, continued growth made more personnel necessary. SEP decided to hire more administrative personnel, which would free him to concentrate on external contacts and product development. SEP eventually realized that the further development of the Lux Perpetua product range was restricted by the standard components of conventional suppliers, and therefore decided to develop his own components. Together with Sander Plast, a local producer of plastic components, he developed a range of modules. His aim in designing these modules was to meet the interests and capabilities of the various actors as much as possible. A range of lamps could be assembled from the modules without the extensive use of tools and machinery. This was well-received by the therapy workshops, which, for training purposes, preferred this type of component. However, there were also benefits for Lux Perpetua. Unit production time was reduced, and substantial investment in specialized machinery was made unneces-sary. Furthermore, it was possible to postpone assembly, which reduced both storage and opportunity costs. It also increased flexibility vis-à-vis buyers, since it made it easier to adjust to changes in demand. In addition, it gave Lux Perpetua an advantage over competitors who relied on more standardized components. Finally, it enabled Lux Perpetua to jump over a link in the value-adding chain and deal

directly with suppliers, which saved costs. The drawback to all this was a loss of flexibility. Lux Perpetua cut itself off from part of the components market, as part of the product range had to build on in-house components. However, due to the flexible design, this was not seen as crucial.

The more the firm prospered, the more SEP found the work tiresome. He became increasingly bogged down in problem-solving activities outside his field of interest, and the daily administration was fast becoming the dominant part of his work load. He therefore decided to sell Lux Perpetua. SEP reorganized the firm to make it easier for an investor to take over. A formal organizational structure was developed, and responsibility was delegated to present employees. Lux Perpetua was formally divided into three areas: Product planning, product development, and sales management.

In 1988, the firm was sold to its present owner and manager, Jørgen Havemann (JH). JH has an MBA in marketing and administrative experience from a previous job in a larger firm. He was therefore able to use his administative experience to strengthen and document the procedures for coordination, including more clearly-defined areas of responsibility and functional specialization. JH wanted to continue the organizational setup. Unlike SEP, JH had no objection to some degree of financial commitment. In 1988, Multilak, a lampshade lacquerer, ran into financial difficulties. Along with two employees, JH decided to invest in the firm and succeeded in saving it.

Other changes took place after the reorganization and takeover by the new manager. The previous sales executive left the firm, and was replaced by Per Gissel (PG). PG had worked for a large lamp producer and used his experience from this job to establish contact with a Swedish distributor, with whom a formal contract was later signed.

During the past few years, the international turnover and profitability of Lux Perpetua in general has declined. In 1992, the Swedish distributor regretted that he was unable to meet the terms of the contract and asked to be released from it, and continue the relationship on a more informal basis. In addition, the Finnish intermediary closed down and had to be replaced by a new one.

Organization of exports - collaboration with intermediaries

Exports to the Scandinavian markets were organized early on primarily as "piggybacking". Maxam, a producer and retailer, acted as export agent, and sold the products through their distribution network. Lux Perpetua took care of delivery, and maintained contact with retailers through regular meetings twice a year. Maxam changed hands, however, and decided to shift to another area of business. SEP contacted his largest Norwegian customer, who agreed to represent Lux Perpetua in the Norwegian market. The Swedish market was covered by Lux Perpetua from Denmark. The relationship towards foreign distributors and customers was generally characterized by openness. SEP put it like this:

> *"Most agents are interested in keeping a fair relationship to both suppliers and customers; the supplier is also a resource in terms of being a specialist in his field. We therefore had contacts with our customers 1-2 times a year, where we discussed product assortment and exchanged information on competitors products, etc."*

[Svend-Erik Poulsen]

Lux Perpetua: Relations to Swedlux A/S

Today, Lux Perpetua exports directly to customers in Sweden through Swedlux A/S, which, as regards the organization of production, is very similar to Lux Perpetua. Like Lux Perpetua, Swedlux uses therapy workshops for assembling tasks, and produces via suppliers. The firm is situated in Kinnahult and is owned by Ingemar Andersson (IA), the former manager of a large Swedish lamp manufacturer. Swedlux was established in 1990, and today has three employees, with a turnover of SEK 10.5 million. The lamps are designed by IA and produced by Danish and Swedish suppliers. The product range consists of a limited number of standard models, made from turned wood, in a variety of colours, according to current trends in interior decoration. Swedlux works closely with both Danish and Swedish suppliers in developing new features and production processes. IA is especially interested in

172

lamp design, which he describes as a process of translating general fashion trends into lamp designs. IA describes this process in the following way:

> *"When you look at fashion shows and magazines of interior decoration you get a clear feeling of a shared pattern of colors, fabrics and design. I simply try to capture this impression and translate it into a lamp design."*
>
> [Ingemar Andersson]

IA studies fashion and other areas where new colours and styles are presented. Next, ideas are discussed with suppliers and applied in designs. The Kinna area has a tradition for cabinet- making, which the firm makes good use of. For example, together with a cabinet-maker and a painter, IA has revived an old technique for "marbelling" turned wood which was used by cabinet-makers in the 16th and 17th centuries. Geographical proximity is not the only criterion for deciding which suppliers to use in developing products and production processes, however. One of the latest product lines, a lamp series for childrens´ rooms, was developed together with a Danish industrial cabinet-maker.

Swedlux sell lamps in Sweden, Norway, Finland and Germany. Exports account for about 50 per cent of the turnover. IKEA is the single largest customer, contributing 35 per cent of the turnover. The second largest customer is a Finnish chain of furniture retailers, which takes 20 per cent of the sales. The remaining 45 per cent are divided between several Swedish and foreign buyers, primarily furniture outlets, lamp retailers and electricians. IA does not export to Denmark, because:

> *"Danish taste, when it comes to lighting and interior decoration, is very distant from the rest of Scandinavia, and wooden lamps are close to impossible to sell to the Danes."*
>
> [Ingemar Andersson]

Both customers and suppliers are visited frequently, during which time ideas are exchanged and later tested at fairs or directly in shops.

Swedlux: Relations to Lux Perpetua

The relationship to Lux Perpetua was initated at the Göteborg fair in 1990. PG, the sales executive at Lux Perpetua, knew IA from his previous job. Swedlux and Lux Perpetua signed a contract which obliged Swedlux to market the complete range of Lux Perpetua products in Sweden. Sales have been disappointing, however, and the contract was terminated at the end of 1991, when IA regretted that he was unable to meet the terms of the contract. This did not mean the end of the relationship, however. Today, Swedlux sells only a limited range of products, and Lux Perpetua is allowed to display their products at the prestigious Swedish lamp fair in Göteborg from the Swedlux stand. Furthermore, Swedlux has supported Lux Perpetua in their attempts to enter the German market by introducing JH to some of their own customers. As regards the Lux Perpetua range, however, Swedlux limits their sales activity to the Swedish market.

IA contacts PG, and JH and visits Lux Perpetua once or twice a year, before the lamp season begins, where he is shown their new products. IA normally chooses the newest lamps, together with other models which have earlier proven successful in Sweden. These are displayed in January at the large fairs, where purchasers from retail chains and single shops go to select products for the coming season. The Swedlux-Lux Perpetua relationship differs from that of other suppliers. In contrast to these, Lux Perpetua does not use Swedlux as a provider of market information, and does not adapt their designs to Swedlux's ideas and insights into Swedish tradition and trends in interior decoration. Rather, Lux Perpetua is strongly product-oriented. IA expresses this as follows:

> *"It is very typical ... when PG and JH are visiting us, we go out and study lamp retailers, and they always look for lamps which are closest to their own products, rather than trying to figure out what is the overall trend displayed in the store ... We think very differently and often have communication problems."*

[Ingemar Andersson]

Lux Perpetua: Relations to Thor A. Ljungman

In Norway, Lux Perpetua sells its products through Thor A. Ljungman, a large Norwegian importer and designer of lamps and a wholesaler of sanitary articles. Thor A. Ljungman was established in 1965 as a trading agency in sanitary articles, but has gradually developed into selling lamps. Today, lamps make up two thirds of the total turnover. The firm is situated in Skyta, a few kilometres from Oslo, and has a turnover of NOK 50 milion. It is owned and co-managed by Thor A. Ljungman (TAL).

The firm employs 40 persons, covering sales, marketing, design, purchasing, storage, and administrative tasks. Sales are carried out through a staff of provision-based salesmen, who travel all over Norway. Customers are mainly Norwegian lamp stores and retail outlets. In recent years, the distribution of lamps has changed from being mainly based on a number of retail outlets to being increasingly dominated by the large retail chains. Today, approximately 50 per cent of all lamps purchased in Norway are sold through supermarkets. Hand in hand with this development, customers are increasingly seeing lamps as just another commodity, to be replaced in the same way as curtains, carpets, etc., when they redecorate. Thus, lamp design and the development of new lamp assortments has become more important, and this has influenced the way lamps are displayed in retail outlets. The firm keeps up with design fashions through collaborating with a number of producers in Norway and Denmark, as well as in a number of other countries. Thor A. Ljungman imports lamps to the value of approximately NOK 18 million, almost half of which (NOK 8m) come from Denmark. 80 per cent of the lamps are sold under the firm´s own brand name, the remaining 20 per cent being other producers´ products, including Lux Perpetua, which makes up approximately 3 per cent of total turnover.

The relationship with Lux Perpetua was initiated by SEP, who contacted the firm shortly after starting his own firm. TAL was interested in the lamps on condition that he had exclusive rights to them. An agreement was eventually reached whereby TAL received exclusive rights to sell the lamps in exchange for buying a certain minimum number of lamps each year. Shortly before selling Lux Perpetua, SEP contacted TAL to ask whether he was interested in a closer relationship and in becoming a trading agent in Norway. TAL agreed, on condition that this would not affect his existing business, since he wanted to carry on with the development of his own product range. They reached an agreement to the effect that Thor A. Ljungman could continue selling to other wholesalers, and that, besides selling Lux Perpetua products, the firm would also keep a stock of Lux Perpetua products, so that Lux Perpetua could refer Norwegian customers directly to Thor A. Ljungman. It was also agreed that this closer collaboration would include joint product development.

> *"The part of the agreement including joint lamp development was especially interesting for us, because of the changing market conditions and because SEP is a person with a strong creative talent."*
>
> [Thor A. Ljungman]

The relationship went well from the start, but the sale of Lux Perpetua products has dropped about 50 per cent over the past three years. There have been several reasons for this. One is the devaluation of the Norwegian crown, which pushed up Lux Perpetua prices. Danalux, another Danish supplier to Thor A. Ljungman, was able to maintain its sales figures in spite of the devaluation, however.

TAL attributes the main reason for the steady decline to the fact that the Lux Perpetua product range is out of touch with the tastes of Norwegian customers, only minor changes having been made to lamp design and packaging in recent years. Unlike other suppliers of lamps and lamp components and the original intentions of both SEP and TAL, Lux Perpetua does not involve Thor A. Ljungman in their product development efforts, and in general has not been interested in the changing conditions in the Norwegian market. In general, TAL finds that Lux Perpetua offer only little support.

> *"As an example: When the Norwegian crown was devaluated, we contacted our suppliers and asked them to lower their prices in order to maintain the present activity level. I made arrangements with my two other Danish suppliers. One said: Name your acceptable price level. Lux Perpetua, however, resisted, on the grounds that he could not afford this. I then told him that we would have to import a series of spot lamps which would collide with the Lux Perpetua product range in order to maintain our position on*

the Norwegian market. Lux Perpetua accepted this, provided that their lamps still would be in our catalouge."

[Thor A. Ljungman]

ANALYSIS OF THE LUX PERPETUA CASE

A snapshot view of the Lux Perpetua resource chain reveals a complex web with many actors and many types of relations, stretching over several organizational borders.

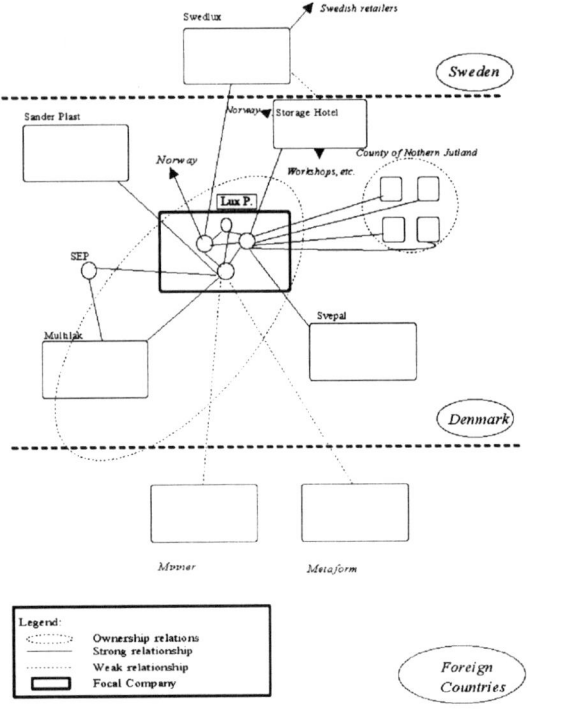

Figure 6.1.: The Lux Perpetua focal network

As figure 6.1 shows, Lux Perpetua is characterized by a high degree of externaliza-tion. Most of the business activities are subcontracted to specialized firms with which Lux Perpetua collaborates extensively. The allocation and direction of resources does not follow organizational boundaries in terms of hierarchical resource control, nor market signals in terms of price. Furthermore, there are no legal contracts between the actors. Despite this, Lux Perpetua is able to coordinate a relatively stable web of relations. Large parts of the Lux Perpetua resource chain consist of closely connected but independent firms, coordinating transactions among themsleves on a continuous and long-term basis.

The Lux Perpetua case clearly illustrates the central role played by personal relations in configuring and managing a resource chain. SEP's personal network has

178

survived firm closure and job change, and he has been able to reestablish activities which were earlier carried out for his employer, in a new organizational setting. Moreover, Lux Perpetua has offered a fairly stable pattern of demand to the other participants in the resource chain without demanding increased control over their resources in return. Each enterprise is still regarded as an independent decision unit, with the right to terminate collaboration if conditions make this necessary.

To a large degree, the development is systemic. The resource chain has been continuously reconfigured in line with the development in activity patterns. Suppliers and customers have specialized in dealing with Lux Perpetua products, and have developed an assortment of skills in doing so. Relations are not stable, however, but change over time. Organizational settings differ, and so do role expectations. Consequently, the contextual setting in which actors find themselves influences their cognition of status and role within the resource chain. Their cognition of their own role and the roles of others also clearly influences the communication and organizing processes. Previous organizational set-ups are founded on specific relations and communication patterns, and changes in these also lead to changes in activity on a more general level.

The organization of the Lux Perpetua resource chain is therefore characterized by a web of mutual obligations and shared practices, rather than an authoritarian body legitimized by a formal structure and/or some form of resource dependency. This demands a specific management style, characterized by openness and extensive communication, for galvanizing the organizational setup into concerted activity. These patterns are gradually developed through the accumulation of personal experience and trial-and-error processes. They are also deeply idiosyncratic. The change of managers has therefore also meant a change in management style. As a result of the reorganization and task specialization, and perhaps underlined by the background and concepts of the new manager, the organization of the resource chain is changing from a loosely coupled, self-organizing arena for conducting activity into a tightly coupled hierarchical setting, resembling the managerial experiences of the new manager. An effective bureaucracy functions through the minute divison of labour enforced by rules and regulations. Although this makes for an ordered universe inside Lux Perpetua, it also handicaps adaption to external relations. The organizational boundaries become visible, as areas of responsibility are clearly defined, and coordination is supported by rule-like systems. Informality is suceeded by formality, communication by lines of standardized information. This change in organizational practice is incompatible with the established routines, however, as they are based on incommensurable principles, including different roles, positions, coordination principles, etc., in relation to the organization of activity. Consequently, the resource chain is faced with problems which are becoming increasingly difficult to deal with within the present set-up. The firm is being pressed by forces which relate to both supply and demand conditions.

Suppliers are becoming increasingly dissatisfied with their position as "pure" subcontractors in arm´s length relations. They are starting to feel uncomfortable about the large proportion of their total turnover contributed by Lux Perpetua products, as they regard this as a threat to their independency and economic wellbeing. Consequently, they want to engage in a closer dialogue with Lux Perpetua, both in order to commit Lux Perpetua to their products and ideas and to obtain a deeper insight into the future demand situation.

With regard to demand, distributors associated with the firm point to its lack of adaptability to changed demand conditions. They claim that production is no longer innovative, and that, due to its lack of adjustment, the firm is falling behind major competitors in foreign markets. This also seems to be reflected in the export turnover, which has decreased in recent years. Within the resource chain, suppliers and distributors are becoming increasingly dissatisfied with what see as an arm´s length relationship with Lux Perpetua. Consequently, these firms downplay their involvement with Lux Perpetua, and turn their attention to other relations, leaving Lux Perpetua less and less space to maneuver in. Lux Perpetua, on the other hand, interprets this fall in interest as a sign of disloyalty and as threatening the market position of the firm. This would seem to indicate a looming conflict between Lux Perpetua and its resource chain partners.

CHAPTER 7

Hydro-X A/S

Hydro-X is a small-sized producer of alkaline liquid for the prevention of scale and corrosion in steam boilers, central and district heating plants, condensers, and any industrial plant liable to scale formation. The firm is situated near Hjallerup, in northern Denmark. It was founded in Copenhagen in 1940 by the father of the present manager and co-owner, Ole Kristensen (OK), who took over the firm in 1964. During the 1970s, the physical facilities gradually became too small for the firm, and OK started looking for new premises in order to expand production capacity. Unable to find any at a reasonable price in Copenhagen, in 1977 he decided to move the firm to Hjallerup.

The firm has 16 employees, 5 of whom are in marketing, production planning and administration. Two persons are employed in a fully automated chemical plant, and the remaining personnel work as service consultants. The number of employees has slowly increased over the past 10 years. Besides OK, his wife and two sons also work full-time in the firm. The firm is owned by OK and his mother, who took over his father's shares. She owns two thirds of the firm, while the remaining one third is controlled by OK.

Water treatment

The need for water treatment products arises from the ability of water to corrode certain metals. Layers of scale form in water distribution systems, causing various kinds of insulation problems, such as reduced heat exchange or cooling ability, which increases power use and decreases the life of the plant. In some water systems, such as pressure vessels, where insulation problems can be dangerous, inspection and cleaning is mandatory by law. Thus, the need for cleaning both district heating and cooling systems is supported by leglislation as well as by reduced efficiency in industrial production.

Products and markets

The Hydro-X alkaline liquid differs from other water treatment products by being based on organic compounds. Other water treatment systems use one or more active compounds, such as caustic soda, trisodium phosfate, and sodium sulphite. These have various side-effects, however. Caustic soda can interact with different iron alloys, causing metal fatigue. The Hydro-X liquid combines the physical and chemical abilities of the added compounds, and achieves a similar effect to purely chemically-based liquids, but without the damaging side-effects. However, the compounds in the liquid must be combined according to the type of feedwater used.

Treating water with the Hydro-X alkaline is a complicated task which, apart from the liquid itself, also requires the testing of the water system in order to identify the cause(s) of corrosion. Water samples are taken and thoroughly analyzed, and the proper dosing of the chemicals is calculated on the basis of this analysis. This requires specialized knowledge of flow equipment, as well as a thorough knowledge of chemicals. Moreover, heating, steam and cooling systems are often integrated parts of continuous-flow production systems, where any halt in production is extremely costly. Treatment therefore has to be swift and accurate, allowing only a small margin of failure. In general, therefore, customers prefer to buy this service from a water treatment company, rather than trying to do the job themselves. In this sense, Hydro-X can be seen as offering a method for the solving of scale and corrosion problems, rather than being the producer of an alkaline liquid. OK puts it like this:

"We have attempted to position a concept and a brand name. Hydro-X is identical with a specific quality, a method for solving a problem for the customer."

"The most important message to deliver to our customers is one that ensures that their system is continuously controlled by professionals."

[Ole Kristensen]

Denmark is serviced by a staff of consultants, who pay regular visits to customers in order to evaluate the general condition of their systems, using different types of analyses.

The marketing task is divided between OK and one of his employees. OK concentrates on international markets, while the sales manager takes care of the domestic market. Internationally, service contracts are offered through a network of independent distributors, which are trained and equipped by Hydro-X.

Industrial customers are both small and large companies. The large companies (e.g. breweries and food processing firms) often control an international network of production plants. Hydro-X has therefore seen an international sales potential in establishing a network of distributors offering an identical service worldwide, in order to follow these firms abroad.

Hydro-X water treatment services are offered in more than 37 countries worldwide. As such, more than 70 per cent of total turnover is generated through foreign sales. The firm had a turnover of DKK 13.5 million in 1993, and expects this figure to exceed DKK 14 million in 1994.

The firm has gradually spread its activities to a number of countries over the past 30 years and developed its international engagement in several respects. During the 1960s and early 1970s, the firm expanded into all the Scandinavian countries and most West European countries. The firm has established relationships with

183

intermediaries in a number of African, Middle Eastern and Asian countries, and also has links in two Latin American countries.

It has been the explicit policy of the firm only to enter a limited number of markets at one time. OK explained it like this:

> *"I have always had the rule of thumb never to enter more than two markets a year. It always takes a lot of effort and a large amount of time to start up a new intermediary"*

[Ole Kristensen]

The firm has tried different ways of entering markets. For example, it established a Norwegian subsiduary in 1981, based on a contact to an intermediary. This did not prove successful, however, and the subsidiary was closed in 1987.

EXTERNAL RELATIONS

Hydro-X has a number of external relations, both as regards servicing, marketing and the development of products and production processes. Some of these relations serve a number of different purposes, being reconfigured and used for specific tasks in which Hydro-X plays a number of different roles. This is evident in the following presentation of Hydro-X's focal network, which includes relations to suppliers, peers, and foreign intermediaries.

Relations to Suppliers

Both chemicals, dosing pumps and measurement equipment are necessary inputs in water treatment services. The chemicals used are all standard compounds, and are bought on the spot market. Normally, Hydro-X purchases its chemicals from Superfos Chemicals. Dosing pumps are purchased jointly with AVF Waterbehande-ling, a Dutch water treatment company which also represents Hydro-X in The Netherlands. The firms jointly purchase specially designed dosing pumps from Prominent, a German manufacturer of pumps. The measurement equipment used by consultants has been specially made by Hydria, a producer of measuring equipment. Total purchases amount to DKK 5 million a year.

The Danish Board of District Heating - a marketing and knowledge network
Hydro-X participates actively in a district heating information network, set up by the "Danish Board of District Heating" (DBDH), which includes 40 firms, all of which have experience in district heating and international business. This organization was established in 1978 to coordinate work on district heating plants.

The original purpose of DBDH was to organize promotion campaigns for Danish district heating technology abroad. It has since also expanded into other areas, however.

Danish district heating is unique in that it works with low-temperature water. In comparsion, other district heating systems, e.g. in Germany, the USA and Russia, operate with temperatures up to 150 degrees celcius. Danish producers of district heating equipment have collaborated in developing a product concept which allows district heating systems to function at lower temperatures, which in turn saves energy costs. The concept consists of a range of components, including insulated pipes, specially designed pumps, heat exchangers, etc. Together, these components form an interdependent system for district heating. This interdependence has provided the rationale for joint product development, including joint marketing activities, export promotion, and, to some extent, the organization of international activities. Thus, members of the DBDH network share foreign intermediaries to a large extent, and regularly exchange information with each other.

DBDH covers a wide range of skills and products, including consulting engineers, advisors, planners, contractors, and supervisors. The association has connections to a number of other organizations involved in the development and distribution of knowledge about district heating, including the European Institute for Environmental Energy, the Danish Technological Institute, and a training school for district heating personnel. These connections are used regularly by board members, who are thus able to draw on other members in relation to specific projects. OK gives the following picture:

> *"As the board includes a number of consulting engineers who have conncetions to the World Development Bank (WDB), we are always informed concerning the projects taken on here. [As an example] In relation to a planned modernization of the district heating systems in large Polish cities, a group of consulting engineers who knew each other from DBDH formed a task group which developed a feasibility study of the area. This was sponsored by the Danish state. The study was used as documentation in an application to the WDB. The project was undertaken and later these engineers participated in the detail projecting, but now as separate firms... In the WDB, there are strict rules that forbid consulting engineers to participate in more than one phase of such a project. Moreover, you are not allowed to state the type of product to be used, only the specifications of the components. Here, however, the consultant engineers are capable of coming up with specifications that are met only by Danish valves. This is, in itself, not peculiar, as the Danish model of district heating is unique."*
> ..

> [Ole Kristensen]

Members of DBDH visit markets and hold seminars on the Danish model of district heating for potential buyers and other key persons. At these presentations, the producers present their individual products as parts of a complete concept, in which the discrete components mutually support each other. These seminars are a vital part of the worldwide promotion of Danish district heating technology.

Organization of exports: relations to foreign intermediaries
Hydro-X's basic philosophy is to sell a principle - a method for solving corrosion problems - rather than "just" an alkaline liquid. Hydro-X attempts to market its services homogeneously worldwide, in order to attract multinational firms operating in numerous countries. The basic idea is that customers should be able to receive the same service in all countries.

186

"It may sound a bit bold to wave the flag and say: "We sell worldwide from Hjallerup". On the other hand, the world is shrinking. What we attempt to sell is a trademark, which represents a similar service worldwide. When a customer buys our product in Singapore, he should be able to receive the same type of service as he would get in Denmark."

[Ole Kristensen]

This means that the service must continuously conform to specific and narrowly defined standards. This requires the worldwide communication and implementation of a number of routines, or shared ideas, for treating water distribution systems homogeneously. Offering water treatment services worldwide through a network of independent distributors thus represents a significant challenge for the firm's policy concerning its international market intermediaries. This can be illustrated in figure 7.3 below.

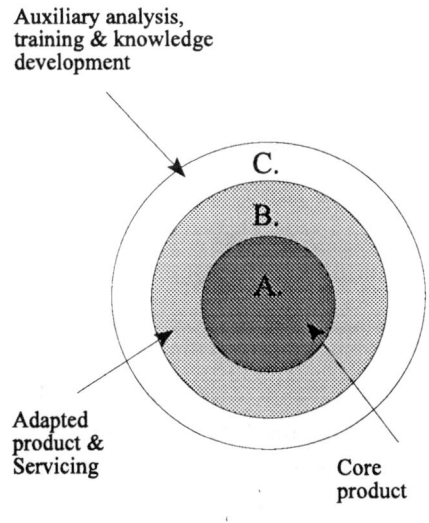

Figure 7.3: An extented definition of the Hydro-X Product

While the core product, (A), is a standard product, the (B) & (C) levels must be adapted to local needs, which requires a great deal of consistency and homogeneity in the methods used by intermediaries. Furthermore, the accuracy and swiftness of the treatment depends on the knowledge of the local intermediaries concerning production methods and water qualities. These skills must be coordinated and developed on an ongoing basis, as illustrated by the (C) level in figure 7.3.

Hydro-X achieves this by actively encouraging intermediaries to adopt the firm's standards. OK spends a large amount of time visiting market intermediaries and developing relations through training, problem-solving, etc. Typically, a relation takes 3-5 years to develop, during which time the intermediary participates in various training seminars, and OK visits the intermediary regularly. When mutual agreement has been established, however, the contacts become less frequent and more related to specific activities.

> *"Our way of cooperating changes over time. It's hard work the first two years, because we must provide training, and there are always some individual problems which we have to help an intermediary with. Later, relations become routinized."*
>
> [Ole Kristensen]

In all, these activities add up to more than 180 travel days a year. In addition, Hydro-X functions as a meeting place for the intermediaries, and this takes up another 130 days of OK's time a year. This underlines the amount of time that OK uses in developing an intermediary relationship.

These market relations are a vital asset for Hydro-X. OK sees the main task here as providing intermediaries with a thorough grounding in the firm's product concept. Thus the firm does not dwell too much on lack of qualifications - what is more important is their attitude towards cooperation and learning the methods and standards of the firm.

> *"We attempt to eliminate problems with troublesome intermediaries before they arise by sorting out potential intermediaries by the aid of economic information. At the end of the day we are, however, dealing with people. You can have a large and well-known firm to represent you through an*

unmotivated employee - and then it is all worth nothing. Also, diplomas are not in themselves qualifying. The essential question is whether the person has got the entreprenuerial spirit demanded. These are qualities which are much better evaluated when the potential intermediary visits us."

[Ole Kristensen]

Hydro-X runs a training programme for both potential and active distributors in order to teach them the fundamentals of water treatment and to update their knowledge of production plants and chemicals. This training programme is obligatory, and is specified in detail in the contract between intermediaries and Hydro-X. These training seminars are also used for evaluating intermediaries and their commitment to the product.

Training takes place at Hydro-X, and new knowledge in the field of water treatment is constantly being incorporated into the training programme. These seminars not only disseminate knowledge of water treatment, but also foster the development of a common technical language through which shared water treatment problems can be addressed, as well as further the development of specific routines for solving them.

Hydro-X also offers advice on intermediaries' organizational set-ups, e.g. with regard to marketing, etc. Independent distributors often devote a specific department to the Hydro-X service network, with a staff of field consultants. OK offers advice on this type of sales organization. Secondly, the seminars function as workshops for the distributors, where experiences can be shared with others and specific problems discussed. Last but not least, the seminars have a social function, bringing together the social and technical relations of actors scattered all over the world.

The next step in the development of a relationship involves frequent visits during the first few months in order to provide support, clear up misunderstandings, and help in implementing the product concept. Typically, one person in the intermediary is responsible for direct contact to Hydro-X, and it is his job to communicate the basic principles to the field consultants. OK helps out by conducting training seminars at the intermediary.

This development is not only furthered by research results, but is also the consequence of joint problem-solving. Distributors use Hydro-X as a consultant when they run up against problems which they can't solve using their own resources, or which cannot be handled by telephone. Occasionally (typically once or twice a year), therefore, OK is personally involved in direct problem-solving together with the intermediary. The results of this are then reported and add to the general knowledge base of the firm.

> *"When intermediaries experience serious problems in relation to selling our product and tell us about it, then we immediately give this problem first priority. The rationale for doing so is that, in general, we always learn something by meeting problems which cannot be solved through our standard repertoire. When we meet such a problem, we have a considerable number of contacts which can be drawn on to help us identify the causes of the problem. The knowledge we obtain by solving these problems may later become useful and be integrated in our training programme. It costs a large sum to solve these problems, but must be considered as an investment."*
>
> [Ole Kristensen]

Another means by which Hydro-X knits the distribution network closer together is through a worldwide computer network for ordering chemicals and standardizing sales material and various types of business correspondence. This network also serves as an on-line service for solving specific problems related to water analysis. For example, the chemical composition of a sample of water can be keyed into the network, enabling any network member to help out and/or gain knowledge from solutions to similar problems. Hydro-X engages actively in this, and uses these specific problems as a base for developing their own knowledge of corrosion problems and other areas relevant to water treatment, thereby updating their knowledge bank.

Thirdly, Hydro-X has achieved ISO 9002 certification, which it uses in evaluating and defining standards for new distributors. This fits in well with Hydro-X's overall strategy of standardizing their services worldwide, and has also helped the firm in specifying their training programme and making demands on intermediaries concerning customer service.

In the following, the relations to and organizational set-ups of two intermediaries will be examined more closely.

Collaboration with HyXo Oy

HyXo Oy is a small Finnish firm, situated in Kerava, 30 kilometres north of Helsinki. The firm specializes in waste water treatment and water treatment services in water works. HyXo manufactures and imports a number of components and instruments for these purposes.

HyXo Oy was established in 1968 by Höyrytys Oy, a firm specializing in steam generators for greenhouses. The firm had a lot of problems with corrosion, however, and was looking for a product to prevent scale and corrosion. Around 1966, initial contact was made to Hydro-X via a Finnish intermediary. However, in 1968, Höyrytys Oy took over the marketing of Hydro-X and set up HyXo Oy as an independent firm with assistance from OK, who, together with Eurowater, was looking for an intermediary to represent their products on the Finnish market. Today, Höyrytys Oy and HyXo Oy are approximately equal in size and turnover. As Höyrytys Oy specializes in the production of boilers, the firms naturally use each other as sales representatives, and share a considerable knowledge base. Today, the firms are situated in the same building.

HyXo's turnover has fluctuated a great deal, due to Finland's economic problems at the beginning of the nineties, which forced a lot of Finnish firms to decrease or terminate their production activities. The economic situation in Finland has stabilized somewhat, however, and with it HyXo's annual turnover. The firm had a turnover of FIM 16.5 million in 1993, and expects this to increase to FIM 20 million in 1994. The firm is family owned, and has been so for two generations.

Today, HyXo Oy employs 25 persons, including the manager and present owner, Harry Viiala, and four other persons, who work in administration. There are 14 employees in the marketing and sales department, and 6 in production. The firm also owns a production outlet in Oulo, approximately 1,000 kilometres north of Helsinki, which produces a range of boilers.

HyXo's sales and marketing department is organized around the firm's business activities. Half of the sales and marketing personnel have an educational background as mechanical engineers. One group of sales persons - all engineers - mainly work as field consultants with Hydro-X products.

The main product lines are: measuring and control equipment, dosing pumps, water treatment products, and water treatment services. HyXo produces various types of pumps and a number of units for waterwork use. The major part of HyXo's product range is supplied from a number of foreign producers, including Hydro-X.

HyXo Oy only produces dosing units itself, and even this is declining as high-quality specialized products become increasingly available from foreign suppliers. Today, HyXo Oy imports products from a number of domestic and foreign suppliers, and functions as market intermediary for these producers.

Typical customers are water works and various kinds of processing firms, who use feedwater at various stages in the production process. Besides this, HyXo delivers water processing and analytical equipment to a number of firms offering water treatment services, or which have water treatment as an integrated part of their business activities.

Most of the product assortment is sold to customers in Finland, but HyXo also exports to Russia, Turkey, Poland and Estonia. Moreover, the firm has set up a sales joint venture in Estonia together with a former intermediary.

OK helped in developing the organization and routines for water treatment services, including regular customer visits, training of personnel, etc., and established contact to Eurowater, which produces a range of filters and some additives which complement those produced by Hydro-X. This gave Hydro-X considerable influence over the organization and development of HyXo Oy, and a number of additional

Mkt Journals.

MEISENBOCK

(c) 1985

International Small Business
Journal + Bibliography.

Library staff- Particularly about
Scandinavian approach
to Small Firms.

Product taken as one piece — goes
up abroad Directly — tremendous
control over Distribution channels —

Suggested Reading : 'How to Buy and Sell overseas'

P31, P66

activities have been organized along the same lines. During this period, OK became a close friend of the Viiala family. Today, HV and OK visit each other regularly, and are usually in contact once a month.

The water treatment programme, including regular visits to customers, has been important in developing long-term customer relations, and has helped the company in selling its other products. Today, the sales organization is therefore seen as the most valuable asset in the fight against competition.

All the company's sales consultants have been on training seminars in Denmark, and their training is regularly updated. OK visits HyXo Oy twice a year, in order to meet and hold seminars for new employees and potential and new customers. Occasionally, OK has also been involved in establishing contact to customers. His role here has been to convince the customer about the capabilities of the Hydro-X product.

Today, the coordination and division of labour between HyXo Oy and Hydro-X is more or less routinized, which means that there is very little communication concerning everyday operations. HyXo Oy uses Hydro-X for training and product promotion purposes, and they also exchange information with Hydro-X about special problems, particularly those which cannot be solved by the chemists themselves. This happens rarely, however, since HyXo Oy has accumulated considerable experience about water treatment problems.

Hydro-X and HyXo Oy have established a joint venture in Estonia. OK and HV regularly exchange information on this, and coordinate their efforts in order to support and develop the market position of the Estonian subsidiary. HyXo Oy takes care of elementary problems, only involving OK in the more strategic issues. The Estonian market is currently experiencing a period of rapid growth, and HyXo Oy is in weekly contact with the management of the Estonian company.

Collaboration with AVF Waterbehandeling
AVF (short for "Amsterdam File Company") Waterbehandeling specializes in chemical water treatment for the prevention of scale and corrosion in various types

of water boilers, water cooling systems, and water distribution systems for horticultural use. The firm is situated in Zwanenburg in the western part of Holland, a few kilometres from Amsterdam. AVF products have a range of different purposes: cleaning, water treatment, irrigation, and additives to oil for oil-fired boilers. All chemical additives, except water softeners for boiler water, are produced by AVF. The turnover amounts to NLG 4 million, which is spread equally among the product lines.

The firm has relations to approximately 1,000 customers. These can be split into two main groups: Horticulture and industry, which account for 40 and 60 per cent of total turnover respectively. The group of industrial users can be further divided into food and non-food companies. Relations to customers are normally long-term. Typically, AVF is contacted by customers who have discovered scale and corrosion in their systems, either through system malfunctioning or through the state-controlled inspection of pressure vessels. In these cases, customers turn to the system inspectors or to other specialists for advice concerning treatment. They advise customers to contact a water treatment company for an analysis of the water. These visits are often the starting point of a service contract.

AVF has 12 employees, including the co-owner and manager of the firm, Paul Kok (PK), and his brother. The firm also employs a chemist who specializes in corrosion and water treatment. In all, there are five employees involved in production, administrative tasks and laboratory work, while the rest are travelling consultants, who take care of water analysis and treatment at the customers' premises.

AVF has water treatment service contracts with more than 700 customers, whom they visit monthly. The analysis of feedwater in water systems is a complicated task. Each case is different. The water differs from one system to another, and often comes from various sources, such as drinking water reservoirs, canal water, condensed water, and natural spring water. The firm has met this challenge through contracts with a number of sub-suppliers, who operate 12 company cars equipped with small laboratories. In addition, the firm has invested more than NLG 300,000 in computerized, analytical equipment, and a laboratory for dealing with more complicated analyses. Furthermore, AVF is considering using on-line computers in water analysis, which is expected to reduce the time spent at each customer by approximately two thirds, thus increasing efficiency substantially. The number of laboratory analyses of water sediments has tripled over the last two years, and the firm is therefore seriously considering employing another chemist and expand the capacity of the laboratory.

AVF is a family-owned firm and has been so for 50 years. The present manager, PK, has been in the firm for ten years. Before that, he was international manager of a large company in a completely different area of business. PK wanted to give his family life a higher priority, however, and his mother and brother asked him to take over the management of the family firm, he accepted. When PK started at AVF, the firm only had 3 employees, mostly involved in boiler cleaning, and an annual turnover of NLG 300,000, which was steadily declining. After analysing the caused of this decline, he found that the main reason for the loss of customers was that the firm's technology in the area of chemical treatment of corrosion and scale was out of date.

He therefore decided to update the knowledge base of the firm, and got in touch with a retired corrosion engineer, who had worked for Shell Oil and in the fertilizer division of another firm. PK and his brother hired the engineer for two years, to teach them the basics of and latest developments in chemical water treatment. After this, PK hired a water treatment chemist, who taught the brothers the principles of water samples, feedwater analysis, etc. These two new additions to the firm also helped to update the water treatment product programme. This included the development of a number of new products and procedures, tailored to meet the needs of specific customers. One example of this was the development of a special water treatment procedure for drip systems, used in greenhouses for the nourishment of plants grown on substrates. AVF has applied for a European patent for this chemical process, and expects this to be granted in 1994.

The initiatives proved successful. AVF started to win back former customers, and managed to double the turnover several times over during the following years. In 1990, the firm had an annual turnover of NLG 1 million, which enabled it to set up a laboratory for water analysis and employ qualified personnel, thereby further expanding the knowledge base of the firm.

Relations to Hydro-X

The firm also needed a product which could help it win back its customers in the food industry. As a result of the development in hygienic standards and legislation in this line of business, food producers demand that their suppliers are certified according to the international DIN norm[16]. Acquiring a DIN certification is a costly and time-consuming affair, however, and AVF badly needed to use the resources necessary for this development elsewhere. When PK and his partners realized that it would be too costly to develop this product and obtain the necessary certifications themselves, they began to look for an external supplier. The retired corrosion engineer had earlier met OK at a scientific congress on water treatment in Düsseldorf, and they had arranged to meet again in Denmark. The engineer visited OK in Denmark after the conference, and was therefore familiar with Hydro-X's products and certifications. The Hydro-X product uses tannin as an oxygen scavenger, which makes it suitable in relation to disinfection or evaporation in food production. Consequently, he arranged a meeting between OK and PK. Hydro-X had previously tried to gain access to the Dutch market, but with limited success, and they were therefore interested in finding a competent partner with an established network of contacts to industry and key decision-makers. OK visited PK in 1990, and found that the business concepts of the two firms had many similarities, and that their methods for water treatment were largely compatible.

After this meeting, they agreed on the terms and principles for the partnership. AVF was to represent Hydro-X on similar conditions to other market intermediaries, except that contracts and the standard training procedures were considered unnecessary, since the Dutch firm's guidelines and procedures were already more strict than those used by Hydro-X.

---

[16]   Deutsche Industrie Norm

"... I told him that our goal would be 20,000 litres in, let's say, 4-5 years time... I could not guarantee how much effort we would put into the whole thing, because ... we were doing so and so. The only thing we could assure him was that we needed such a product. That if we could not buy it from Hydro-X or somebody else, we would have developed it ourselves, and then we had to postpone the whole thing for another 5 years, so that's what we made clear to him. And we made one appointment - A gentleman's agreement, that we would never imitate the product and that I will never do. Especially not with Hydro-X."

[Paul Kok]

The relationship between the two firms has gradually developed to include a number of other areas of cooperation as well. Since AVF's knowledge base is, in some respects, even larger than Hydro-X's, it has been considered unnecessary for AVF to participate in the training seminars in Denmark. AVF sent a chemist to a seminar three years ago, but as he did not learn anything new, AVF merely visits Hydro-X to learn about product development and for business discussions in general.

Thanks to the Hydro-X product, AVF has succeeded in winning back a number of its former customers in the food industry, and has been able to achieve its sales target. Today, AVF keeps 3,000 litres of the Hydro-X water treatment product in stock. Additional supplies are ordered automatically on a pre-printed sheet, which is faxed to Hydro-X. Apart from this, PK is in weekly contact with Hydro-X, during which the two firms swap market information.

Today, there are other reasons for maintaining the relationship with Hydro-X than the Hydro-X product. AVF is capable of producing it itself, but has chosen not to because of the mutual benefits of its relationship with Hydro-X. The relationship gives both companies access to a number of competencies scattered around the focal network of each actor, which are combined and utilized in a number of joint projects, as well as being used in individual projects in each company.

The number of projects in which the two firms are involved has gradually expanded to include joint market development and purchasing, as well as joint efforts in product development and problem-solving. The following examples illustrate this collaborative process. AVF has developed a product range of low-priced dosing pumps together with Prominent, a German producer of dosing pumps. AVF purchases these jointly with Hydro-X in order to obtain discounts. Also, Hydro-X has assisted AVF in establishing relations to HECO, a Danish supplier of water filters, and has introduced AVF to other members of the Danish District Heating Society.

> *"Both Hydro-X and HECO are members of the Danish Board of District Heating. In Denmark you have 40 years of experience on District Heating. In Holland we have none at all. Yes, we do now. But due to that contact, we have been introduced to ABB... We exchange knowledge with them, and if they have a problem, they come to us."*
>
> [Paul Kok]

In addition, both Hydro-X, HECO, another supplier and AVF have joined forces to pay the stand costs connected with the Aquatech exhibition in Holland.

AVF and Hydro-X also occasionally exchange information on the solving of specific water treatment problems.

> *".. On exchanging information on corrosion problems, we have discussions once in a while. Ole says: "Look I got this stainless steel system, I got this problem". We tell him: "Send us a sample of the water, and let's have a look at it." And the other way around when we have a certain corrosion problem with Hydro-X..*
>
> *For instance, we have a big company making conductive root. Conductive root is used for tapes, video tapes, for all kinds of filtering... It is a worldwide Dutch company who is the biggest producer in this kind of stuff. They wanted us to have a look at their water, because they had a big corrosion problem in their condense system, which is all stainless steel - but it was still rotting. They have been thinking of changing (the water treatment) to us now for more than a year. And we thought that there was*

a good chance to get this customer, but we are not sure, so then we call Ole and we say "Ole, what do you think ? we think it could be done" ... We made them an offer for getting the water treatment 6 months for free, just so they can see six months result or not with Hydro-X. Ole come especially down .. Schripol in the morning, he is here at 9, we go to the company, we have the whole discussion with technical service, we look together at the system once more, we go over every detail, and we read what we already got on paper, the whole bloody thing."

[Paul Kok]

PK also uses his contact to Hydro-X and their net of international relations in new projects involving market contacts in third countries. For example, one of AVF's customers - a technical installation company - is modernizing a large horticultural plant in Romania. The horticultural plant consists of 26 hectares of greenhouses, supplied by one power station. This system had immense corrosion problems, and the company therefore asked AVF to help them solve this problem. AVF has asked Hydro-X to participate, as they have an intermediary in Bulgaria who can take care of the initial following-up.

This sort of collaboration enables both firms to get involved in activities and gain access to knowledge which would be beyond their capacity as individual firms. The organization of activities is characterized by shared expectations of the relationship and mutual trust through recognizable behaviour. PK puts it like this:

"Because our connection is open, we don't have to hide anything and he doesn't have to hide anything. The only attitude is that where we can help each other, we shall help each other. Because we have all to fight the big ones and we have all to fight to enlarge our market, which is more or less a - what I would say - a replacement market. When we come in, the big ones lose a customer !"

[Paul Kok]

ANALYSIS OF THE CASE

The internationalization of Hydro-X has been made possible by the possession of a unique knowledge of chemical water treatment. This ownership advantage has gradually lost its importance in the firm's relations to intermediaries, however, as the intermediaries have themselves obtained knowledge of product methods, and have used the firms connected with Hydro-X's product service to develop this knowledge. It has since been replaced by a "network advantage". This change of advantage can be seen in figure 7.5. From having an ownership advantage, the firm today has a "knowledge network" advantage from being in the middle of the ongoing information exchange between the intermediaries.

As has been shown, despite its small size, Hydro-X has managed to develop and market a brand name worldwide, based on relations to a number of foreign intermediaries. These relations have mainly been established through the efforts of OK, including a massive personal interface and intensive training programmes, through which intermediaries have gradually learned to practise water treatment the "Hydro-X way". In addition, the seminars have served to build up a shared grammar of concepts and practices, which rationalizes the daily organizing of activity and inclusion of external services.

The focal network of Hydro-X is shown in figure 7.5 below.

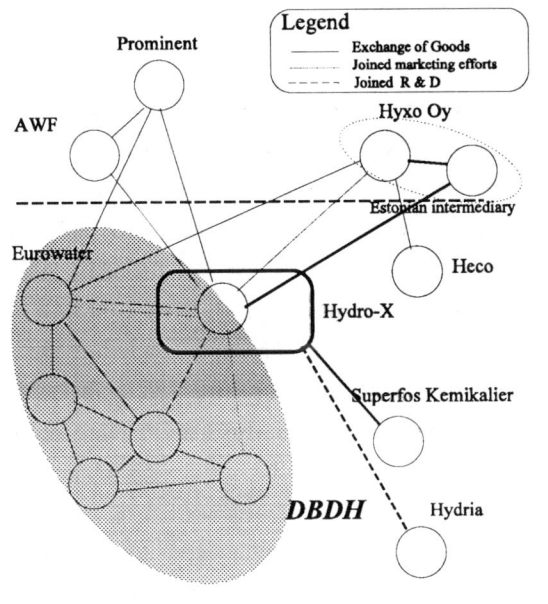

Figure 7.5: The focal network of Hydro-X

As shown in figure 7.5., the focal network of Hydro-X is characterized by a large degree of shared division of labour, which means that the distribution of tasks is not fixed, and that various activities are carried out by resource chain participants in an ongoing sequence. The actors participate in various activities and include each other on a variable basis. Thus, intermediaries are suppliers in some contexts and joint venture partners in others. Also, Hydro-X functions as a bridge to other organizations. As a result, the network is characterized by the fluid rather than the rigid positions of actors. It is difficult for any one actor to obtain advantages and accumulate gain at the expense of others. Rather, gain tends to be distributed among the network actors.

Through interaction with intermediaries, the knowledge base of Hydro-X is constantly renewed. Thanks to its position in the network, and the fact that its resources are closely related to those of its market participants (through the development of shared routines and a shared frame for solving various water treatment problems), Hydro-X is able to maintain its global market position.

Thus, by setting up a value-creating exchange system, in which all parties can participate according to their own capabilities, Hydro-X has actively shaped its own environment. The basis of this knowledge network lies in the development of a number of specific skills. Thus, the Hydro-X case clearly adheres to the resource chain metaphor developed earlier. In this case, the specific skills consist of the specialized knowledge of the intermediary, while the core skill of Hydro-X is its knowledge of chemical water treatment. Through interaction, this skills lead to the development of shared skills, both as regards the development of new procedures for water treatment and the routinization of activity, thus reducing organizing complexity.

However, there are inherent weaknesses in this type of organization. First, while it is clear that OK has been able to build a relationship based on trust between Hydro-X and its intermediaries, this trust is vested in the personal relations between OK and his contact persons. Today, OK spends more than half his time travelling and visiting agents. This massive personal interface will become increasingly difficult to maintain, since OK also has other responsibilities, both of a personal nature and towards the firm. Moreover, OK hopes to stop his travelling activities within 8 years. Hydro-X must either find someone else to take over, therefore, or consider changing the organizational set-up. However, with the computerization of the network, personal presence may, to some extent, be replacable by a computerized presence.

CHAPTER 8

Analysis of the case studies

In the preceding chapters, four different examples of export organization involving SMEs and foreign intermediaries have been presented and analyzed. Each case represents a unique pattern of events leading to the organization of international activity, and each has contributed to a more detailed understanding of the international division of labour and coordination of activity in SMEs. Together, the cases provide a picture of multi-layered and complex patterns of interactions, in which the organization of activities stretches across national as well as organizational boundaries.

The aim of the present chapter is to go beyond the idiosyncracies of each individual case to develop a more general framework for understanding the organization and development of SMEs international activity. An attempt is made to identify and abstract identical strands or patterns from the cases and to broaden and modify the conceptual framework of the organization and development of SMEs international activity developed in chapter three.

This serves several purposes, which can be summarized in the following three main themes. These are dealt with in this and the following chapter.

♦   First, it leads to the development of "ideal types" or models, which condense to more general concepts, and abstracts what has been learned from the preceding cases. This can be used, challenged and improved in subsequent studies of these or related phenomena.

♦   Next, the modelling will serve as a platform for challenging the perspectives of conventional theories of the internationalization and international organization of firms.

♦ Finally, the analysis discusses the ability of the conceptual framework developed in chapter three to capture the studied phenomena.

Unlike statistical analysis of quantitative data, there is no formalized approach to guide the researcher in analyzing data from field studies. Much depends on the investigator's own way of thinking, together with the proper presentation of the material and careful consideration of alternative interpretations (Yin, 1989). The approach used in the following resembles what Yin (op. cit.) describes as *pattern matching*, which relies on theoretical propositions, or *the constant comparative method*, as described by Glaser & Strauss (1967). It is an attempt to match the field data with the theoretical frame, and use the results obtained to broaden this comparison to include more general theories of the field, here the field of international business. This approach owes much to Popper's (1965) ideas of falsification, the general idea being that theoretical development advances most quickly by constantly challenging and modifying exisiting theoretical doctrines.

First, a number of the characteristics relating to the configuration of international activity are outlined. Next, the organizational approaches of the four case studies are dealt with, and finally, the patterns of development of the firms' international activity are discussed. The conclusions of the analysis are used to discuss the usability of and possible improvements to the theoretical understandings represented in the conceptual framework. In addition, they are used in chapter nine as a basis for discussing the implications of the present study for the theory of international organization and development of business activity.

1. Configuration of international activity

The conceptual framework of this study implies that a central task of the SME is to legitimize its activity in order to generate commitment from external resource controllers. This was generally supported by the cases, where all firms were established on the basis of low fixed costs. All firms have initially based their activities on coordinating external resources in such a way as to generate a profit. The case studies revealed a number of characteristics which added to the understanding of this process.

1.1.   Mobilization of personal ties in establishing international resource chain activity

In chapter three, it was suggested that personal ties and the reputation of the SME entrepreneur from previous interactions also play a key role in the configuration of international resource chains. This occurs either through local ties, linking the actor to other resource controllers, or international ties from previous business activity directly related to the actor. It was also suggested that these were often a result of the career paths of the entrepreneur, thus representing a socio-cognitive community organized around a work domain, or *profession*. Personal ties are used very differently in configuring international resource chains. For example, Nordex Food was established on the basis of relations to former suppliers and customers. These gave access to their resources and relations on the strength of their past experiences with the actors involved, which convinced them that business opportunities could be developed. In other words, it was knowledge of each other's reliability as a business partner, rather than access to a resource, which enabled Nordex Foods to maintain business relations to its international partners.

In the Lux Perpetua case, contact was clearly activity-based. SEP used his national and international contacts to purchasers and producers in the lamp trading business to configure a business deal. He was then able to go to other resource controllers and show them the possibilities.

There is an interesting point in relation to the Lux Perpetua and Nordex Food cases. Both cases demonstrate the importance of personal relations, but there was also an element of market power in the case of Nordex Food. At Lux Perpetua, SEP configured the resource chain by combining the resources and activites of diverse actors and establishing a new economic space in which to maneuver. This space was already present in Nordex Food, however, as powerful actors had an interest in maintaining an alternative resource chain linking the Danish dairy industry and the end-user market in the Middle East.

All cases demonstrate the key role of traditional practices in collaboration between firms. Existing practices generated through past activities and experiences form a resource base for others to utilize. In the HWH case, the manager was able to draw on sub-suppliers and configure a supply chain, as well as establish relations with intermediaries, based on a few personal contacts, which is typical of Danish producers of agricultural machinery. This was also clearly demonstrated in the Lux Perpetua case, as well as in the Nordex Food and Hydro-X cases, where relations to a small number of actors functioned as bridges to other resource holders, and where existing practices influenced the configuration of new ones. Together, these findings suggest that the interpersonal experiences of different actors play a vital role in the configuration of both national and international business activity.

The cases points to the central function of trade fairs in the development of international activity. Trade fairs are important in two respects: a) A number of the contacts established here are later used in the configuration phase of the international resource chain; and b) they serve as information clearing points for dispersed international intermediary networks. It is at these fairs that face-to-face communication between business partners takes place. It is also here that information spreads rapidly and the reputation of a potential business partner can be checked. The fairs are used for different purposes in the establishment phase. They are meeting places where existing bonds are strengthened and new bonds developed. In addition, they offer easy access to new information. All cases demonstrate a heavy use of fairs in this respect. Hydro-X, HWH, Nordex Food and Lux Perpetua all use fairs for finding and evaluating potential intermediaries. For Nordex Food in particular, the weekly fairs of ethnic wholesalers are an important source of information about changes in ownership and new competitors. For Lux Perpetua and its intermediaries, fairs are an important arena for the presentation of new lamp collections and the collection of information about new lamp trends.

So far, the use of personal bonds in the configuration of activity has only been discussed in relation to the establishment of firms. However, direct and personal interface among actors is also used in the ongoing configuration of new activities. They are used, among other things, to draw actors into other activities, thereby adding to the complexity of inter-firm activities. The variation and extent of these activities underlines the flexibility of the roles undertaken by the actors in the organizational setup. The organization of activity resembles not so much stable chains of added value as what has elsewhere been called dynamic specialization (Karnøe, 1991). In all cases, the activities of the individual actor form part of several resource chains and serve different purposes in relation to these. Moreover, resource chains are constantly being modified and new ones created. In contrast to this changing nature of organization, personal relations among actors seem to be characterized by a pattern of stable and long-term commitment. In the HWH case, for example, the supplier relation to Homburg Machinehandel was changed into an intermediary relation. The relation between Nordex Food and Gula Huset also involved a change in roles, with Gula Huset acting as a consultant for Finnish retail chains and using Nordex Food as a supplier of private brands in competition with other producers. The opposite occurred at Hydro-X, where AVF, in addition to being an intermediary, also started supplying dosing pumps to Hydro-X.

1.2. Intermediaries are committed to collaborative projects involving the skills of each partner

A central point in the conceptual framework relates to how SMEs commit other firms to participate in and devote resources to a joint venture. A possible answer to this question is indicated in the case studies. It seems that SMEs persuade intermediaries and suppliers to participate in joint ventures in which both parties contribute resources, so that start-up costs are shared. This approach has been demonstrated elsewhere (Petersen, 1994). Moreover, rather than committing intermediaries to standardized goods, SMEs usually offer a product concept together with the necessary skills and production capacity, which allows the intermediaries to influence the product themselves and complement their own skills with those offered by SMEs. Analogous to studies of consumer-driven innovations (Von Hippel, 1978), the cases suggest that both customers and intermediaries play an active role in specifying product features. Thus, the relationship can be characterized more as the joint problem-solving activities of customers, intermediaries and SMEs, than the control of an ongoing flow of commoditites.

Studies show that, in general, SMEs are highly flexible. SMEs often produce products which are either a) adapted to the specific needs of the intermediary/customer, or b) developed together with the intermediary or the customer. One study of export firms in eastern Jutland revealed that more than 57 per cent offered modifiable products (Christensen, 1988). This has been confirmed by parallel studies of export firms in northern Jutland (Andersen & Dahl, 1991; Bohn et al., 1989; Bohn & Sørensen, 1990).

The case studies also demonstrate the importance of the actors' understanding of their own role and that of others in this process. In situations where managers are replaced, as in Lux Perpetua, or where joint problem-solving efforts are given less priority, as in HWH, the relationship becomes severely handicapped and can even be dissolved.

This approach is markedly different from the traditional textbook view, which largely discusses the exportation of standardized products. According to this view of the organization of international activity, the intermediary does little more than sell the product and administer the various product, payment and promotion flows between producer and buyer (Keegan, 1985; Cundiff & Hilger, 1988). The fact is, however, that intermediaries are often actively involved in defining both the product and the market approach, which not only enables them to adapt the product to their own product profile, but, at the same time, also allows the SME to learn from the development process.

The project-based configuration of the resource chain of activity implies that it involves a substantial dialogue. The nature of this process gives both the SME and the intermediary a chance to assess the reliability and competence of a potential partner, which is a prerequisite for the development of mutual trust. In the absence of a formal agreement, both parties are forced to demonstrate their capabilities and willingness to cooperate. Also, due to the sequential development of activities, both partners have ample time to reconsider their commitment.

The pattern outlined above can be clearly seen in the Nordex case, where the product assortment aimed at the Turkish segment was the outcome of a joint product development between Nordex Food and the Turkish wholesaler. The distribution arrangement with the Dutch wholesaler was also the result of a joint project, and Gula Huset's request for a Port Salut cheese also clearly demonstrates that exchange patterns are far from fixed, and that new projects evolve over time. Similarly, in the Lux Perpetua case, SEP persuaded both Thor Ljungman and Swedlux to join collaborative arrangements involving product development. In the HWH case, the product was adapted to meet customer needs, and the marketing efforts were therefore also largely left to the intermediary. Unlike the other cases, the Hydro-X liquid can be considered a standard product. Hydro-X offers intensive training in order to standardize the water treatment methods used by intermediaries. Here, however, the relationship developed as a result of marketing the Hydro-X product was subsequently used in the development of collaborative projects. These include market entry projects in Romania together with the Dutch intermediary, AVF, and the establishment of an intermediary in Estonia together with the Finnish intermediary, Hyxo Oy.

In accordance with these characteristics, the configuration of resource chains regarding activities emerges through interaction, rather than being ex ante defined. This often results in an intensive dialogue, in which the partners try to coordinate their mutual needs, by redefining the collaborative project to fit the range of skills available. This fit, or coherence, of resources can be discussed in a number of respects (Nørreklit, 1994), e.g. fitting the diverse skills of actors in various situations. Thus, skill coherence can be viewed in relation to technology, financial capabilities, etc. Common to all cases, however, is that it is necessary to create a structure in which recurrent activities can take place.

In this sense, business opportunities are mutually identified through processes of trial and error. In the Nordex Food case, the relation to Hoers Agenturen involved the fit of mutual interests in collecting payments from customers. In the Hydro-X case, the fit to AVF involved definitions of work domains, whereas the Lux Perpetua case involved the fit of creative skills among actors situated in essentially different market areas.

1.3 Competence similarity & development possibility in resource chain configuration

Another finding of the study is that SMEs tend to search for intermediaries which are similar in size, competence profile, and definition of work domains to themselves. This may seem paradoxical, since, from the point of view of traditional management theory, these can be seen as generic competitors. There seem to be three main reasons for this collaboration. First, firms which share these characteristics are likely to possess, or have access to complementary resources, which makes mutual learning possible. In the Lux Perpetua case, for example, lamp producers search for other producers with similar views on lamp design as themselves. Second, firms which have similar definitions of work domain and skills find it easier to communicate and develop shared meaning. Third, if both firms are small, they are more likely to see each other as allies than potential competitors. Thus, Hydro-X and AVF agree to assist each other in business activities which can help them defend their market position against larger firms.

What has been earlier referred to as the entrepreneurial function of the SME seems to play a significant role here, since it is on the basis of the subjective world view of the entrepreneur that the competence profile of the SME is controlled and the profiles of other actors are interpreted. These principles of judgment are often tacit and difficult for SME managers to explain. When asked how they choose a potential partner, they are either unable to explain or can only vaguely define their criteria for selecting candidates for further dialogue.

The cases illustrate a number of incidents which underline the importance of the entrepreneur in defining and maintaining a specific configuration of activities and authority structures to ease the creation of shared meaning.

With regard to Lux Perpetua, SEP originally searched for firms with an interest in joint product development, and which were willing to participate in administrative tasks through daily dialogue and on the basis of small fixed costs. In this way, SEP hoped to gain access to firms which were flexible and which could contribute to the development of work practices and lamp designs. When the firm was taken over by

JH, however, a new approach was taken, in which management looked for firms willing to adopt practices centrally defined by Lux Perpetua. Thus, existing definitions of activities, role structures, etc., were replaced by others which eroded the position and role of the intermediaries, which, in consequence, are gradually losing confidence in the relationship.

Similarly, HW believes that the core competence of HWH lies in its ability to produce easily repairable, high quality appliances for tractors, and thus looks for intermediaries which appreciate the quality of the HWH product and are able to repair appliances using standard components. However, this definition seems to conflict with the institutionalized business approach followed by local tractor dealers in Holland, and, to some degree, also conflicts with Norwegian methods. Consequently, these efforts have had only limited success.

In the Hydro-X case, OK has defined the service offered as "quality through knowledge and continuous control". On this basis, he has searched for firms with similar attitudes towards the importance of technical know-how in boiler water treatment. However, the strategy that Hydro-X follows differs in some respects from the ones outlined above. Rather than searching for potential intermediaries with some knowledge of the product process, Hydro-X looks for intermediaries without any process knowledge, but which are willing and able to learn about water treatment process and eager to enter this area. Thus, instead of utilizing an exisiting knowledge base, Hydro-X prefers to shape the knowledge profile of their intermediaries, which enables them to develop a shared understanding, and saves them having to "unlearn" principles of water treatment which are inferior to the Hydro-X method. This pattern can clearly be seen in the HyXo Oy relation, for example, but is also present in the other relations.

In the Nordex Food case, JU searches for intermediaries with a cultural competence similar to his own, e.g. Hoers Agenturen, since management believes this to be central to maintaining and developing their position in the ethnic market. However, there are some similarities between Hydro-X and Nordex Food as regards developing the competence profile of their intermediaries.

Similar competence profiles do not presuppose shared objectives, however. In support of Weick's model in figure 3.4, a number of intermediaries have committed resources to the development of resource chains for other reasons than those of the SME, and the relation is seen as a means of achieving different targets than those defined by the SME. It seems, therefore, that shared values and goals are not necessary for the development of organized behaviour and the development of shared codes among resource chain participants, as postulated elsewhere (Iyer, 1992).

The above points can be briefly summarized as follows: Through the utilization of personal ties, the SME manager/entrepreneur forms international resource chains by configuring those in possession of resources and skills into open-ended collaborative projects. This creates an interlocked structure characterized by mutual reciprocity, in which a coordinating function is needed in order to maintain the activity. This is dealt with in the following section.

2. Organization and management of international resource chains

In chapter 1, it was stated that the assumed complexity of international markets would increase the possibilities for opportunistic behaviour by intermediaries, thus leading to market failure. One of the central questions in the internationalization of Danish SMEs, therefore, concerns their ability to organize cross-border activities on a massive scale without running the risk of market failure.

What the cases suggest is that an owner structure is not a sine qua non of administrative ability. Patterns of organization are formed because individual activities are reciprocally interlocked into interpersonal business practices, which makes concerted action possible. However, the cases also show that this mode of organizing and managing activities differs radically from textbook models of hierarchical administration in at least two vital respects. Firstly, aligning the resources of the SME with those of others in an international resource chain activity is an ongoing process. As suggested by the theoretical framework, rationalization emerges through a shared grammar rather than through the command structure of administrative hierarchies. The basic task of the bureaucracy, as pointed out by Simon (1948) and Gailbraith (1977), is to reduce ambiguity by simplifying data flows to organizational decision-makers. In one sense, a shared grammar fulfils similar functions, though in a different way. Analogous to the learning curve effect, the development of shared grammars can be described as the discarding of redundant interpretations, which allows for a simplified and less ambiguous picture of joint activity (Weick, 1991). Thus, the grammar is a coding device, in which acts, words, and other media of communication are ascribed a contextual, iconic meaning, allowing complex patterns of interaction to take place on the basis of the interchange of a minimum of information.

Secondly, the cases indicate that collaborative management is an essential characteristic of activities in international resource chains. According to this principle, activities are negotiated rather than decided unanimously in one decision centre. Reciprocity is the key to an understanding of this process. This is analogous to the coalition model of organization suggested by Cyert & March, and the conditions for interlocked behaviour suggested by Weick, which were discussed in chapter three as instrumental and consummatory acts. The success of the case firms in collaborating and developing shared skills is clearly related to the degree to which they have followed this principle. Thus, while Hydro-X and Nordex Food have obtained support for their organization of international activity by offering reciprocal benefits, HWH and Lux Perpetua, where these mechanisms are absent, have failed to persuade intermediaries to accept their definition of the marketing tasks. Together, these cases lend support to the idea that reciprocity is socially constructed rather than externally imposed. Reciprocity presupposes the existence of a collective "mind" in which such reciprocal acts can be conceived, offered and received. In an ongoing relationship, norms of reciprocity are developed in line with actors' increasing knowledge of each other. As shared skills emerge, so does an understanding of each other's needs and wants. As idiosyncratic knowledge increases, the relationship becomes heterogeneous, which in turn changes the norms of reciprocity. In this sense, reciprocity is not a static mechanism determined by market forces, but an ongoing exchange which evolves over time.

2.1 Development of a shared grammar

According to the conceptual framework, the organization and management of the resource chain presupposes the construction and institutionalization of a shared grammar, which in turn allows rationalized conduct and the development of routinization. The notion that the development of shared meaning is a prerequisite for concerted action is strongly confirmed by the cases. An ongoing dialogue serves the purpose of framing the activity and legitimizing the role of the SME in integrating the skills of the resource chain participants. In the Lux Perpetua case, daily contact to SEP, and, later, the development of standard components both helped in developing a shared frame of reference in which coordination could be routinized. In order to be properly understood and received, communication between actors often expresses - and requires - past shared experiences. In the Hydro-X case, technical codes for pH values and measurement methods are communicated in very brief exchanges. Training seminars and frequent visits by OK seem to have served a similar purpose. This pattern is also found in the Nordex Food case, where frequent socialization helps to develop and maintain shared interpretations and correct any misunderstandigns. This is also reflected in the daily communication, which is abrupt and where a few words trigger an array of interlocked behaviour. The development of communication patterns can be portrayed as in figure 8.1.

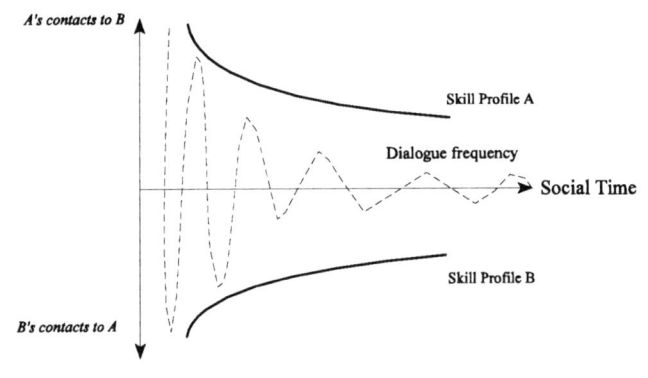

Figure 8.1: Idealized pattern of dialogue intensity over time

The X axis in figure 8.1 relates to the dialogue frequency, which is seen as the number of contacts multiplied by their average length measured in chronological time. This relates directly to the activities undertaken in the resource chain. The Y axis measures relational time, which thus sees time as a social phenomenon, dependent on the context in which it is measured. Thus attributes of time, such as "short" and "long", reflect the past, present and future of the relationship (Mietela & Törnross, 1993).

Figure 8.1. suggests that the frequency of the dialogue between SME and intermediary essentially constitutes a process of mutual learning, socialization and internalization, where shared communicative frames are developed. In the early phases of a relationship, mutual understanding is amplified, and this later serves as the basis for generating the dialogue. Thus, the development of a shared grammar can be said to occur in three phases, analogous to the dialogue discussion above: I) An initiation phase, where different frames are tested and the identity of the relationship partner is assessed; II) A learning phase, where a shared grammar is gradually developed and rationalized as redundant interpretive frames are discarded by the actors. This phase demands frequent contact, since misunderstandings must be cleared up and shared definitions of business situations, etc., elaborated. Finally, III) a calibrating phase, where the dialogue becomes dependent on the shared understandings developed earlier. This, then, is the basic building block of the development of shared routines in the SME-intermediary relationship.

The pattern outlined in figure 8.1. can be identified in, for example, the Nordex Food case, where established communicative patterns to intermediaries are built on experience gathered over a period of time, and thus represent a type of sunk costs. A similar state of affairs exist in the Hydro-X case.

2.2. Legitimization of authority in international resource chains: Mobilizing coordination

A central aspect of the analysis relates to how SMEs legitimize their role in setting the agenda for resource chain activity and how they persuade other actors in the resource chain to accept their understanding of the situation. Unlike organizational hierarchies, where coordination is scheduled and supported by a given set of rules and sanctions, resource mobilization in international resource chains is an ongoing process. Once established, however, resource chain relationships become important for the actors because they provide them with simplified routines for coping with the equivocality of their surroundings.

Strategies[17] for coordination all depend on the development of shared patterns of meaning, where each actor is aware of the dispositions and resources of other actors with whom he interrelates. Thus, rather than relying on administrative structure, coordination is achieved by means of a role system, in which each actor automatically coordinates his resources with those of other actors. These interactions at the dyadic level of the resource chain add up to the complex activity pattern found at the interconnected level, which is perhaps most vividly illustrated in the Lux Perpetua focal network.

The case studies revealed that dialogues, through various strategies of communication, form the foundation of coordination. Although various strategies are used and combined in different ways, a number of core components can be identified, similar to the coordination techniques discussed elsewhere in organization literature (Mintzberg, 1983; Lorenzioni & Ornati, 1988; Metcalfe, 1981). These components are briefly outlined and explained below:

> **Formalization** relates to the process by which written agreements and routines are introduced into the relationship in order to specify the roles and obligations of each actor. In highly formalized settings, these are either used as frames of reference or to justify specific behaviour or demand specific actions from others.

> **Socialization** is the strategy of developing mutual agreements through the establishment of personal bonds. Here, personal friendship plays an important role in legitimizing the coordinative function of the SME in the resource chain.

> **Learning** is the process by which the SMEs studied persuade intermediaries

---

17   The concept of strategy has numerous meanings in business literature. It is therefore appropriate to define the term more specifically. By strategy is here meant the way in which actors combine means and ends. This definition resembles what Mintzberg (1987) calls a world view or pattern.

to accept the concepts and procedures related to their definition of the activity and adhere to these through seminars and other forms of training.

Mutual adjustment refers to the strategy by which SMEs and intermediaries jointly coordinate activities in an ongoing dialogue, and where frames are tested and rejected by both actors in a trial-and-error process.

Shared experience-gathering relates to a strategy in which intermediaries and SMEs join forces, e.g. in problem- solving, and through these activities develop shared codes of conduct.

The generic strategies are used in varying degrees in the resource chains studied. An attempt to illustrate the profile of each SME in this respect is shown in figure 8.2. below. In the figure, the various strategies have been ranked on an ordinal scale in relation to each case. The result is computed as four profiles of coordination strategies.

Coordination Strategies in
Resource Chains

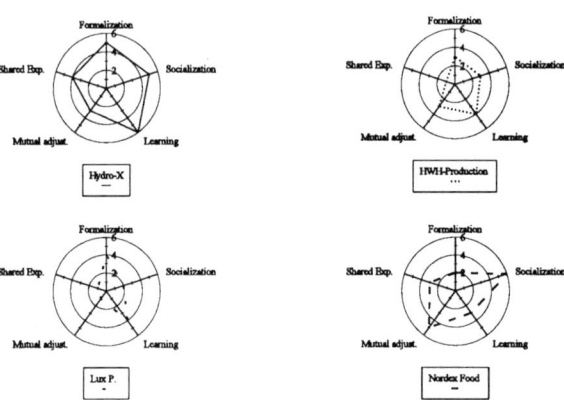

Figure 8.2: Coordination Strategy Profiles

Figure 8.2 reveals that the profiles of the coordination strategies followed are all very different, which precludes generalization. However, it does show that the firms which are the most successful in their international activities are also those which have made the biggest effort to develop and maintain shared grammars through intense communication. On the other hand, Lux Perpetua and HWH, which were both characterized by weak and problematic relations to their intermediaries, are also those with the smallest coordination efforts.

The pattern of coordination in the international resource chain found in this study suggests that each action is modified by a preceding action, rather than being coordinated in a given structure. Thus, actors constantly learn from interaction with other actors by modifying their frame of reference. This is perhaps the core of the coordinative ability of networks.

2.3. Open division of labour

The division of labour between SMEs and intermediaries in the cases is more often based on competence than tasks, which means that actors can carry out widely different tasks and thus play different roles in the collaboration.

The distribution of tasks thus reflects more a division of knowledge than a division of labour. Contrary to traditional conceptions of the division of labour, competence-based specialization does not give a once-and-for-all division of tasks and areas of responsibility. The division of tasks between organizations is fluid, and is determined on an on-going basis. A competence-based division of labour rather reflects a complementarity: a partnership which builds on the maintenance and development of a shared grammar, and which simplifies the processes of mutual adaptation.

This type of intersubjective adaptation clearly hinges on personal bonds between actors which have been developed over time and which represent a large store of tacit knowledge in both actors. For the same reason, it is difficult to move patterns of coordination to an institutional level, where the interpersonal interface is substituted by standardized rules and regulations. This is why SMEs have built-in growth problems, and it also explains why the economic growth of an economy is not necessarily reflected in the growth of firms. Rather, the degree of internationalization of an economy consisting mainly of SMEs depends on the number of SMEs with cross-border activities.

As shown in a number of examples, SMEs can use intermediaries as suppliers and vice versa. In addition, SMEs can be used as sub-suppliers in relation to activities carried out by intermediaries. Thus, the division of labour does not imply a fixed pattern in any form. What does seems to be relatively stable, however, is the actor dialogue, which is necessary to ensure that firms are constantly aware of each other's competencies and resources in relation to new activities.

An illuminating example of the dynamic nature of the division of labour can be found in the relation of Hydro-X to its Dutch intermediary, AVF. The development of this relation with regard to the tasks carried out by the actors in different resource chain activities is illustrated in figure 8.3 below.

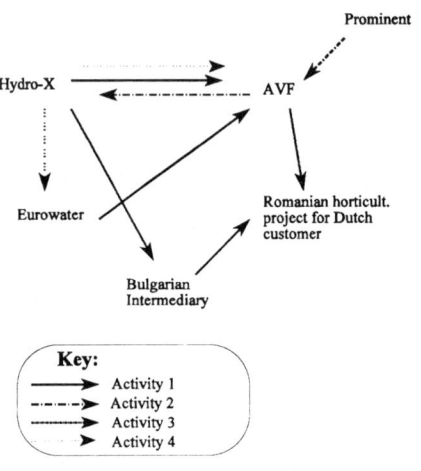

Figure 8.3: Open division of labour: The configuration of competences in various tasks

Figure 8.3 shows four activities, represented by four different arrows, where the roles of Hydro-X and of AVF differ substantially. Activity 1 represents the selling of the Hydro-X product to the Dutch customers. Here, Hydro-X is an exporter and AVF functions as intermediary, offering the Hydro-X service according to agreed specifications. In activity 2, AVF and Hydro-X collaborate in purchasing the Prominent pumps. Here, the flow of goods is reversed, since Hydro-X takes on the role of customer in relation to AVF. Activity 3 illustrates the collaborative project between AVF and Hydro-X regarding the horticultural venture in Romania. Here, Hydro-X is both an intermediary and consultant to AVF and the Bulgarian intermediary. In activity 4, Hydro-X also acts as consultant to AVF and introduces Eurowater, a Hydro-X affiliate, to AVF. Together, these four situations reveal the transitory nature of the division of labour, since resources are mobilized and configured differently in each case, calling for different task performances and different adjustments to performed activities.

2.4 Interconnectedness of relations

In chapter three, interconnectedness was defined as the interdependence of relationships. Interdependence is the result of actions in one relation affecting, or being the consequence of, actions in another relation. In this sense, the combination of relations in the individual SME represents both a business opportunity and a structural constraint on independent resource allocation, analogous to the model outlined in chapter three.

Interconnectedness can be structurally related to the exchange of physical goods, or sequentially related to the learning processes of resource chain actors. In the latter case, interconnectedness becomes institutionalized in business practices as past events form the basis for new activities.

In all the cases studied, there were situations where the interconnectedness of relations played an important role. In the Lux Perpetua case, the large degree of externalization, both of production and administrative tasks, clearly displays some of the aspects of interconnectedness mentioned above. Going from the assembly of lamps from standard components to the utilization of specially designed components both reflects the skills and possibilities of the existing relationship and affects the subsequent development of work practices in Swedlux and the therapy workshops. The practices of the intermediaries were also affected by the decision to produce a special type of packaging for the lamps. This allowed the lamps to be displayed in blister packages, which made them more attractive to supermarkets.

As seen in the Nordex Food case, the development of business practices towards ethnic wholesalers led to new routines for handling the transfer of goods as well as new payment methods and socialization policies. These routines have gradually evolved into a system of interconnected practices for conducting business, but they have also imposed structural constraints on the firm. For example, the firm's limited storage and production capacity means that feta cheese must be ordered on a weekly basis. Moreover, the scheduling of JU's business trips also puts a number of constraints on the way new relationships are fitted into the present frame of activity. This is perhaps most clearly demonstrated by the difficulties which the European sales division has experienced in selling to European retail chains.

Both the Nordex Food and Hydro-X cases demonstrate that patterns of interconnectedness are not necessarily restricted to the configuration and management of existing resource chains, but can go beyond these. In both cases, the existence of already institutionalized business practices imposes certain roles on SME actors. In the case of Nordex Food, the business practices of the ethnic wholesalers took time and effort to understand and adapt to. Faced by the existing role and status of ethnic wholesalers, the firm changed its product assortment in order to meet their needs, and this led to the alteration and establishment of a number of relations to suppliers of dairy products and other producers, e.g. sausages makers. In the Hydro-X case, Danish district heating technology, which allows for the transmission of low-temperature feedwater for heating and other purposes, can be seen as a technological trajectory or paradigm, analogous to Dosi (1982). The cleaning of heating systems is dependent on the components which make up the system. Thus, the effectiveness of the Hydro-X service is dependent on their knowledge of the characteristics and effects of these components. As the Hydro-X liquid has been developed in the context of Danish district heating technology, the firm tries to persuade intermediaries to buy the filters and components of other Danish firms, since it has full knowledge of the efficiency and side-effects of these components in relation to the Hydro-X liquid.

Another example of relationship interconnectedness is the personal ties of network actors. The personal knowledge and experience of one actor is used to assess the trustworthiness of another actor. There were several examples of this in the cases, e.g. the initiation of relations to AVF in the Hydro-X case, the Nordex Food case the initial relations has informed the development of business practices in terms of payment practices and business ethics which subsequently has influenced the formation of relations to ethnic wholesalers, and in the HWH case, the relation to Homburg Machinehandel builds on the personal bonds developed during a supplier relationship.

3. Development of international resource chains

In general, the four cases studied show patterns of development which differ from the internationalization model developed earlier. Rather than describing a gradually developing pattern of international commitment, the firms all seem to have capitalized on an already existing knowledge base. This is inconsistent with the incremental pattern outlined in this theory. In some cases, the development of international activity has "leap-frogged", and the firms in question have gone straight from exporting to direct foreign investments, or have started up in psychologically as well as geographically distant markets. Together, these findings suggest that the development of knowledge and the development of international activity may be linked in a different way than that suggested by the internationalization model. In the following, a number of proposals derived from the study are presented.

3.1 Internationalization of resource chains as instantaneous or precarious arrangements of international activity

The cases can be compared with respect to the development in export turnover. This is illustrated in figure 8.4 below.

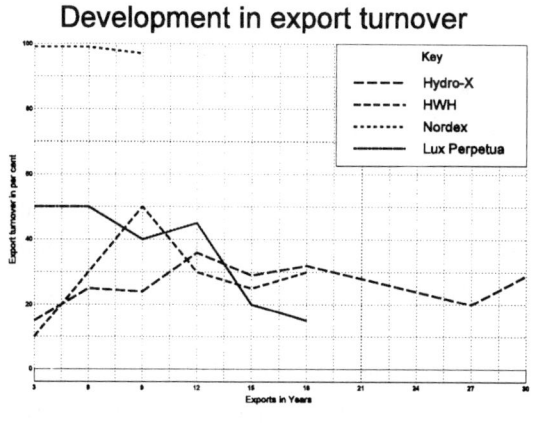

Figure 8.4: Development in Export Ratio

223

The above figure shows a different pattern than that of increasing involvement through specialization and foreign market commitment. Foreign market entry and exit seems to be more widespread and less problematic for the firms studied than is generally assumed in internationalization literature.

Both patterns found seems to support the network model of internationalization developed by Johanson & Mattson (1986). According to this, the firm's internationalization must be seen in relation to the internationalization of markets. Thus, where markets are strongly interconnected as a result of business relationships developed through historical exchange, actors tend to specialize around core skills and rely on national as well as international suppliers for compleementary products and services.

There seem to be two internationalization patterns present in the material studied, which reflects the degree to which activities are interrelated in the network: Instantaneous and precarious internationalization. In the former, which is characterized by tightly coupled relations, the activities of individual actors strongly depend on each other. The systemic nature of the components promote what is here called instant internationalization. The interrelation of product components leads to a situation in which the introduction of one product automatically leads to the introduction of another, where several foreign markets are entered in the same year, or shortly after the establishment of the firm, and where the export ratio is high from the start. Here, the internationalizing SME is pulled outwards by its relations to other firms. Precarious internationalization is found in more loosely coupled networks, where participation in activities is of a more temporary nature, where the export ratio shows a more fluctuating pattern, and where foreign market entry and exit are an established business practice.

Thus, the internationalization patterns found correspond to the internationalization of the various actors with which the firm has relationships and how these relationships are constituted. In Hydro-X and Nordex Food, R&D and production relationships were found in a national context. The internationalization of these firms clearly relates to the proximity and importance of relations to other Danish firms within their institutional context. The production and export of feta cheese largely depends on the capabilities and knowledge of Danish dairy producers, as well as on the skills

224

developed jointly with market intermediaries. Similarly, the development of the Hydro-X product is closely related to other producers of components with know-how of district heating. In both cases, the institutional environment supports the internationalization of the firms: Either directly, as in the case of Hydro-X, where collective efforts towards international market expansion are organized by DBDH, or more subtly, as in Nordex Food, where established practices of exporting feta cheese to the Middle East led to the internationalization of this firm.

Although the importance of the institutional context in shaping the internationaliza-tion paths of these two firms cannot be denied, it should also be emphasized that are not alone in this. The importance of the institutional context has changed during internationalization, as have the firms themselves, from imitating existing business practices to developing their own internationalization profile. Thus, they have themselves become producers of business practices which are imitated by others.

The precarious pattern of internationalization can be seen in both HWH Production and Lux Perpetua. This strategy is characterized by internationalization flexibility. Small firms following this strategy make sure that they can exit markets again at little cost (this seems to agree with an Italian survey of SME exporters, which showed that less than 15 per cent of the firms studied exported continuously over a period of 5 years, Bonaccorsi, 1992). Moreover, resources are not irreversibly allocated to particular markets and particular products; the SME can draw on external resources and coallign these with its own resources in the event of new opportunities arising. However, the cases do demonstrates that SMEs, rather than terminating relationships, maintain them at a low level of activity, reactivating them when conditions are more favourable.

The instant pattern of internationalization is characterized by widespread internatio-nal specialization in the division of labour. Here, the business environment is comprised of trajectories of strong interdependence, where existing business patterns instantaneously connect the SME to a extensive net of international contacts. Thus, the firm does not have to depend on the gradual development of international competences, but can capitalize on existing routes developed by others.

It is important to emphasize here that internationalization does not constitute a basic change in the way the SME organizes business activity. Rather than seeing internationalization as a process of development, firms attempt to organize international activity along the same principles used in other business activities.

The central task for SMEs is not to enter new markets, but to build up stable relations to these markets. As the SME is dependent on externally-controlled resources, the ability to collaborate and build up stable relations to intermediaries thus becomes of major importance.

3.2   Networks as competence generators: the institutional context as a lever for the development of international competence

The case studies suggest that the learning and memorizing process associated with internationalization is located in relationships, thereby forming an institutional memory. Decisions concerning internationalization are not adequately described by the model of the individual firm seeking to optimize the allocation of ownership-controlled resources. Rather, internationalization is an outcome of the interconnected and interpenetrated firm, which is both a reflection and motor of institutional production and legitimization. The institutional context retains business practices and distributes these among a number of actors. This knowledge exists independently of the single firm, which can use it to configure its international activities and in general draw on it, and which, through its action, also adds to it. Knowledge in relationships is more adequately described as an activity than as an entity, analogous to Nelson & Winther's (1982) discussion of organizations as remembering by doing.

In the Hydro-X case, the international business practices of DBDH enabled OK to adapt his own business and thus utilize the experiences and connections of other DBDH members. At the same time, OK added to these relations by establishing relations in new markets and involving other members and business affiliates.

Lux Perpetua was established on the basis of both national and international relations from previous business activities. One important actor in the internationalization of Lux Perpetua is Maxam, which had earlier been active in the Swedish and

Norwegian markets. SEP was acquainted with a number of the sales persons in this firm, and subsequently used these contacts in establishing the international activities of Lux Perpetua.

The cases demonstrate that institutional contexts are capable of successfully shaping and reshaping international organizational patterns. This demonstrates the importance of business contexts as fields of international competence. The case studies point to personal ties as the basic building block of complex patterns of international resource chain organizing and reorganizing. Personal ties survive organizational contexts, and entrepreneurs are able to establish action patterns through their connections in this network. Thus, the interpersonal practices of individuals add up to a complex pattern of actions. In this sense, the knowledge network rests on some form of cognitive interdependence. Actors know the locations, rather than the details, of shared experiences, and rely on one another to supply the missing links (Weick & Roberts, 1993).

The central role of personal ties in maintaining and developing patterns of organization are not only evident in the formation of international activity. The cases also demonstrated that structural changes, e.g. internalization efforts in the form of foreign investments in sales subsidiaries, are in fact carried out in order to preserve existing personal ties. This was most evident in the Nordex Food case, where Nordex Food UK was established as a direct result of the closure of their intermediary. Nordex Food was thus able to hire the former employees of this intermediary by establishing a sales subsidiary. Similarly, the relationship between Nordex Food and Hoers Agenturen may end in a joint venture, with Nordex Food investing in the Dutch intermediary.

3.3 Role development in international resource chains

As firms interact, they develop shared skills. The development of international resource chains is thus also a mutual learning process. In the initial phases of a relationship, SMEs and intermediaries function as reservoirs of practice and new insights for each other. However, the more knowledge partners acquire, the more this is likely to change, thus new roles appear in the relationship. The dynamics of this process are illustrated in figure 8.5.

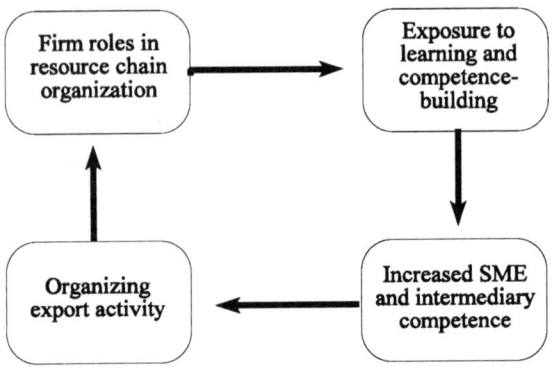

Figure 8.5: Dynamics of learning and resource chain organization

The organization of activity in the international resource chain includes the performance of specific activities by each actor. Consequently, the relationship between SME and intermediary can be described as a set of roles enacted over time as the resource chain is configured. The configuration and occupation of this role-set is clearly related to the competences and knowledge of each actor. However, the organization of activities is also a learning process. SMEs and intermediaries gradually acquire knowledge and adopt each others skills where applicable. Eventually, the basis for the division of tasks and responsibilities disappears. The learning process thus requires changes in the organization of activity. From the point of view of the SME, this means that role expectations changes.

The more SMEs and intermediaries want and/or become capable of carrying out activities previously carried out by the other firm, the more their expectations of each other's roles changes. Lorenzioni & Ornati (1988) have described this as a development process from supply or intermediary management to strategic partnerships. In the present study, this development pattern is found in the Hydro-X case, where intermediaries gradually become more involved in the Hydro-X concept development, technical improvements, etc. However, the cases also clearly demonstrate that the process is not inevitable. Intermediaries and/or SMEs may be unwilling to adjust to the change in skills and role expectations. This is obvious in both the Lux Perpetua and HWH cases, where these firms' role expectations did not coincide with those of their intermediaries. In these cases, communication between SME and intermediary was erratic, and the partners often concealed information from each other and/or failed to include each other fully in important decisions on the future of the relationship. Moreover, the competences of the SME and/or intermediary may become obsolete. This has been discussed especially in relation to strategic alliances, which have been described as a competitive race for learning (Hamel, 1990). Following this, collaboration is essentially an interpartner learning process aimed at acquiring the competences of others in order to outcompete them or make their presence unnecessary.

4. The conceptual framework revisited

The practices of international activity described here reflect unique ways of organizing, which have developed historically. They reflect the dynamic interplay of collective socializing of institutional frameworks, and individuals´ use of these frameworks in the formation of strategies for new and consistent ways of organizing activities. These processes follow their own paths and form distinct business approaches. However, as demonstrated in the above analysis, there are a number of shared elements which together provide a more general understanding of SMEs as international business organizers. The most significant of these seem to relate to the collaborative ability of SMEs in forming or participating in virtual organizations, where the activities and resources of each firm are combined in project-based, flexible organizational forms. These organizational forms are virtual in the sense that, rather than reflecting one form of activity, they reflect a potential reservoir of activities with almost instant access, as the discrete dyadic relations are connected by different types of project generators.

The connectedness of SMEs in numerous activities seems to underline the transient nature of the organization of activities in these networks. Networks of SMEs are characterized by a knowledge-based specialization, rather than a form of technological specialization, where the skills of the individual actor are related to the skills of numerous other actors. Thus, the skills of each actor are related to production activities through shared routines.

The conceptual framework has largely been supported by the cases studied, and refined accordingly. However, some of the expectations either failed to materialize or were challenged by the case results. In the following section these are briefly outlined.

It was expected that the development of international relations would lead to various demands on the firm which would be increasingly difficult to meet. This was not supported by the cases, however. On the contrary, all attempts to find patterns of automatic evolution, with built-in challenges to the internationalizing firm, proved in vain. Rather, the cases showed that, while firms may share an institutional background, the challenges and opportunities facing the firm during its internationalization process are largely a product of its own enactments of reality.

Another expectation which was rejected was the idea that business systems are largely separated by national institutions and that this is reflected in the internationalization of the SME. The cases all pointed to the existence of professions and other types of socioeconomic or socio-cognitive communities which stretch across national borders. All the cases demonstrated that firms were able to utilize personal relations either directly or as bridges to international suppliers and customers. Also, the shared practices of the actor networks involved in, for example, the production of lamps or the manufacture and distribution of agricultural machinery, emphasizes the similarities of the actors involved rather than their dissimilarities.

5.   SMEs as international business organizers: Towards a business system approach

It seems obvious that several of the axioms underpinning the conventional view of the organization of export activities are unable to capture the peculiar forms of organization illustrated in the cases presented here. The findings suggest that the business logics of SMEs differ radically from the conventional view of organization in economics and business textbooks. Instead of a fixed pattern of roles distributed among producers, intermediaries and end users, the cases show that the division of

230

tasks and roles in the international division of labour are far from settled. The analysis of the cases has demonstrated that the ways in which SMEs organize their international activities are not easily captured by general descriptions and clear-cut concepts.

The production systems in which the SMEs participate reveal a picture of diverse skills held together by shared grammars. The grammar allows for the relatively easy reconfiguring of inter-organizational relationships into alternative resource chains.

Resource chains express an extensive division of labour and collaboration in relation to the conclusion of specific tasks. The activities carried out by the single firm are joined with the activities of other firms in patterns which stretch across the boundaries of the single unit. In this way, the internal organization of the single unit also signals that it is part of a larger system.

Because of the extensive division of labour and large degree of interorganizational coordination in changing resource chain configurations, the mediation of activities is frequent and ad hoc. These processes of coordination are not easily pre-planned or left to formalized structures of organization. The opaque processes of organization require flexibility, with a large degree of personal communication and dialogue. Through these collaborative activities, shared patterns of meaning gradually develop, as subjective interpretations become externalized, institutionalized, and internalized in everyday interaction. In this sense, the process of coordination among involved actors is also a process of mutual learning. The insights obtained by the single actor adds to his general interpretation of reality, and influences his acts in other relationships as well. Thus all actors are arenas, where fragments of knowledge are accumulated, combined, and used in unique ways. The division of labour in the resource chain is constantly evolving, with the result that actors combine in different constellations, and are thus constantly involved in a process of learning and unlearning. New practices are adopted and old practices are erased, or perhaps preserved for future constellations.

It is in this context that the abilities of SMEs to establish, maintain and develop international activities must be understood. The development of shared interpretive schemes strengthens the possibilities of collaboration, and with it a higher degree of specialization in the division of labour. From the perspective of the individual firm, increasingly specialized actors allows for a larger degree of externalization, which in turn strengthens the adjustment possibilities of inter-unit relationships. The large degree of specialization and division of labour among firms which are connected by a shared grammar in networks can, according to Chandler (1962, 1977), lead to external advantages of scale and scope (Storper & Harrison, 1991; Brusco, 1982). Network economies of scope can be said to exist when the production process is fragmented, such that, while the scope of the business network as a whole is wide, the scope of the individual units is relatively narrow.

The nature of the business context of the firm seems at odds with the traditional role of management as described in the literature. In SMEs, managers are often directly involved in production activities themselves, and resources are often dependent on external resource controllers. Consequently, the role of the manager lies more in negotiating and participating directly in production activities, rather than planning and giving direction from a distance.

An important task of the SME manager follows from the characteristics of the resource chains outlined above. Since SMEs participate in various activities which are only partly under their control, the maintenance of flexibility becomes an important parameter. It is therefore also important to remain independent and small, sinces both are prerequisites of flexibility. In this sense, the production system represents a trajectory for the single firm which is not easy to escape. Since SMEs lack the means to control external resource holders, they are only able to keep resource chains together by remaining attractive to external resource controllers as potential partners. This again calls for a large degree of flexibility (Kristensen, 1994). This makes the growth difficult, however, because it is mainly possible only through the extension of the operational core. For most SMEs, growth through the mass production principles of large firms is an insurmountable barrier, as this process is not so much a question of gradual readjustment as one of leap-frogging. SMEs are therefore not expected to develop similar organizational patterns to large firms through internationalization. Whereas the large firm needs to protect its specialized core by stabilizing demand and supply conditions, the business rationale of the SME is essentially different. From an SME viewpoint, it is more interesting to identify collaborative partners, and it is only rarely relevant to consider forward or backward vertical integration, as this handicaps their ability to readjust to the diverse demands of their surroundings.

This only confirms the earlier statement about the nature of SMEs: Small firms are not infant large firms. SMEs represent an essentially different way of organizing activity than large firms. Hopefully, this study has demonstrated what must come as a surprise to some commentators of the role of Denmark in a globalizing economy: The practices followed by SMEs can function equally well in an increasingly internationalized economy as in a purely national one. The opportunities of and threats to the industrial structure should not be viewed solely in the light of arguments of efficiency based on advantages of scale. A more visionary debate on the concept of efficiency is therefore called for, one which also includes learning and adjustment as important aspects of efficiency rather than solely focusing on variable costs.

CHAPTER 9

Theoretical and practical implications of the study

The purpose of this chapter is - based on the case analyses in the preceeding chapter - to elaborate some of implications of the study for both international business theory and business practitioners. The chapter starts by reviewing some of the theories briefly outlined in chapter one. This time, however, the discussion will revolve around the basic assumptions of these theories and the extent to which they are supported by the present study. Finally, some normative implications for business practitioners concerning international collaboration and the development of international resource chains are outlined.

1. Implications for Theory

Chapter 1 discussed the theoretical underpinning of dominant opinion on the competitiveness of Danish industry, which was mainly based on rationalistic arguments of economic theory. Previous chapters have offered insights from an empirical viewpoint, and have revealed a number of the practices used in the Danish context. The time has now come to discuss these findings in terms of the theoretical frameworks in order to determine their applicability to the studied phenomena.

In the following section, the basic premises of the two main schools of thought in international business will be challenged. The aim here is to see whether the traditional theoretical framework used in international business studies could have explained the organization of international activity found in the present case studies.

The analysis discusses the underlying assumptions of these theoretical traditions and the extent to which they are verified or falsified by the study. Thus, the chapter will attempt to point out some of the weaknesses of present internationalization theory and indicate some of the ways in which the theoretical framework can be improved.

1.1 Market Failure: Two Theoretical Explanations

The question of how international firms overcome the disadvantage of "foreignness" has occupied researchers ever since the concept of market failure (Hymer, 1976; Buckley & Casson, 1976) was introduced as an explanatory factor for the existence of multinational firms. At present, there are two schools of thought, both of which stress knowledge disadvantage as a central concept in understanding international organization and development: The internalization approach and the internationalization approach. Although these traditions are often distinguished from each other (Bradley, 1991; Strandskov, 1994), and have developed independently, they also have similarities. These relate to their common focus on knowledge development and their parallel adaption of Simon's (1948, 1958) model of the boundedly rational decision-maker. These similarities can also be seen in the various attempts to integrate the two schools into a unified framework (Anderson & Gatignon, 1986; Ried, 1983). Thus, two of the central scholars of the internationalization approach recently claimed that their theory essentially reflects transaction costs in motion (Johanson & Vahlne, 1990).

As pointed out by Strandskov (1994), however, the theories differ from each other in their emphasis on different explanatory variables. In the following, therefore, these two theoretical traditions will be treated separately, despite the fact that they have a number of concepts in common.

1.1.1 The Transaction Cost Framework

Transaction cost theory takes a starting point in the single **transaction**[18] and focuses

---

[18] According to Williamson, a transaction occurs, when a product or service is transferred across a "technologically separable interface" (Williamson, 1985, p.1) .

on the economic efficiency of mechanisms, or governance structures, which emerge to coordinate and control transactions (Williamson, 1981). Transaction costs are contingent on three types of factors: *Asset specificity,* which relates to the degree to which investments are made in order to conduct transactions, *transaction frequency,* which refers to the volume of transactions, and *uncertainty,* which derives from the limited mental capabilities of decision-markers.

According to Williamson, transaction cost analysis is an examination of the comparative costs of planning, adapting and monitoring task completion under alternative governance structures. Governance structures are essentially different types of rules for coordinating and controlling tasks legitimized by a contract, which specifies the principles for transacting and the consequences of non-observance.

Williamson attempts to explain the emergence of organizations from an efficiency point of view. In situations of perfect competition, the market is assumed to be the most efficient organization for the allocation of resources. Perfect competition is rarely "perfect", however, which leads to market failure, i.e. the costs of leaving governance to the market exceeds the costs of administrative governance.

Williamson's framework provides the basis for a variety of research on the organization of international activity and the choice of foreign market entry mode (Anderson & Gatignon, 1986; Klein et al., 1990; Root, 1987; Hollesen, 1991; Ried, 1983; Petersen, 1994). It is assumed that the intermediary plays an instrumental role. Seen from the transaction cost viewpoint, the aim of the intermediary is to involve both exporter and customer in transaction-specific activity at the lowest possible cost in order to maximize its own gain. The pursuit of self-interest is thus only curbed by the existence of competition, which is also what makes the perfect market the most efficient governance structure. This means that, in cases where asset dedication can be minimized (either because of a low degree of asset specificity or a large-numbers-bargain situation), externalization is the most efficient way to organize transactions, while the presence of factors causing market failure suggests that internalization is the most efficient way.

In this framework, the externalization and internalization of transactions are equated

236

with intermediaries and sales subsidiaries (or other governance structures involving ownership control) respectively. Any asset-specific investment and/or increase in transaction frequency will increase market failure, thus pushing the exporting firm towards the internalization of activities. Anderson & Gatignon (1986) outline four constructs which determine the optimal degree of control from a transaction cost point of view. The conditions which are expected to influence the choice of entry mode are:

i) Transaction-Specific Assets

The first construct in the framework relates to the dedication of investments to the needs of specific customers. When the degree of asset specificity is low, competitive pressures will force intermediaries to perform effectively. Dedication of assets also increases entry barriers, however, and decreases the number of potential competitors as well as increasing the dependence of the market entrant. This increases the risk of market failure and justifies the internalization of cross-border transactions. Transaction-specific assets are associated with investments in i) proprietary knowledge and/or products which are only transferrable to intermediaries after intensive training, ii) products where the direct interface to the end user plays a substantial role in product adaption, development or modification, and iii) products which are in the early stages of their product life cycle.

ii) External Uncertainty

The second construct addresses the unpredictability of the firm´s environment. In markets characterized by a high degree of uncertainty, firms are, ceterus paribus, expected to shift the burden of risk to outsiders. Market control is therefore unaffected by external uncertainty, since exit costs are low. However, in cases where asset specificity is involved, flexibility is lost, and the unpredictability of the environment increases intermediaries' opportunities to behave opportunistically. In such cases, therefore, market volatility is expected to increase market failure, thus strengthening the propensity to internalize. External uncertainty can be caused by demand and/or supply instability, political risks, competitive pressures, etc.

iii) Internal Uncertainty

The third construct involves the inability of the market entrant to determine intermediary performance from output measures. In these cases, firms are expected to safeguard themselves against opportunistic behaviour, since the monitoring of inputs is easier than the specification of performance (see also Alchain & Demsetz, 1972). Moreover, internal uncertainty is expected to decrease as the firm acquires more international experience. Thus, the more experienced the firm is, the more aggressively it is expected to pursue international business opportunities, and the closer it is expected to be situated to the customer. International experience is therefore expected to be positively related to internalization. Internal uncertainty is thus related to international experience and the socio-cultural distance between the host country and the firm's own country.

iv) Free-riding Potential

The last construct concerns the idea that firms which invest in brand promotion are more exposed to free-riding, either through discrediting the entrant's brand in favour of another brand, or through capitalizing on the reputation of the brand without incurring the costs of maintaining it.

1.1.2 The transaction cost framework in relation to the findings of the cases
The four constructs developed above can be interpreted in a transaction cost framework by the aid of the theoretical constructs outlined above.

It is possible to find some form of transaction-specific assets in at least three cases, which, following the framework developed by Anderson & Gatignon, indicates market failure and thus suggests internalization. In the Hydro-X case, there is a massive transfer of proprietary knowledge to the intermediary, incurring training costs which are financed by Hydro-X. Both the HWH and Nordex Food cases involve customized products, with the consequent development of idiosyncratic relations to intermediaries.

238

The second construct, external uncertainty[19], is present in all cases in the form of unstable demand conditions, either caused by fluctuating patterns of demand as a result of exchange rate instability (HWH, Nordlux) or by political intervention in business conditions in general (Nordlux, Hydro-X). External uncertainty is connected with asset specificity in two cases: HWH and Hydro-X.

The third construct relates to management's international experience. In all cases, managers have considerable experience of foreign market conditions, and in two of the cases, managers are away on business for more than 80 days a year (Hydro-X, Nordex Food). It therefore seems reasonable to observe that management has strong or moderate international experience. In addition, the socio-cultural distance between home and host country is substantial in relation to the international market profile of both Hydro-X and Nordex Food.

Finally, a free-riding potential was found in firms which have invested in a brand name. This applies especially to Nordex Food and Hydro-X, which have both invested substantial resources, as well as their market reputation, in specific brand names.

Clearly, more or less all the firms have experienced what Anderson & Gatignon (op. cit.) describe as market failure. It seems obvious that internalization can be expected in all cases, though most strongly in the Hydro-X case. The question is, therefore: why has it not taken place? From a transaction cost point of view, two explanations are possible. The first relates to transaction frequency and goes more or less like this: the fixed costs associated with forward market integration cannot be spread over a sufficently large sales volume, and it is therefore not possible to reap the economies-of-scale-related benefits of a specialized marketing function. Consequently, small firms are unable to internalize and, although exposed to opportunistic behaviour, are forced to externalize their activities instead (Rugman, 1982; Klein et al., 1990; Ried, 1983; Hollesen, 1991). As explained by Klein et al.:

---

[19]   Environmental uncertainty has been dealt with in contingency theory. Here, "uncertainty" is defined, analogous to Thompson (1967), as fluctuating supply and demand (input & output) conditions which change in a non-predictable manner.

"Because increasing foreign integration requires a more complex and specific governance structure, greater fixed costs are inevitable. To cover such fixed costs, greater volumes are required. If channel volume for the product line is not extremely high but economies of scale are still facilitated through use of an integrated channel, the firm is expected to serve the foreign market from its home base." (Klein et al., p. 198)

Thus, following this argumentation, internalization can mainly be expected in markets characterized by idiosyncratic investments, intermediaries with strong bargaining power, and a high transaction frequency. Although this argumentation is not supported by some of the cases, it not challenged either. However, in the Nordex Food case, it is possible to find intermediaries with a sales volume which would justify internalization from a transaction cost viewpoint. For example, Nordex Food products account for more than half the total sales of the Dutch intermediary Evers Agenturen. Although Nordex Food has devoted a number of assets to this relationship, including specialized administrative procedures and procedures for visiting customers, this has not led to internalization. The potential loss of an intermediary in the UK market resulted in assets being recouped by internalizing transactions through the establishment of a sales subsidiary.

A second explanation relates to the development of safeguarding mechanisms in terms of credible commitments on behalf of market entrants and intermediaries. Petersen (1994) has outlined a taxonomy of safeguarding mechanisms in a recent study of a sample of Danish exporting firms. Safeguarding mechanisms were also found in the cases studied here, but contrary to expectations, these were not developed or decided ex ante in relation to the specific transaction. Rather, they were organized through a reputational system, in which information is exchanged between business partners and used in assessing the credibility of potential and actual business partners. Thus, one way of guarding against opportunism is through knowledge of the reputational system, which is only possible by acting honestly. Here, it can be argued that this is what is meant by acting with guile. If this is the case, however, then it equates honesty with opportunistic behaviour, since it helps the actor build up a position of trust which can be exploited at some future point. With this, the transaction cost framework has reached a point where it is no longer empirically testable.

1.1.3 The transaction cost theory of international organization: A critique

In sum, the cases challenge rather than support the transaction cost framework. The basic assumption - that firms internalize activities which they are able to perform at lower cost, and only use external relations for transactions where other producers have an advantage - is not supported by the findings presented. While some factors can be interpreted as credible commitment, these can just as well be interpreted in a theoretical framework which does not include safeguards against opportunism. Thus, the shared division of labour and shared transaction-specific assets can equally well reflect the use of joint investments and patterns of collaboration as defences against moral hazard. The case studies point more to some limitations of the transaction cost framework in relation to the analysis of entry mode decisions by foreign entrants (which is due to the basic premises of the framework). These are discussed in the following.

A major objection to the transaction cost framework in relation to the present analysis is its implicit assumption that economic exchange mainly concerns commodities with given utility value. In neoclassical economics, efficiency is obtained through optimal allocation. However, as pointed out by several scholars, this assumption is clearly problematic, as firms operate in a world characterized by change and unforeseeable events. Thus, efficiency is equated with allocation rather than a dynamically changing economy (Pasinetti, 1981).

As pointed out earlier, the superiority of the hierarchy is first and foremost due to its ability to diminish the impact of information, thus reducing the complexity of decision-making, since decisions are backed up by authority, and conflicting interests stemming from vertical competition are absent. However, it can be argued that there is a trade-off between efficiency and the ability to learn, as efficiency is based on reducing complexity, while learning stems from the interaction of complex and multiple world views. Integration will tend to reduce or exclude the interaction of integrated units from the broader set of potential users and producers (Lundvall, 1993). Thus, far from removing uncertainty, in a dynamic environment, internal

241

uncertainty in the hierarchy is merely replaced by another type of uncertainty. As the potential for conflict due to diverging interests and world views is reduced, so is the possiblity for learning. This has been discuseed in project management literature as a trade-off between operational and contextual uncertainty (Christensen & Kreiner, 1991). According to these authors, projects (and business activities in general in a world of uncertainty) have a built-in discrepancy between the need to learn about changing environmental conditions and the need for control. Thus, a strong emphasis on efficient allocation through the hierarchy hinders the ability to interact and learn. This argument is more in line with the situation in the cases, in which a premium is put on flexibility and learning rather than input-output efficiency. This also underlines the use of flexible entry mode arrangements and the need for SMEs and intermediaries to pool resources in collaborative product and process innovations.

Another appeal is the strong emphasis on asset-specific investments. In the cases, however, these are connected with a number of complementary investment made by the market intermediaries. In the Hydro-X case, the training costs incurred by Hydro-X were matched by intermediaries' travelling and labour costs of personnel attending training seminars in Denmark. In the Nordex Food and HWH cases, marketing costs were shared between the SME and the intermediary. Thus, transaction-specific assets can be used as a basis for acting opportunistically by foreign entrants as well as by foreign intermediaries (Petersen & Pedersen, 1992; Strandskov, 1994).

The focus of the transaction cost framework is on the costs associated with different entry modes rather than the expected gain. Thus, the relation between an exporter and an intermediary becomes a zero-sum game, where the emphasis is on cost control rather than the development possibilities associated with mutual learning and the mutual gain that can be obtained through the interconnection of diverse clusters of relations.

1.2 The internationalization theory

The internationalization model was discussed earlier, in chapter three. The discussion here will focus on its value as an alternative framework for analyzing the cases. The main premise of the internationalization model is briefly recapitulated below.

Briefly, the internationalization model is based on the idea that the organization of international activity occurs in stages, where activities are increasingly internalized. Consequently, firms are expected to start out as exporters, and gradually expand their activities to include cross-border transactions. Moreover, international activity is expected to start in a market where the psychic distance is small, and then gradually expand to increasingly distant markets. This is a trial-and-error process: as managers gain knowledge, their risk perception gradually decreases, thus encouraging them to commit more resources to international business activity. This can be expressed in the following way (Johanson & Vahlne, 1977, p. 30):

$R'_i =$ Maximum tolerable market (market i) risk = f (firm's resource position, firm's risk approach)

$R_i =$ Existing market risk situation $= C_i * U_i$
where $C_i =$ existing market commitment
$U_i =$ existing market uncertainty

$\triangle R_i =$ incremental risk implied by an incremental addition to operations on market i

Scale-increasing decisions are assumed to affect the size of C_i but not the size of U_i so that

$$\triangle R_i = U_i * \triangle C_i > 0$$

Uncertainty-reducing decisions are assumed to affect U_i primarily so that

$$\triangle R_i = U_i (C_i + \triangle C_i) + \triangle C_i * U_i < 0$$

Following of Johanson & Vahlne's framework, the international commitment can be divided into A) scale-increasing decisions, which furthers market commitment, and B) uncertainty-reducing decisions, which decrease risk perception. Internationalization is expected to be initiated by scale-increasing decisions up to R^*_i. However, increasing market commitment by increasing scale will leave the firm more exposed to the business conditions in foreign markets, thus strengthening the need for reducing risk perception. Scale-increasing market commitment is therefore expected to be followed by uncertainty-reducing market commitment, achieved through

243

forward integration with the foreign market environment. This again allows for a larger market commitment, which leads to a new situation of imbalance. From this, it follows that internationalization can be described as the gradual correction of imbalance between the existing market risk situation and the maximum tolerable market risk.

1.2.1 The Uppsala internationalization model in relation to the findings of the cases
Generally speaking, the patterns of internationalization in the cases are similar to the pattern described above. In the Nordex Food case, for example, scale investments in production capacity reflects developments in the perception of foreign market risk. And in both the Hydro-X and HWH cases, the gradual commitment of resources follows the gradual acknowledgment of foreign market opportunities. However, commitment decisions are not necessarily based on the assumption that uncertainty is reduced through forward integration. Furthermore, the assumption of socio-cultural distance is challenged in the Nordex Food case, as well as the Hydro-X case.

In sum, the cases largely confirm the assumption that internationalization describes a pattern of decisions which gradually builds up the international competence of the actor. International experience is thus expected to further international commitment. There does not seem to be any predefined path for internationalization, however. On the contrary, the cases show that perceptions of risk and the choice of action does not follow any universal means-ends frame. Thus, risk is not universally associated with any concept of distance, and neither does risk reduction lead to a specific pattern of unilateral organization. Rather, the cases represent a variety of strategies, though which SMEs, in collaboration with intermediaries and other resource holders in unique organizational arrangements, have succeeded in overcoming problems of uncertainty and resource specialization.

In a broader perspective, the network in which the firm participates can be seen as a learning system. Novel practices and business opportunities are constantly generated by actors in their relationships to other actors. In some cases, these patterns are imitated by a broader community and gain status as part of the shared knowledge of the business network, which in turn influences the development of relations among actors in a given business area. One example of such a practice was found in the Hydro-X case, where the increasing use of laptop computers by field consultants is likely to modify the relations between customers, field consultants and producers of chemicals.

The assumption that the network is a learning system points to a different concept of knowledge than that found in the theory of business internationalization presented here. Internationalization theory implicitly sees the decision-maker as an intendedly rational calculator, though handicapped by a limited mental capacity. In this theoretical universe, reality is objectively given and the states which reality may attain are finite. Thus, knowledge is equated with information processing capability, and the process of optimal (or satisfactory, given actors with limited rationality[20]) decision-making becomes a problem of Bayesian calculation (Hayek, 1945).

Decision-makers are thus distinguished by their ability to partition information and compute probabilities, and to assess probable outcomes using this method. Learning thus becomes a process of updating the present probability distribution, analogous to what has been described as the process of detecting and correcting errors in relation to a given set of operating procedures (Argyris & Schön, 1978; Morgan, 1986).

The present study ascribes a different role to knowledge and decision-making, however. First, the role of decision-making does not seem to be as central as assumed in conventional theory. Rather than expressing rational calculation,

> *"Decision-making is a highly contextual, sacred activity, surrounded by myth and ritual and as much concerned with the interpretive order as with specificies of particular choices."* (March, 1989, p.651)

In other words, decisions are made from an existing definition of the situation, rather than from a confrontation with reality. Environmental changes are incorporated into

---

[20]   The difference between optimal and satisfactory decision-making is explained in chapter 3, footnote 16.

the existing framework of reality and activities adopted accordingly. Existing world views thus have an interia of their own.

Secondly, knowledge plays a more active role in the cases. Rather than it being a question of information-processing capacity, knowledge is seen as the ability to typify novel situations from past experiences, thus assigning meaning, and with this, action, to reality (Fast, 1992 & 1993; Weick, 1979 & 1991). Here, knowledge becomes a metaphorical framework in which business opportunities are constructed through processes of enactment. Consequently, the interpretive schemes of actors (or the collective of actors known as the firm, or network of firms) developed from past experiences are essentially a knowledge differential (Nelson, 1991) or a distinctive competence of the firm (Dosi & Marengo, 1993). The organization of international activity found in the case studies therefore reflects the development of interpretive frames in which shared representations are found in an information code or technical language which makes collective action possible.

As the organizing of international activities proceeds, interpretive schemes come to represent an asset for the actors involved, since it allows rational interacting. Interpretive frames developed during the organization of an activity thus also influence the subsequent development of activities. Once established, SMEs attempt to incorporate new relations into existing frameworks, adapting to the idiosyncracies of these relations either by extending existing schemes or by introducing new actors into existing patterns of communication. As the internationalization of the firm proceeds, however, these patterns become increasingly diverse and therefore more complex. Compared with the internationalization process of larger firms, SMEs are unable to reduce this complexity by supplementing these efforts with substantial investments in subsidiaries. Therefore they try to reduce complexity by other means - either through increasing standardization of the shared code (Hydro-X), or through partitioning tasks into new functions, thus adhering to the internationalization processes of larger firms. Other firms lack the ability to adapt to the diversity of intermediaries, and find that their internationalization efforts are hampered, because working relationships are difficult to establish (Nordlux) or maintain (HWH).

246

1.2.2 *The Uppsala internationalization model revisted: A Critique*

The present study raises two objections to the internationalization model, both of which suggest that a modification is necessary in relation to the international activities of SMEs.

Firstly, it seems clear that the gradual vertical integration of market relations is certainly not the only route to organizational efficiency. By equating authority with ownership, the internationalization model is only partly able to capture the organization processes of small firms. A broader approach to the concept of authority is clearly called for.

Secondly, the focus on internal competence and resource gathering is only partly relevant. Resources and competences are developed together with other firms, and these play an active role in the organization of international activity. Thus, the division of labour and coordination of tasks are not the results of a centrally controlled plan, but of ongoing organization, in which both SMEs and external resource controllers play an active role.

2. Managerial implications of the Study

From a managerial viewpoint, the possibilities and problems of international organization and development are similar to those of any cross-border activity, whether across national, regional, or industrial boundaries. In all these cases, managers may face a business environment which differs from the one they are used to, and which cannot be given meaning through the existing framework of means and ends. The key word here is diversity. A major task for any international SME manager is therefore the management of diversity. In general, the diversity of business environments has a Janus-like quality: it offers business opportunities as well as challenges. International success thus depends on meeting the challenges while at the same time exploiting the opportunities of being in a resource chain, where diverse networks are combined.

Business opportunities related to differences between nations has been a hot issue in international trade theory for a number of years. Trade theories have been mainly concerned with the different factor costs of producing commodities with given utility-value characteristics, however. Only recently has mainstream theory begun to discuss business opportunities related to national differences in knowledge or competence (Porter, 1991), despite the fact that national differences in competence has been an issue for several decades (Dahmén, 1950). Such differences are consistent with the "strength of weak ties" argument developed by Granovetter (1973): In networks where actors are connected through a multitude of relations, interaction and mutual learning is common, and skills are therefore dispersed among a number of individuals. This gives a relatively smaller knowledge differential compared with actors from diverse networks. Thus, new information and ideas are typically spread through the weak ties which bridge geographical, cultural or otherwise separated clusters of actors. The central role of the SME manager in this is to identify knowledge diversity and find out how it can be used in his own networks. This is the central act of entrepreneurial innovation as described by Hayek (1945) and Kirzner (1973). This cases demonstrated this mechanism in a number of respects: In the HWH case, experiences from the buyer-seller interface with Danish municipalities led to a product which could be adapted to the needs of a Swedish customer; in the Hydro-X case, experiences with corrosion and scale obtained from one local business environment could be transferred to situations in other markets; in the Nordex Food case, experiences from ethnic wholesalers in one country led to business opportunities with wholesalers in other countries, etc.

There are also problems connected with the increasing diversity of business operations, however. Increasing diversification also leads to increasing international complexity, and it becomes more and more difficult to maintain a coherent base of activities. Management should therefore consider a trade-off between rationalization and diversification.

The cases point to a vital aspect of business management: The ability to establish, maintain and develop a fit between the capabilities of the firm and the demands of the market. In all four cases, the knowledge acquired from dyadic exchange relationships has been used to develop abilities for subsequent exchange activities in other relationships. The implication of the case studies is that effective marketing

248

management hinges on the ability to interpret resource utilization in various contexts and communicate this to other customers, thereby producing a competitive advantage vis-à-vis competitors. In this sense, previous exchange relationships are used as stepping-stones for subsequent exchange. The firm becomes an arena for the exchange of knowledge. Its market rationale becomes the procuring of resources in a world of imperfect knowledge.

The firm must think of itself as a configuration of internal and external relations, in which ownership-controlled resources have contextual rather than absolute value. It is through this market-bound configuration of internal and external resources that the firm acquires its ability to generate new activity. This means that the potential of new relations must be assessed by their contribution to the generation of new activity, either by maintaining or expanding the degree of coherence among the firm's relationships. It is the constant renewal of knowledge of resource utilization which constitutes the basis of the firm's business activities.

From this point of view, balancing the diversity of existing exchange relationships and utilizing the potential changes stemming from the introduction of new relationships becomes a crucial management task. In fact, this marks a balance between innovation and rationalization. Existing relations form the strategic frame from which new activities can be generated. The more stability introduced into this frame through, for example, the interorganizational specialization of assets and other means of mutual adaptation, the greater the certainty, which in turn allows for more mutual predictability, and possibly scale-economic benefits derived from cost efficiency.

On the other hand, specialization necessitates the structuralization of activity, since resources are devoted to a smaller number of potential exchange possibilities. This introduces rigidity into exchange, which obstructs both flexible production patterns and innovation. In view of the fact that these aspects have clearly characterized business conditions over the past few decades, and that increasing competition forces firms to constantly improve existing procedures, it is important to avoid resource dependency.

Moreover, specialization is the opposite of generalization. Too much adaptation to the idiosyncracies of one exchange relationship adversely affects other relationships. Here, the relationship context can be managed by means of multiple sourcing and the avoidance of customer dependence. Management must therefore be aware of the possibilities of learning through market interaction. What is important, therefore, is not careful planning based on the present state of knowledge. Rather, the firm must be open and prepared to alter present beliefs in the light of experience gathered through market interaction. Thus, strategy can be described as a frame which emerges during interaction, allowing changes due to the alteration of knowledge (Mintzberg, 1987; Morgan, 1993). The important task for management can thus be described as the organization and development of the resource network of the firm.

It is important to understand, however, that the strength of an international position builds on the mutual advantages of a continuing relationship. A central task of the SME manager is therefore to contribute to the development of his external resource base. One way of doing this is to use the intermediary in activities involving shared commitment and/or to participate in similar activities of the intermediary. Another is to establish forums where knowledge can be exchanged among the resource chain participants. These may take the form of training seminars and traineeships, where employees are based at local intermediaries and vice versa, as in the case of Hydro-X, or informal, regular business meetings, as in the case of Nordex Food. These are some of the main means of achieving coherence and maintaining relationships found in the cases studied. Similar means have been reported in a survey of Danish exporters. Here, it was found that a number of exporters use local reimbursement, e.g. employing personnel based at the intermediary (Petersen, 1994).

2.1 Organizing for network coherence

In order to benefit from market resources, management must develop an organizational structure capable of handling the diverging needs of stability and innovation. This applies to both the internal and external organization of activity. Two interrelated structural aspects of organization can be summoned to shed light on this discussion: i) the division of labour; and ii) coordination and means of authority.

2.1.1 Division of labour

In the context of the configuration of network coherence, the division of labour is a question of "make-or-buy" decisions, relating to which activities should be produced in-house and which should be subcontracted. Transaction cost theory has approached this through the concept of market failure (Williamsson, 1975). According to this concept, only those activities which are general in nature, and for which a number of suppliers (or buyers) can be found, should be placed outside hierarchical control. The question of resource dependency is an important one, as this may imply substantial bargaining power on the part of resource holders. On the other hand, a prerequisite for developing the core capabilities of the firm is to engage in activities which are closely linked to these capabilities. The fact that firms do engage in this type of activity, despite the warnings of Williamson and his colleagues, may imply that either a) the basic driving force of human behaviour is not unlimited needs, or b) the community of firms has other means of maintaining order and hindering malfeasance, as suggested by Piore & Sabel (1984). A related question is that of proprietary knowledge. From the standpoint of traditional economics, it could be argued that knowledge (a "public good") should be protected from external relations, because openness means sacrificing the rationale of the company (Reve, 1988). The idea of proprietary knowledge implies that some of the firm's knowledge can be hidden, and as such constitutes a unique position which can be exploited. From the point of view presented here, however, knowledge only has value in relation to activity. If knowledge is not incorporated or used, it loses significance. Knowledge not related to activity is knowledge not used. Safeguarding against malfeasance can thus be seen in the creation of exit barriers, where the development of cross skills and patterns of reciprocity leads to further investments in reciprocity. Thus, safeguarding is seen as an ongoing process whereby actors gain more through continuing the relationship than by terminating it.

Network-related knowledge is not proprietary, but is owned jointly by the exchange parties, and in this sense is different from other types of resources. It is a type of social capital which is shared among a group of actors, none of whom has exclusive ownership to it (Burt, 1993). If an actor leaves the network, the connection to this knowledge ia lost. The continuancy of a relationship depends on some form of reciprocity. SMEs are part of the social capital of the intermediary and vice versa.

This also implies that SMEs and intermediaries have conflicting as well as complementary interests. An emphasis on promoting complementary interests or offsetting conflicting interests marks an important dividing line in organization literature. Thus, a substantial part of the literature focuses on potential areas of conflict between exporters and foreign intermediaries, and how exporters can safeguard themselves against the opportunistic behaviour of intermediaries and increase control over their marketing activities (Iyer, 1992; Keegan, 1985; Bradley, 1991). An alternative approach to the relationship between intermediaries and exporters contends that it should be seen more as a plus-sum than a zero-sum game (Håkansson, 1992). Here, the focus is on the complementary interests of exporters and intermediaries and how these can be developed. These viewpoints are juxtaposed with their view on the economic efficiency of external versus internal organizational arrangements, which essentially stems from diverging concepts of economic efficiency. If economic efficiency is equated with rationalization and stability, then arrangements which routinize information flows and reduce information complexity must clearly be seen as the most efficient. If, however, economic efficiency is equated with adaption and innovation, then organizational arrangements which promote flexibility and recurrent learning through diversity are clearly preferred. However, the present study suggests that this distinction is at best only partly valid. External relations may show both flexibility and routinization. Thus, economic efficiency in terms of rationalization does not presuppose internalization. The analysis of the cases clearly demonstrates that other means of achieving stability are available.

2.1.2 Coordination and means of authority

The degree to which tasks are internalized or externalized influences both the coordination and direction of activity, which in turn relates to the means by which power is legitimized (Weber, 1961). For the sake of simplification, we can speak of three idealized regulative situations:

1) *Market-based regulation*, where coordination and control are based on (and limited by) the principles of the market. Here, activity is coordinated through the entrepreneurial coupling of actors, which must be renewed with each new activity.

252

This type of organization is possible if the tasks are sufficiently simple or can be easily communicated. A prerequisite for the latter is the existence of some sort of communicative device, incorporated in a group of economic actors. Configuration and coordination within a profession is one example of this, where specific codes of conduct have been internalized through tradition, training programmes, etc. This can be seen in the configuration of an orchestra, a football team, or a group of dockers loading a ship. The legitimacy of direction is underpinned by the ability to carry out a task in which specific resources can be activated (and rewarded).

2) At the opposite end of the scale are *rule-based organizations*, where tasks are either extremely complex, tightly coupled, or which for other reasons must be kept in-house. This applies, for example, to highly complex or hegemonic organizations, such as parts of the military, nuclear power plants, or religious movements. Here, coordination is achieved through the scheduling of activity, and authority is underpinned by the position in the regulating structure.

3) Most organizations, however, are *intermediary forms*, where the task, or the extent to which resources are controlled in-house, necessitates the supply and coordination of additional relationships. In this type of relation, interdependency underpins coordination. Thus, coordination is regulated through negotiation and cross-organizational agreements (Cyert & March, 1963), which are developed over time as skills are calibrated in an ongoing network dialogue. Interdependency also implies some sort of structure in external relations. This leads to the emergence of specific positions in an activity pattern, which may underpin authority. The above examples are shown in table 9.1 below.

Table 9.1:Three configurations of organizational structure

Division of Labour	Coordination	Means of Authority
Internalized	Administratively Scheduled	Rule-Based
Intermediate form	Negotiated	Position-Based
Externalized	Market-Regulated	Activity-Based

A major implication of the above, as regards the design of an organizational structure to underpin the dynamic stability of a resource network, is that none of the extremes enables the market to be configured or to function as desired. Extreme internalization shuts the market out, while extreme externalization precludes market differential, compared with the configurations of other actors.

2.2 A framework for assessing network position, relationship coherence and strategic action

In strategic analysis, it is common to compare internal strengths and weaknesses with external threats and opportunities in order to see whether there is sufficient fit between the structure and the strategy (Chandler, 1977). We will follow a similar line of thinking here, systematically analyzing networks as activity structures in which actors obtain specific positions of strategic significance, and relating this to the position of the firm in terms of relationship coherence. Finally, an analysis of this type can lead to the assessment of appropiate strategic action. Here, we will discuss some basic types of strategy within this framework.

2.2.1 Assessing relationship coherence

One way of evaluating the current state and potential of the configuration and coherence of market resources is to systematically evaluate the relationships from two perspectives: 1) The relative fit of the single relationship to the remaining relationships, and 2) The question of whether the most salient feature of the relationship is efficiency or innovation. Together, these dimensions form the framework shown in figure 9.2.

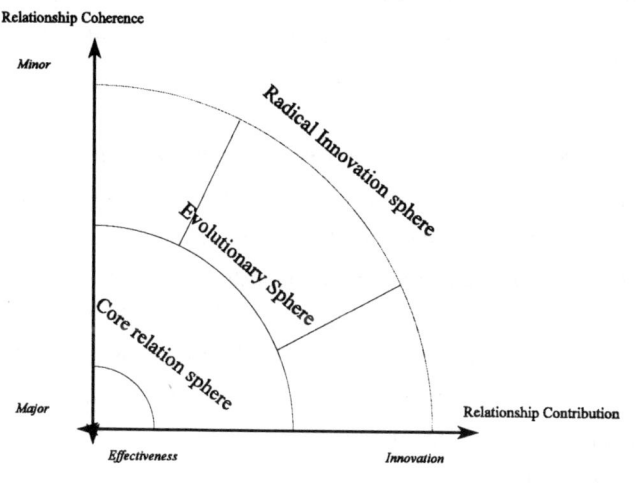

Figure 9.2: Framework for assessing the extent of Network Coherence

The *core relation sphere* contains relationship activities based on task repetition, where the activities can be handled within the present sphere of activity. The *evolutionary sphere* includes activities which imply a change in the present way of doing things, either through new methods or through applying existing methods to new areas of activity. This implies the development of the knowledge base within the frame of activity. The *radical innovation sphere* contains relationships which cannot be handled within the present frame of relationship coherence, and, as such, can represent a threat to it.

The exchange relations can be plotted onto this frame, and have a number of valuable implications for other business relations. The ideal picture is a clustering around the boundary between the evolutionary and the core sphere, with none or only a few of the relationships in the extreme positions. Clusterings in these areas indicate weaknesses in the present market configuration. A large number of relationships in the top left of the figure indicates production inertia, where a large degree of specialization can hinder the ability to innovate. On the other hand, a clustering in the top right sector may imply a small common base from which activity can be carried out, thus signifying the erosion or absence of a core

255

competence, which threatens the legitimacy of the firm as an exchange partner. Relationships placed in the bottom left and bottom right of the figure indicate relations which do not contribute to coherence or for which novelty is substantial compared with the total number of relations.

There are two important aspects of this type of analysis compared with standard strategic analysis and action methods. First, it is important to understand that a change in a firm's position may simultaneously affect its access to relationship resources. Optimization of a firm's resource allocation at the expense of the network may lead to long- or short-term destruction of the basis of the firm's strength. This has, for example, been described in the case of the American automobile industry. Here, the use of arm's-length supplier systems by GM pressed the resources of suppliers to such an extent that they were no longer able to invest in modernized production equipment, and in the long run became ineffective (see Porter, 1983, for more details). Second, changing one position may (especially in networks which are transparent and obviously defined by all actors) lead to counter-measures, and eventually change the entire activity pattern. The configuration of a network may both represent a balance and an indication of room for change.

In analyses of this type it is important to evaluate the stability and potential of a present position, and, if necessary, assign strategic action. A number of strategies for achieving network coherence can be suggested.

Managing resource chain coherence
One oft-mentioned problem of the management of foreign intermediaries is the lack of controllability attached to this market entry mode (Root, 1987; Young et al., 1989).

This is somewhat contradicted by the findings of the present investigation. Here, it is argued that a main problem of intermediary management is that managers fail to recognize that intermediaries are independent firms with interests of their own, not just providers of administrative ability whose interests can be controlled and/or sacrificed to the interests of the exporting firm. Such attempts to achieve control are costly and can - and often do - fail.

It has earlier been argued that the central function of the SME is to coallign knowledge of needs and resources. When these coincide, the SME can engage in value-creation. Access to both factors depends on a position in relation to possible exchange actors, which again depends on the existence of a context. A prerequisite for establishing such a context, however, is that the SME recognizes that the interests of all parties are best served by supporting those activities of the intermediary which best promote the interests of the SME. In this matter a zero-sum game of achieving control may be turned into a plus-sum game of coallignment, where complementary activities are given first priority.

The present study has suggested that, essentially, this context consists of a shared grammar, which is regualarly updated and communicated to the SME's exchange partner. Thus, conventional understandings of organizational management to the contrary, there is more to the management of resource chains than just the transfer of information. In the context of resource chains, communication is an act of exchanging symbols which relates to, and presupposes the existence of, some sort of shared grammar.

What is essentially being argued here is that resource chain management is an act of communication, and that this act is based on other actors' ability to relate to the communicative acts of SME management. However, this is not to suggest that all problems of organizing international resource chain activity are communication problems. Often, however, communicative solutions may be less demanding in terms of economic or administrative resources, compared with such alternatives as vertical integration.

On the basis of the present study, it now seems possible to identify both successful and problematic cycles of communicative management in this respect. Both Hydro-X and Nordex Food had successful cycles of communicative management. This is illustrated in figure 9.3 below:

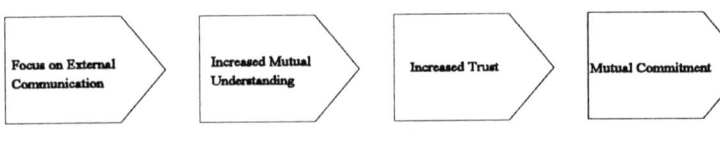

Figure 9.3: Effective Resource Chain Management

In both cases, management were externally oriented, and a lot of time and effort was put into dealing swiftly with intermediaries' problems and relating to their needs (see also figure 8.2). This also strengthened the firms' ability to meet these need in advance, which again smoothed coordination. This in turn increases the mutual trust of the resource chain partners, since here, trust is seen as the ability to meet the expectations of others. Finally, trust leads to the mutual commitment of partners, strengthening their ability to organize joint activity.

A parallel cycle can be identified in firms experiencing problems in organizing resource chains. In the HWH Production and Nordlux cases, there was a lack of communication to intermediaries for various reasons. In the HWH case, communications to foreign intermediaries were disturbed by the inconsistency of signals coming from the competing business logics of the firm, while at Nordlux, the change of management led to a radical change in the way the firm relates to intermediaries and suppliers. In these cases, the communicative cycle of management can be shown as follows:

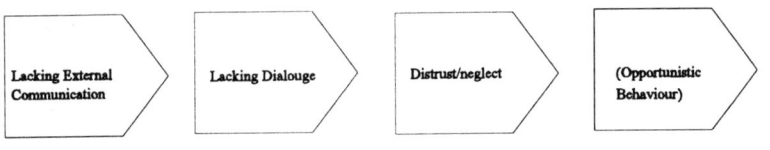

Figure 9.4 Ineffective communication in resource chains

The lack of dialogue makes intermediaries more apt to reduce interaction with the SME and increase interaction with other exchange parties. The more intermediaries adapt to the grammars of other exchange partners, the less they are able to understand the actions of the SME in question. This may exacerbate the loss of trust, which again can lead to the neglect of the SME, and may even cause opportunistic behaviour.

Based on the present analysis, it is possible to identify a number of communicative strategies for establishing shared grammars, as shown in section 8.2.2. These strategies can be evaluated in relation to the analytical frame presented in figure 9.2. From this framework, the position of the firm can be changed in two basic ways: Either through an extension or contraction of the present exchange party, or through the reconfiguration of existing relationships. These strategies are shown in table 9.2 below, according to their relevance for the two action patterns.

Table 9.2: Coordination strategies and generic types of action in network strategies

	Extension/Contraction	Reconfiguration
Formalization	o	x
Socialization	xx	xx
Learning	xx	x
Mutual adjustment	x	xx
Shared experience gathering	x	xx

As can be seen from the table, the communication strategies which are relevant to the extension or contraction of resource chain are those in which the SME plays a sender role and the foreign intermediary a receiving role. Thus, strategies such as socialization and learning are both characterized by the SME as actively promoting a specific vision or idea. In cases of reconfiguration, both SMEs and intermediaries are active in defining the content of the dialogue. This applies to strategies such as socialization, mutual adjustment and shared experience gathering.

3. Concluding remarks

In chapter 1, the purpose of the study was defined as: "A study of the practices by which SMEs participate in and develop their position within the international division of labour". It was also noted that little is known beyond the descriptive level.

In this chapter, it has been shown that traditional theory of the competitiveness of SMEs has serious deficiencies.

The present study has attempted to remedy this by suggesting ways in which SMEs can participate in and develop their international activities. The previous chapter outlined a number of suggestions which together add to the understanding of the business logic followed by SMEs in managing and developing their international activities.

However, one of the most important findings of the study is that present theoretical perspectives offer little insight into the international practices of SMEs. This thesis should be seen more as an interim report in an ongoing study of SME practices. The concepts and models presented in the present framework represent no more than a first step in identifying the way in which the business logic of SMEs are developed and how they reflect the systemic nature of their context. Subsequent investigations are needed, and hopefully these can build on the present findings or replace them with other, more adequate understandings of the organizing processes studied.

Some areas of the theoretical framework have only been vaguely discussed. One of these is the role of national business systems in the organization of international activity, which clearly needs more clarification. It has been suggested that national business systems only play a minor role in the organization of professions. Several of the cases showed that professions cross regional as well as national boundaries. Notwithstanding, there are clearly areas in which national business systems do play a significant role, and these need further investigation. One such area may be the role of the Danish financial system vis-à-vis other financial systems in supporting the international activities of SMEs. This requires a more comparative analytical framework, however. Another "avenue" which needs further investigation consists of the processes through which changes in one context affect relationships in others. This also calls for a different methodological approach than the one used in the present study. Processes are best studied by means of a longitudinal research design.

The study also reveals a gap between the administrative concepts of present management theory and the practices of SME managers. Normative theory building, which takes a departure in the realities of SMEs, addressing their problems in relation to the development of international affairs, is clearly needed here.

Finally, the implications of this study for industrial policy have yet to be spelled out. Although the efforts and hopes of politicians and commentators have mainly been concentrated on the possibilities of large firms, there does seem to be a change towards a more nuanced industrial policy, in recognition of the fact that small firms can be just as important for economic growth as large firms.

There is obviously a need for more investigation and development in this area. Hopefully, this study has drawn attention to this need and stimulated, if not provoked, others to study SMEs and their organization of international activities.

References

Aharoni, Y. (1966):"The Foreign Investment Decision Process", Boston, Mass., Harvard University Press

Alchain, A. A. & H. Demsetz (1972):"Production, Information Costs and Economic Organization", American Economic Review 62, pp. 777-795

Aldrich, H. & D. A. Whetten (1981):"Organization-Sets, Action-Sets and Networks: making most out of Simplicity" in P. C. Nyström & W. H. Starbuck (eds.):"Handbook of organizational Design", Oxford University Press

Alvessson, M. & H. Wilmott (1989):"Critical Theory and The Sciences of management", Working paper R:4, University of Stockholm

Andersen, I, F. Borum, P.H. Kristensen & P. Karnøe (1992):"Om kunsten at bedrive Feltstudier - En erfaringsbaseret forskningsmetodik", Samfundslitteratur

Andersen, P. (1994):"Managing market Resources", Working paper, The Århus School of Business

Andersen, P. & J. Dahl (1991):"Internationalisering af Erhvervslivet i Dronninglund Kommune", Gruppen for International Erhvervsøkonomi, Aalborg Universitetscenter

Andersen, P. & P. R. Christensen (1993): "Managing Internationalization in Loosely Coupled Businesss System", Working Paper presented at the EIBA-Conference, Lisboa

Andersen, P. & P. R. Christensen (1994): "Internationalization of Loosely Coupled Business Systems - The Danish Case", Forthcoming in P.H. Kristensen (ed.): "Strategies and patterns of Change in the Danish Business System"

Andersen, P., H. Anderson, A. Halinen & V. Havila (1994): "Tackling the Dynamics of Business Networks", presented at the 11. IMP workshop, Groningen, The Netherlands

Andersen, H. (ed) (1990):"Videnskabsteori og Metodelære", Samfundslitteratur

Andersen, I. (ed) (1990): "Valg af organisations-sociologiske metoder - et kombinationsperspektiv", Samfundslitteratur

Anderson, E. & Gatignon (1986):"Modes of Foreign Entry: A Transaction Cost Aanalysis and Propositions", Journal of International Business Studies, 17(3), Fall, pp 1-26

Andersson, S.(1981): "Positivism kontra Hermenutik", Uddevalla, Korpen

Ansoff, I. (1966):"Corporate Strategy: An Aanalytical Approach to Business Policy for Growth and Expansion", MC-Graw Hill

Arbnor, I. & Bjerke B.(1977): "Företagsekonomisk Metodlära", Studentlitteratur, Lund

Argyris, C., R. Putnam & D. M. Smith (1987):"Action Science", Jossey-Bass

Argyris, C. & D. Schön (1978):"Organizational Learning: A Theory of Action Perspective", Addison Wesley

Arrow, K. J. (1974):"The Limits of organization", Norton & Company, New York

Astley W. G. & A.H. Van de Ven. (1983): "Central Perspectives and Debates in Organization Theory", Administrative Science Quarterly , pp 245-273

Astley, W. G. (1984):"Toward an Appreciation of Collective Strategy", Academy of Management Review, Vol. 9, No. 3, pp. 526-535

Bain, J.S. (1959):"Industrial Organization", New York, Wiley

Bartlett, C. A & S. Ghosal (1989):"Managing Across Borders: The Transnational Solution", Cambridge, Mass., Harvard University Press

Benson, K. (1975):"The interorganizational network as a political economy", Administrative Science Quarterly 20, pp 229-249

Benson, K. (1977) "Organizations: A Dialectical View", Administrative Science Quarterly 22, pp. 1- 21

Berger, P. & T. Luckman (1967):"The social Construction of Reality", New York Doubleday

Blankenburg, D. & J. Johanson (1992): "Managing Network Connections in International Business", Scandinavian International Business Review, Vol. 1, No. 1, pp 5-19

Blau, P. M. (1964):"Exchange and Power in Social Life", Wiley & Sons

Blaug, M. (1980):"The Methodology of Economics", Cambridge University Press

Bogdan, R. & S. J. Taylor (1975): "Introduction to qualitative research methods", John Wiley

Bohn, K.R., J. Carlsen, M. Fast & O. J. Sørensen (1989):"Virksomhedens Internationalisering - En undersøgelse af 20 Virksomheder i Hadsund Kommune", Gruppen for International Erhvervsøkonomi, Aalborg Universitet

Bohn, K.R. & O. J. Sørensen (1990):"Internationalisering af Erhvervslivet i Pandrup Kommune",Gruppen for International Erhvervsøkonomi, Aalborg Universitet

Bonaccorsi, A.(1992):"On the relationship between firm Size and Export Intensity", Journal of International Business Studies, Forth Quarter, pp. 605-635

Bradley, F. (1991):"International Marketing Strategy", Prentice-Hall International

Brunsson, N. (1981): "Företagsekonomi - Avbilding eller språkbilding", Nils Brunsson (ed): "Företagsekonomi - Sanning eller Moral", Studentlitteratur Lund

Brusco, S. (1982): "The Emilian Model: Productive decentralization and social Integration", Cambridge Journal of Economics 6, pp. 167-184

Bruzelius, L. H. & P-H Skärvad (1983):"Integrerad organisationslära", Studentlitteratur

Brytting, T. (1991):"Organizing in The Small Growing Firm - A Grounded Theory Approach", Doctor Dissertation, Stockholm School of Economics

Buckley, P.J. & M. Casson (1976):"The future Multinational Enterprise", Holmes & Meier, London

Burns, T. & G. M. Stalker (1961):"The Management of Innovation", London, Tavistock

Burrell, G. & G. Morgan (1979): "Sociological Paradigms and Organizational Analysis", Heinemann

Burt, R.S. (1993):"The Social Structure of Competition" in Nohria, N. & R. G. Eccles (eds.):"Networks and Organizations", Harvard Business School Press

Cavusgil, T.S. (1981):"On the Internationalization process of Firms", European Research, Vol 8., pp. 273-281

Cavusgil, T. S. (1984):"Differences among Exporting firms based on their Degree of Internationa-lization", Journal of Business Research, (12)

Chandler, A. D. Jr. (1962):"Strategy and Structure - Chapters in the History of the American Enterprise", The MIT Press

Chandler, A. D. Jr. (1977):"The Visible Hand The Managerial Revolution in America" , Belknap Press, Harvard

Child, J. (1972): "Organizational Structure, Environment and Performance: The role of Strategic Choice", Sociology (6), pp 1-22

Christensen, S. & K. Kreiner (1991):"Projektledelse i løst koblede systemer", Jurist og Økonomforbundets Forlag

Christensen , P. R. (1987):"Industriel Fleksibilitet og lokalisering i et netværksperspektiv", NordREFO, 1987:4, pp. 51-69

Christensen, P. R. (1988):"Østjyllands Eksport - En undersøgelse af servicesektorernes betydning for eksporterhvervene", The Århus School of Business, Dept. of International Business

Christensen, P.R. & L. Lindmark (1991):"In search of Regional Support in Internationalization of Small and Medium-Sized Firms - Anetwork Perspective" Working Paper, presented at the 38th. North American Meeting of the Regional Science Association in New Orleans, Lousiana, november, 7-10 1991

Christensen, P. R., J. Andersson & P. Blenker (1992):"Industriens brug af Underleverandører", Industri & Handelsstyrelsen

Christensen, P. R. & J. Strandskov (1993): "Konkurrence og samarbejdsstrategier i samspil", in S. Hildebrandt (ed.):"Strategi og ledelse - veje og visioner mod år 2000", Systime

Christensen, P.R. (1992):"Ledelse af Virksomhedens Samarbejdsrelationer i et internationalt Perspektiv", in J.P. Ulhøi (ed.): "Virksomhedsledelse i International Belysning"

Coase, R. H.(1937):"The Nature of the Firm", Economica, Vol 4., pp. 386-405

Cohen, M. D., J. C. March & J. P. Olsen: (1972) "A Garbage Can Model of Organizational Choice", Administrative Science Quarterly 17, no. 1. pp 1-25

Cook K. S. & R. M. Emerson (1978):"Power, Equity and Commitment in Exchange Networks", American Sociological Review 43, pp. 721-739

Cook, K. S. & R. M. Emerson (1984):"Exchange Networks and the Analysis of Complex Organizations", Research in Sociology of Organizations (3), pp. 1-30

Cray, D. (1984):"Control and coordination in multinational companies", Journal of International Business Studies, Fall, pp 85-98

Cundiff, E.W. & M. T. Hilger (1988):"Marketing in the International Environment", Prentice-Hall International

Cyert, R. & J. G. March (1963):"A Behavioral Theory of The Firm", Prentice-Hall

Czinkota, M. R. & W. L. Johnston (1983):"Exporting: Does Sales Volume make a Difference ?",

Journal of International Business Studies, Spring/Summer 1983, pp. 147-153

Dahmén, E. (1950):"Entreprenurial activity and the development of Swedish Industry 1919-1939" American Economic Association Translation Series, Homewood

Dandridge, T.C. (1979):"Children are not "Little Grown-Ups" - Small Business Needs its own Organizational Theory", Journal of Small Business Management, April, pp. 53-57

Danmarks Statistik (1992):"Input-Outputtabeller 1989", Danmarks Statistik

Demsetz, H. (1992): "The Emerging Theory of The firm", Acta Universitatis Upsaliensis, Studia Oeconomiae Negotiorum (33)

DiMaggio, O. J. & W. W. Powell (1983):"The Iron Cage Revisited: Institutional Isomorphism and collective rationality in organizational fields", American Sociology Review (35), pp. 147-160

Dimaggio, W. W. & P. J. Powell (eds.) (1991):"The New Institutionalism in organizational analysis", University of Chicago Press

Dogdson, M. (1993):"Technological Collaboration in Industry: Strategy, Policy & Internationalization un innovation", Roultedge, London

Dosi, G. (1982):"Technological paradigms and technological trajectories", Research Policy (11), pp. 147-162

Dosi, G. & L. Marengo (1993):"Some elements of an Evolutionary Theory of Organizational Competences", CCC Working Paper, Berkely Unversity

Douglas, S. P. & C. S. Craig (1989):"Evolution of Global marketing Strategy: Scale, Scope and Synergy", Columbia Journal of World Business, Fall, pp. 47-59

DRI (1993):"Impacts of Trade Liberalisation under the Urguay round", McGraw-Hill

DTI (Danish Technological Institute) (1991):"Eksportundersøgelsen 1991"

Due, J. & J. S. Madsen (1983):"Slip Sociologien Løs - En invitation til 80'ernes Sociologi",

København

Dunning, J.H. (1988):"Explaining International Production", London

Dunning, J.H. (1991):"Dunning on Porter: Reshaping the Diamond of Competitive Advantage", WP 6-91, Business and Economic Studies on European Integration, Copenhagen

Dwyer, F. R., P. H. Schurr & S. Oh (1987):"Developing Buyer-Seller Relationships", Journal of Marketing, (51), pp. 11-27

Easton, G.(1992):"Industrial Networks - A Review", B. Axelsson & G. Easton (eds): "Industrial Networks - A new View of Reality"

Easton, G. & L. Araujo (1992): "Industrial Networks Theory - A literary Critique" Paper presented at the 8th IMP Conference, Lyon 1992

Ekman, R. (1979): "Filosofins Grunder", Esselte Studium

Enderud, H. (1979):"Beslutninger i Organisationer i beslutningsteoretisk Perspektiv", Fremad

Erhvervsredegørelsen (1993)

Erhvervsredegørelsen (1994)

Eriksson, A-K (1993):"Value Creation in Business Relationship - or do relationship benefits exist ?", Working Paper, Uppsala University

Etzioni, A. (1965):"Organizational Control Structure", in James G. March (ed) "Handbook of Organizations", Chicago

Eurostat (1990):"Industrial Stastistics"

Fast, M. (1992): "Subjektivitet og Intersubjektivitet - En udvikling af en hermenutisk forståelse af virksomheders internationalisering som alternativ til mainstream teori", AUC, Denmark

Fast, M. (1993): "Internationalization as a Social Construction", Working Paper, Presented at the

10. IMP conference, Bath (UK)

Finansministeriet (1992):"Finansredegørelse 92", Finansministeriets Publikationscentral

Flyvbjerg, B.(1992):"Magt og Rationalitet", Doctoral Dissertation, Aalborg University

Ford, D. (1982):"The development of Buyer-seller-Relationships in Industrial Markets", in H. Håkansson (ed.): "International Marketing and Purchasing of Industrial Goods"

Ford, R.C., B. R. Armandi & P.H. Charill (1988):"Organization Theory - An Integrative Approach", Harper & Row

Forsgren, M. (1989):"Managing The Internationalization process - The Swedish Case", Routledge (London)

Forsgren, M. & J. Johanson (1992):"Managing Internationalization in Business Networks" in M. Forsgren & J. Johanson (eds.):"Managing Networks in International Business"

Frank, R. , T. Gilovich & D. Regan (1993):"Does Studying Economics Inhibit Co-operation ?", Journal of Economic Perspective, Spring 1993

Freytag, P. & L. Nørreklit (1993):"The Dialouge", Working paper, Presented at the 10. IMP Conference, Bath

Furusten, S. (1992):"Management Books - Guardians of the myth of leadership", Licentiate Thesis, Uppsala University, Dept. of Business Studies

Gailbraith, J.(1977):"Organization Design", Addison-Wesley

Giddens, A. (1984):"The Constitution of Society", Cambridge Polity Press

Glaser, B.G. (1978):"Theoretical Sensisivity: Advances in the Methodology of Grounded Theory", Mill Valley, CA:Sociology Press

Glaser, B.G. & A. L. Strauss (1967): "The Discovery of Grounded Theory ", Aldine de Gruyter

Glaser, B. G. (1978): "Theoretical Sensitivity", The Sociological Press

Glassmann, R.B. (1973):"Persistence and Loose Coupling in Living Systems", Behavioral Science (18) pp. 83-98

Goffman, E. (1959): "The presentation of Self in Everyday Life", Garden City, Doubleday

Gouldner, A. W. (1960):"The Norm of Reciprocity: A Preliminary Statement", American Sociological Review, (25), 2, pp. 161-178

Grabher G. (1993):"Rediscovering the social in the economics of interfirm relations" in G. Grabher (ed.): "The Embedded Firm", Routledge (London)

Granovetter, M. (1973):"The Strenght of Weak Ties - A network Theory Revisited", American Journal of Sociology, Vol 78, no. 3, pp. 3-30

Granovetter, M. (1985):"Economic Actions and Social Structure: A problem of Embeddedness", American Journal of Sociology, November

Greiner, L. E.(1972):"Evolution and Revolution as Organizations Grow", Harvard Business Review, 50, July/August, pp. 37-46

Grøn, J.H. (1985):"Arbejde-Virksomheder-Regioner" Sydjydsk Universitesforlag

Gummesson, E. (1988):"Qualitative Methods in Management research: Case Study Research, Paricipant Observation, Action Research/Action Science and other qualitative Methods used in academic Research and Management Consultancy", Studentlitteratur

Hall, D. J. & M. A. Saias (1980):"Strategy Follows Structure!", Strategic Management Journal, Vol. 1, pp 149-163

Hallén, L. & M. Sandström (1991):"Relationship Atmosphere in International Business", Uppsala University Reprint Series, 1991/6

Hamel, G. (1990):"Competition for Competence and Interpartner Learning within International Strategic Alliances", Strategic Management Journal, vol. 12, pp. 83-103

Hannan, M. T. & J. Freeman (1977):"The population ecology of organizations", American Journal of Sociology 82, pp 929-964

Hansen, K.M. (1990):"Direkte udenlandske investeringer og multinationale selskaber - Transaktionsomkostninger og internationaliseringsprocesser" in Forskningsgruppen Nyere Virksomhedsteori:"Organisering af Økonomiske Aktiviteter", Handelshøjskolens Forlag

Hansen, P.E. & C. Lunding (1993):"Dansk Erhvervsliv", Handelshøjskolens Forlag

Havila, V. (1992):"The Role of the Intermediary in International Business Relationships", Uppsala University, Licentiate Thesis, no. 23

Hawkins, R.(1984):"International Business in Academia: The State of the Field", Journal of International Business Studies, 15 (3), Winter, pp. 13-18

Hayek, A. (1945):"The use of knowledge in Society", American Economic Review, Vol 35, pp. 519-530

Hedaa, L. (1991):"On interorganizational relationships in industrial Marketing", Ph. D. Thesis, Samfundslitteratur

Hedberg, B. (1981): "How Organizations learn and unlearn", In N. Nyström et al.: "Handbook of Organizational Design", Oxford

Hellgren, B.,L. Melin & A. Petterson (1992):"Structure and Change - A contextual Approach", Unpublished Working Paper

Henders, B. (1992):"Positions in Industrial Networks. Marketing Newsprint in The UK", Ph. D. Thesis, Uppsala University

Hennart, J-F (1986): "What is Internalization ?", Weltwirtschaftliches Archiv, Band 122 (heft 4)

Henriksen, L. B. (1992): "Virksomheder i Netværk", Ph.D. Dissertation, AUC

Hippel, E. V. (1990): "Task partitioning: An innovation process variable",Research Policy (19),pp. 407-418

Hofheinz, P. (1993):"Europe's tough new managers", Fortune, September 6.

Hofsteede, G. (1981): Culture's Consequences", Sage Publications

Hollesen, S. (1991):"Virksomhedens skift af afsætningskanaler", Ph.D. Dissertation, The Southern Denmark Business School

Holm, U. , M. Forsgren & J. Johanson (1992):" Internationalization of the second Degree: The emergence of European-Based Centres in Swedish Firms", Reprint Series 1992/28, Uppsala University, Department of Business Studies

Hymer, S.H. (1976):"The International Operation of National Firms: A Study of Foreign Direct Investment", Mit Press, Cambridge, Mass

Håkansson, H.(1982) :"International Marketing and Purchasing of Industrial Goods: An Interaction Approach", Wiley

Håkansson, H. (1992): "Networks as a Mechanism to develop Resources", Working Paper, Uppsala Universitet

Håkansson, H. & B. Axelsson (1989):"Inköp För Konkurrenskraft", Liber

Håkansson, H. & J. Johanson (1988):"Heterogeneity in Industrial Markets and its implications for Marketing" in I. Hägg & F. Wiedersheim-Paul:"Between market and Hierarchy", Uppsala University, Dept. of Business Studies

Håkansson, H. & J. Johanson (1993): "Network as a governance structure" in Grabher, G. (ed): "The embedded Firm", Routledge

Håkansson, H. & I. Snehota (1989): "No Business is an Island: The Network concept of Business Strategy", Scandinavian Journmal of Management, (5), no. 3, pp. 187-200

Håkansson, H. & I. Snehota (1994):"Developing Relationships in Business Networks", Working Paper

Imai, K. I. (1987):"Mobilizing Invisible Assets", Cambridge University Press

272

Imai, K. & Y. Baba (1989):"Systemic Innovation and Cross-Border networks" Working Paper. Presented at the OECD International Seminar on Science, Technology and Economic Growth, 3rd of May 1989

Imai, K. I. & H. Itami (1984): "Interpenetration of Organization and Market", International Journal of industrial Organization 2, 285-310

Industri- & Handelsstyrelsen (1992): "Nye virksomheder og iværksættere i tal 1985-1989." Notatserien, København.

Israel, J. (1973):"Sociologisk Grundbog", Gyldendal, Copenhagen

Iyer, V. (1992):"Managing and Motivating your Agents and Distributors", FT Pitman, London

Jarillo, C. J.(1988):"On Strategic Networks", Strategic Management Journal, No 9,p 31-41

Jensen, T. K. (1991) "Statskundskab som viden for praksis", GRUS 33, AUC

Jick, T. D. (1979):"Mixing qualitative and Quantitative Methods: Triangulation in Action" Administrative Science Quarterly, 24, pp. 602-612

Johannisson, B. (1988):"Business Formation: A Network Approach", Scandinavian Journal of Management, vol 4, no 3/4, pp. 83-99

Johannisson, B. (1990):"Toward a Multidimensional Model of Entrepreneurship: The Case of Achievement Motivation and the Entrepreneur", Entrepreneurship, Theory and Practice, Spring

Johanson, J. & L. Hallén (1989):"Networks of Relationships in International Industrial Marketing" in S. T. Cavusgil (ed.):"Advances in International Marketing", (3),

Johanson, J. & L.-G. Mattson (1986):"Internationalization in Industrial Systems - A Network Approach", Reprint Series, Uppsala University

Johanson J. & J-E Vahlne (1990): "The Mechanism of Internationalization", International Marketing Review, 7(4), pp. 11-24

Johanson, J. & J-E Vahlne: (1977) "The Internationalization Process of the Firm: A Model of Knowledge Development and Increasing Foreign Market Commitment", Journal of International Business Studies, Spring/Summer, pp. 23-32

Johnson, B.(1993):"Institutional Learning" in B-Å Lundvall (ed): "National Systems of Innovation", Pinter Publishers, London

Kallinikos J. (1986):"Networks as webs of signification", Working Paper, Uppsala University

Kamm, J.B. & A. J. Nurick (1993):"The Stages of Team Venture Formation: A Decision -making Model", Entrepreneurship - Theory & Practice, Winter, pp. 17-27

Karnøe, P. (1993):"An analysis of Danish and American Models of innovation", Working paper

Karnøe. P. (1990): "The Danish Wind Turbine Industry: A New Industrial Complex. Paper presented at the workshop:"Ways out the restructuring Race: Problems, experiences and Strategies for Small, Open Countries". Institute for Advanced Studies, Wienna.

Karnøe. P. (1991): "Dansk vindmølleindustri - en overraskende international succes: Innovation, teknologipolitik og industriudvikling." Samfundslitteratur, København

Katz, D. & R. L. Kahn (1966): "The Social Psychology of Organizations", New York

Keegan, W. J. (1985):"Global Marketing Management", Prentice-Hall International

Kinch, N. (1991):"Management - tro och vetande", Tro & Tanke, Svenska Kyrkans Forskningsråd

Kirzner, I. M. (1973):"Competition and Entrepreneurship", The University of Chicago Press

Klein, S., G. L. Frazier & V. J. Roth (1990):"A Transaction Cost Analysis Model of Channel Integration in International Markets", Journal of marketing research (27), pp. 196-208

Knight, F.H. (1921):"Risk, Uncertainty and Profit", Houghton & Mifflin

Knudsen, C.(1984): "Metodologi contra Forskningspraksis", Rapport HA-Center, Copenhagen Business School

Koch, C. A. (1993):"Den Erhvervsøkonomiske Teori er ikke død", Ledelse og Erhvervsøkonomi, 1/93

Kotler, P. (1984):"Marketing Management", Prentice Hall International

Kristensen, P. H. (1986):"Teknologiske Projekter og Organisatoriske Processer", Samfundsøko-nomi og Planlægning, Roskilde University

Kristensen, P. H. (1992):"Industrial Districts in West Jutland, Denmark", in F. Pyke & W. Sengenberger (eds): "Industrial Districts and local Economic Regeneration", Routledge

Kristensen, P. H. (1992): "When labour defines Business Recipes", Working paper, HHK

Kristensen, P. H. (1994):"On the constitution of economic actors in Denmark: Interacting Skill Containers and Project-Coorinators, Working Paper, presented at the EMOT Group 1 workshop, Humboldt University (Berlin)

Kuhn, T.S. (1970): "The structure of Scientific Revolutions", University of Chicago Press

Kvale, S. (1990):"To validate is to question", in S. Kvale (ed.): "Issues of validity in Qualitative Research", Studentlitteratur

Larsson, A. & J.A. Starr (1993):"A Network Model of Organization Formation", Entrepreneurs-hip - Theory & Practice, Winter, pp. 5-15

Lawrence, P. & J. Lorsch (1967):"Organization and Environment", Cambridge Mass

Levitt, B. & J. G. March (1988): "Organizational Learning", Annual review of Sociology, 14: pp 319-340

Levitt, T. (1983): "Globalization of markets", Harvard Business Review, May-June

Lindblom, C. E. (1959):"The science of 'Muddling Through' ", Public Administration Review, Vol. 19, Nr. 2, pp 238-255

Lorenzoni, G. & J.P. Ornati (1988):"Constellations of Firms and New Ventures", Journal of

Business Venturing, Vol 3, no. 1, pp. 41-57

Luhmann, N. (1982):"Autopoiesis - Handlung und Kommunikative Verständigung" Zeitschrift für Soziologie, vol.11, no 4, pp. 366-379

Lundvall, B-Å (1988):"Innovation as an interactive process: From user-producer interaction, to national systems of innovation" in G. Dosi, C. Freeman, R. Nelson, G. Silverberg & L. Scott: "Technical Change and Economic Theory", Pinter Publishers, London

Lundvall, B-Å (1993):"Explaining interfirm cooperation and innovation - limits of the Transaction Cost Approach" in G. Grabher:"The Embedded Firm", Routledge

Lundvall, B-Å, N. M. Olesen & I. Aaen (1984):"Det Landbrugsindustrielle Kompleks", Serie om Industriel Udvikling, Nr. 28, Forskningsrapport, Aalborg Universitetsforlag

Lyman, P.(1984):"Reading, Writing and Word Processing: Toward a Phenomenology of the computer age", Qualitative Sociology, 7 (1/2), pp: 75-89

March, J. G. (1989):"Decisions and Organizations", Blackwell, Oxford

March, J. (1978):"Bounded Rationality, Ambiguity and The Engineering of Choice", Bell Journal of Economics, Vol. 9, nr. 2

March, J. & H. Simon (1993):"Organizations" (orig. 1958), Blackwell

Marshall, A. (1919): "Industry and Trade", Oxford University

Maskell, P. (1992) :"Nyetableringer i Industrien", Handelshøjskolens Forlag

Maslow, A.(1954):"Motivation & Personality", New York, Harper

Mattson, L.-G. (1985):"An Application of a Network Approach to Marketing - Defending and Changing Market Positions" in N. Dholakia & J. Arndt (Eds.):"Changing the Course of marketing: Alternative Paradigms for Widening marketing Theory", Research in Marketing, JAI Press

Mattson, L.-G. & J. Johanson (1992):"Network Positions and Strategic Action - An analytical Framework", in B. Axelsson & G. Easton (eds): "Industrial Networks: A new view of Reality", Routledge

Mayhew , J.(1983):"Culture: Core Concepts under attack", Journal of Economic Issues, Vol. XXI, no. 2

Metcalfe, L. (1981):"Designing Precarious Partnerships "in P. C. Nyström & W. H. Starbuck (eds.):"Handbook of organizational Design", Oxford University Press

Meyer, J. M. & B. Rowan (1977):"Institutionalized Organizations: Formal Structure as Myth and Ceremony", The American Journal of Sociology, Vol. 83, No 2, pp. 340-363

Mietela, A. & J. Å. Törnross (1993):"The Meaning of Time in the study of Industrial Buyer-Seller Relationships", Working Paper, Publications of the Turku School of Economics and Business Administration, 4

Miles, M.B. (1979): "Qualitative Research as an attractive Nusiance", Administrative Science Quarterly, December, vol 24, 590-601

Miles, M. B. & A. M. Huberman (1984): "Qualitative Data Analysis - A sourcebook of new Methods", Sage Publications

Mills, C. W. (1959:1970): "The Sociological Imagination", Penguin Books

Mintzberg, H.(1987): "The Strategy Concept I: Five Ps for Strategy", in Glenn R. Carroll & David Vogel (eds): "Organizational Approaches to Strategy", Cambridge MA

Mintzberg, H. (1979):"The Structure of Organizations", Prentice-Hall International

Mittroff, I. I. & R. H. Killman (1978):"Methodological Approaches to Social Science", Jossey-Bass

Morgan, G. (1993) :"Imaginization", Sage Publications

Morgan, G. (ed.) (1983):"Beyond Method: Strategies for Social Research", Sage

Morgan, G. (1980): "Paradigms Metaphors and Puzzle-Solving in Organization Theory", Administrative Science Quarterly, pp 606-622

Morgan, G. (1986):"Images of Organization", SAGE publications

Morgan, G. & L. Smircich (1980):"The case for Qualitative Research", Academy of management Review, vol 5, (4), pp. 491-500

Møller, K. & H. Pade (eds.) (1988):"Industriel Succes - Konkurrencefaktorer i 9 danske Brancher", Samfundslitteratur

Mønsted, M. (1985):"Små Virksomheder i Rådgivningssystemet", Nyt fra Samfundsvidenskaberne

Nelson, R. (1991):"Why do Firms differ and how does it Matter", Strategic Management Journal (12), pp. 61-74

Nelson, R. & S. G. Winter (1982): "An Evolutionary Theory of Economic Change", Belknap Press

Nielsen, K. (1991):"Industrielle Netværk", PhD. Thesis, Århus University, Dept. of Management

Niss, H. (1992):"Made in Denmark: Nationalitetens betydning i international markedsføring", Aalborg Universitet

North, D. C. (1988):"Final Remarks: Institutional Change and Economic History", Journal of Institutional and Theoretical Economics 145, pp. 238-245

Norus, J. U.(1993):"Bioteknologi i små og mellemstore virksomheder", PhD. Dissertation, Copenhagen Business School

Nørreklit, L. (1993):"Resources and the Firm: An introduction", Working Paper, AUC

Nørreklit, L., S.L. Pedersen, B. Prangsgaard, K. Tuft. (1987): "Aktørsmetoden - En indføring i Erhvervsøkonomisk Projektarbejde", Aalborg Universitetsforlag

Nørreklit, H. (1991): "Virksomhedens problemerkendelse", DJØF Forlag

OECD (1992):"OECD Economic Survey 1991-1992 Series: Denmark", OECD Publications, Paris

OECD (1993):"Globalization of Economic Activities and Small and Medium-sized Enterprises (SME) Development", Department of International Business, The Aarhus School of Business

Ohmae, K.(1987):"Triad Power", Free Press

Ouchi (1982): "Theory Z", Addison Westley, Mass.

Pasinetti, L. (1981):"Structural Change and Economic Growth", Cambridge Univ. Press

Penrose, E. (1959):"The Theory of the Growth of the Firm", New York

Perrow, C. (1986):"Complex organizations - A critical Essay", McGraw-Hill 3. ed.

Perrow, C. (1992):"Small Firm Networks", in Nohria, N. & R. G. Eccles (eds.):"Networks and Organizations", Havard Business School Press

Peters, T. & R. H. Waterman (1982):"In Search of Excellence", Harper & Row

Petersen, B. (1994):"Engaging Suppliers in transaction-specific activity: Empirical evidence of exporting firms", HEC Research Paper

Petersen, B. & T. Pedersen (1992):"Research on the Entry Mode Choice of the firm: How close to a Normative Theory", Working Paper, 20-92, Busines and Economic Studies on European Integration

Pettigrew, A. M. (1990):"Longditudinal Field Research on Change: Theory and Practice", Organization Science (1), 3, pp.

Pfeffer, J. & G. Salancik (1978):"The external control of Organizations - A Resource Dependence perspective", Harper & Row

Piore, M. J. & C. F. Sabel (1984):"The Second Industrial Divide: Possibilites for Prosperity", Basic Books, New York

Popper, K. R.(1965):"The Logic of Scientific Discovery", Harper Torchbooks, New York

Porter, M. E. (1980):"Competitive Strategy: Techniques for Analysing Industries and Competitors", Free Press

Porter, M.E. (1983): "Cases in Competitive Strategy", Free Press

Porter, M. E. (1990):"Competitive Advantage and Nations", Harvard Business Review, (68), April-May pp. 73-93

Porter, M. E. (1985):"Competitive Advantage", Free Press

Porter, M. E. (1990):"The competitive advantage of Nations", Free Press

Putnam, K. Roberts & L. Porter (eds.) (1987): "Handbook of Organizational Communication", Sage Publications

Quelch J., R. Buzzell & E. R. Salama (1990):"The Marketing Challenge of Europe 1992", Addison Wesley, (Reading Mass.)

Rasmussen, E. (1988):"Har en Danmark en fremtid som Industrination ?", Internal Report

Rasmussen, E. (1991):"Den Mindre Industris vækstmuligheder i 90'erne",Mandag Morgen

Rasmussen, E. (1993): "Hvad skal Danmark Leve af ?", Mandag Morgen

Rasmussen, P. N. (1991):"Erhvervslokomotiver og samfundsøkonomisk organisering", Økonomi og Politik, no. 4

Reve, T. (1988): "Toward a Theory of Strategic management", Working paper, Bergen School of Management

Ried, S. (1983):"Firm Internationalization, Transaction Costs and Strategic Choice", International Marketing Review, Winter 1983, pp. 44-56

Reid, S. (1984): "Information acquisition and Export Entry Decision in Small Firms", Journal of

Business Research, (12), pp. 141-157

Root, F. R (1987): "Entry Strategies for International Markets", Lexington Books

Rorty, R. (1979) in S. Kvale:"Issues of valdity in Qualitative research" (1990), Studentlitteratur

Rothwell, R. & W. Zegweld (1985): "Reindustrialization and Technology", Harlow UK

Rugman, A. M., D. J. LeCraw & L. D. Booth (1981):"International Business: Firm and Environment", McGraw-Hill International

Sabel, C. F. (1990):"Studied Trust: Building new forms of Cooperation in a Volatile Economy", Unpublished Working Paper

Sabel, C. F. (1991):"Moebius-Strip Organizations and Open Labour markets: Some consequences of the Reintegration of Conception and Execution in a Volatile Economy", in J. Coleman & P. Bourdieu (eds):"Social Theory for a Changing Society", Boulder:CO, Westview Press

Schutz, A. (1970): "Concept and Theory Formation in The social Sciences", in Emmet & McIntyre: Sociological Theory and philosophical Analysis, Macmillan

Scott, R. W. (1992): "Organizations - Rational, Natural and Open Systems", Third ed., Prentice-Hall International

Scott, R. W. (1987):"Adolescence of Institutional Theory", Administrative Science Quarterly (32), pp. 493-511

Scott. R.W. (1983):"The Organization of Environments: Network, Cultural and Historical Environments" in J.W. Meyer & R.W. Scott (eds.):"Organizational Environments: Ritual and Rationality", SAGE Publications

Sengenberger, W., G. Loveman & M. Piore (1990):"The reemergence of Small Enterprise: Industrial Restructuring in Industrialized Economies", Geneva: International Labour Organization

Sieber, S.D. (1976):"A synopsis and critique of guidlines for qualitative analysis contained in selected textbooks", New York: Center for Project on Social Architecture in Education, Center for Policy Research

Silverman, D. (1971): "The Theory of Organizations", Basic Books

Simon, H. (1973):"Applying Information Technology to Organization Design", Public Administration Review (33) pp. 268-278

Simon, H. (1948):"Administrative Behavior", Prentice-Hall International

Singleman, P. (1972):"Exchange as Symbolic Interaction: convergence between two Theoretical perspectives", American Sociological Review, (37), pp. 414-424

Skinner, B.F. (1953):"Science and Human Behaviour", New York Macmillan

Slipsager, F. (1969):"Virksomhedens Internationale Afsætningskanaler", Nyt Nordisk Forlag, Arnold Busch

Smircich, L. & G. Morgan (1982): "Leadership: The Management of Meaning", Journal of Applied Behavioral Studies, 257-273

Smircich, L. (1983): "Concepts of Culture and Organizational Analysis", Administrative Science Quarterly, (28), pp. 339-358

Smith, A.:(1973 (org. 1776)):"The Wealth of Nations", Doubleday, New York

Smith, P.C. & J. Laage-Hellman (1992):"Small Group analysis in industrial networks", in B. Axelsson and G. Easton: "Industrial Networks: A new View of Reality", Routledge

Snehota, I. (1993):"Market as Network and the Nature of the Market Process", Advances in International Marketing, Vol. 5, pp. 31-41

Snehota, I: (1990):"Notes on a Theory of The Business Enterprise", Doctoral Dissertation, Uppsala University

Snehota, I & H. Håkansson (1989):"No Business is an Island", Scandinavian Journal of Management, (5), 3, 187-200

Strandskov, J. (1987):"Virksomheders Internationalisering", Nyt Nordisk Forlag Arnold Busch

Strandskov, J. (1993):"Studier i danske virksomheders internationaliseringsprocesser I-III", Doctoral Dissertation, The Århus School of Business

Strandskov, J., K. M. Hansen (1988): "Eksporten under Omvurdering - en erhvervsøkonomisk analyse af dansk erhvervslivs internationalisering", Danmarks Sparekasseforening

Strauss A. & R. Corbrin (1990):"Basics of Qualitative Research: Grounded Theory procedures and Techniques", Sage Publications

Stymne, B. (1989):"Information Technology and Competence formation in the Swedish Service Sector: An analysis of Retail Strategy and Development of the Finance Sector", The Economic Research Institute, Stockholm School of Economics

Swedberg, R. & M. Granovetter (1992):"The sociology of Economic Life", Westview Press

Sydow, J. (1992): "On the Management of Strategic Networks", H. Ernste & V.Meier (eds): "Regional development and contemporary industrial response: Extending flexible specialization", Belhaven Press

Sydow, J. (1991):"Changing Managerial Roles in Strategic Networks", Paper Presented at the 7th. IMP conference in Uppsala.

Teece, D. J. (1986):"Transaction Cost Economics and the Multinational Enterprise", Journal of Economic Behaviour and Organization (7), pp. 21-45

The Oxford Concise Dictionary (1990), Oxford

Thompson, J. D.: (1967):"Organizations in Action", McGraw-Hill

Thorelli, H. B. (1986):"Networks: Between Markets and Hierarchies", Strategic Management Journal Vol. 7, pp 37-51

Toffler, A. (1980): "The Third Wave", Morrow

Toyne, B.(1989):"International Exchange: A Foundation for Theory Building in International Business", Journal of International Business Studies (20), 1, pp. 177-186

Turner, B. A. (1981):"Some practical aspects of qualitative data Analysis: One way of organizing the cognitive Processes associated with the generation of Grounded Theory", Quality and Quantity, 15 pp. 225-247

Van de Ven, A. (1985):"Central Problems in the Management of Innovation", Management Science, may, vol 32, No. 5

Veblen, T. (1898):"Why is Economics not an Evolutionary Science", The quarterly Journal of Economics, vol. xii, July

Veblen, T. (1904): "The Theory of Business Enterprise", Scribner & Son

Vestergaard, A. (1992): "In Search of Managerial Linkages", Ph. D. Dissertation, The Århus School of Business

Von Hippel, E. (1987):"Sucessfull Industrial Products from Costumer Ideas", Journal of Marketing, Vol 42, no. 1, pp. 39-49

Wallraff, G. (1989):"Ganz Unten", Sprogforlaget, Copenhagen

Weber, M. (1961):"The Three types of legitimate Rule", in Amitai & Etzioni (eds): "Complex Organizations - A sociological Reader", Holt Rinehart & Winston

Weber, M. (1968): "Economy and Society: An interpretive Sociology", Bedminister Press

Webster, F.R. (1975):"Perceptions of the Industrial Distributor", Industrial marketing Management (4), pp. 257-264

Westley, F.R. (1990):"Middle managers & Strategy: Microdynamics of inclusion", Strategic Mnagement Journal (11), pp. 337-351

Weick K.E.(1976):"Educational Organizations as Loosely Coupled Systems", Administrative Science Quarterly, March pp. 1-11

Weick K. E. (1979):"The social Psychology of Organizing", Addison-Wesley

Weick, K.E. (1987): "Substitutes for Strategy", In Teece, D. J. (ed) "The competitive Challenge", New York, Harper & Row

Weick, K. E (1991).: "The Nontraditional Quality of organizational Learning", Organization Science, vol.2, 1 Feb 1991, pp:116-124

Weick, K. & K. Roberts (1993):"Collective Mind in Organizations: Heedfull Interrelation on Flight Decks", Administrative Science Quarterly, (38), pp. 357-381

Welch, L. S. & R. Loustarinen (1988): "Internationalization: Evolution of a concept", Journal of General Management, 14 (2), Winter, pp. 34-55

Whetten, D. A. (1987):"Organizational Growth and Decline Processes", Annual Review of Sociology, (13), pp. 335-358

Whitley, R. (1984): "The fragmented Stage of Management Studies: Reasons and Consequences", Journal of Management Studies 21, 3, pp 331-348

Whitley, R. (1992): "The social Construction of Organizations and Markets - The comparative analysis of Business Recipes", in Michael Reed & Michael Huges: "Rethinking Organization", SAGE Publications

Whitley, R. (1993): "Business Systems in East Asia", SAGE Publications

Wiedersheim-Paul, F. & J. Johanson (1973):"The internationalization of the Firm - Four Swedish Case studies", Journal of management studies,Vol. 12, october 1975, pp. 306-313

Williamson, O. E. (1981):"The economics of Organization: The transaction Cost Approach", American Journal of Sociology, (87), pp. 548-577

Williamson O. E. (1975):"Markets and Hierarchy: Analysis and Antitrust implications", Free Press

Williamson, O. E. (1985):"The Economic Institutions of Capitalism", Free Press

Wonnacott R. & P. Wonnacott (1988):"Economics 3.ed", McGraw-Hill

Woodward, J. (1966):"Industrial Organization: Theory and Practice", Oxford University Press

Wyckoff, A. W.(1993):"The International Expansion of Productive Networks", The OECD Observer, (180), February/March

Yin R. K. (1991):"Case Study Research", Sage Publications

Young, S., J. Hamill, C. Wheeler & J. R. Davies (1989):"International Market Entry and Development", Prentice-Hall International

Aaby, N.E. & S. F. Slater (1989):"Management Influence on export Performance: A review of the empirical literature 1978-1988", International marketing review, 6(4), pp. 7-22

Zeits, G. (1980):"Interorganizational Dialectics", Administrative Science Quarterly, (25), pp.72-88

Zucker, L. G. (1987):"Institutional Theories of organization", Annual review of Sociology (13), pp. 443-464

Østergaard, U. (1992):"Peasants and Danes: The Danish National Identity and Political Culture" Comparative Studies in Society and History, (34), 1, pp. 3-27